THE 100 WACKIEST ACTION MOVIES

mine's bigger than yours

WRITTEN BY CHRISTOPHER LOMBARDO · JEFF KIRSCHNER

4880 Lower Valley Road · Atglen, PA 19310

Library of Congress Control Number: 2020930731

Designed by Jack Chappell
Cover design by Jack Chappell
Type set in Ammonite/Micro Technic/Futura

ISBN: 978-0-7643-6025-1
Printed in India

Published by Schiffer Publishing, Ltd.
4880 Lower Valley Road
Atglen, PA 19310
Phone: (610) 593-1777; Fax: (610) 593-2002
E-mail: Info@schifferbooks.com
Web: www.schifferbooks.com

IN MEMORY OF PAUL MANCUSO
(1982–2014)

NICO. GINO. MASON.

C. L.

Theirs not to make reply,
Theirs not to reason why,
Theirs but to do and die.

The Charge of the Light Brigade
—Alfred, Lord Tennyson

CONTENTS

CHAPTER FIVE

Revenge Is a Dish Best Served in This Chapter

104

CHAPTER SIX

My Fist, Your Face

124

CHAPTER SEVEN

The Long Arm of the Law

156

CHAPTER EIGHT

Stupor Heroes

184

CHAPTER NINE

Covert Ops

208

FOREWORD

My taste in cinema ranges from Bergman to bat-shit crazy. *Leprechaun in Space*, anyone? So, I'm proud to find two wacky films of mine are included in this book.

We filmmakers are an obsessive lot, driven by a consuming passion that can lead to an Oscar or a Razzie, depending on whether you are Spielberg or Tommy Wiseau. This book plumbs the Wiseau end of the spectrum: films that are so incompetent they metamorphosize into hallowed artifacts of cultural disaster. Yet their directors all started with the best of intentions, confident their low-budget version of a high-budget hit would stand out from the crowd. But somewhere along the journey between lofty vision and delivery to marketplace a little wackiness sets in. With each new ineptitude of plot logic or scene staging, you go "what were they thinking?"

Mine's Bigger Than Yours covers nine genre subsets. The first, "Ain't That a Kick in the Head," offers an array of hilariously incompetent pugilism pictures. Taekwondo teacher Y. K. Kim had never acted or made a movie before, but that did not stop him from mortgaging his Taekwondo school to finance an action picture with himself as the star. The result was *Miami Connection*, thus creating a new martial arts category—Rock Band vs. Rival Rock Band allied with Cocaine Biker Ninjas. Speaking from experience (*Strike of the Panther*), ninjas are popular in low-budget films because their standard costume allows waves of fist fodder to be played by the same group of stuntmen. *Miami Connection* is seriously bad in every department but radiates an infectious goofy joy that has earned it cult status.

Another ninja movie—*Ninja Holocaust*—showcases the skills of prolific Hong Kong director Godfrey Ho, who turned out eighty movies in ten years. He pioneered the Frankenstein technique of low-budget production. He would sew the best parts of two older or unfinished films together, then shoot linking scenes intended to unite the unrelated plot strands, but they only added to the confusion. *Ninja Holocaust* combines softcore with kung fu, thus ensuring the exploitation audience maximum carnage and nudity. Special highlight: sex on a rowing machine. In his *Robocop* rip-off, *Robo Vampire*, Mr. Ho throws Chinese hopping vampires, a Thai drug war movie, and a ghost girl in a see-through nightie into the blender. Ho is truly the Ed Wood of Eighties Asian Cinema.

Pistol-packin', karate-choppin', kick-ass women have their own section, including such gems as *Hustler Squad* and *Lady Terminator*. *Too Hot to Handle*, starring leggy platinum blonde Cheri Caffaro as a scuzzy female James Bond with sadomasochistic urges, earned her some exploitation notoriety over five such films, but she was unable to cross over into mainstream roles. However, stars like George Clooney, Arnold Schwarzenegger (*Batman & Robin*), and Jennifer Garner (*Elektra)* were not immune to a walk on the wacky side. But it's no surprise to find movies from Charles Bronson, Dolph Lundgren, Chuck

Norris, and Steven Seagal listed here. Seagal's iconic line in *Hard to Kill*: "I know what you're thinking. Mine's bigger than yours..." provided the inspiration for the book's title.

Dialogue howlers are among many traits shared by these films. "Now that Tom is dead, I want to use his body to create an android-like robot..." would be a challenge for Meryl Streep. Over-the-top villains abound, such as 1978's *Mr. No Legs*, where a mob badass, played by a real-life amputee, dispatches victims from his motorized wheelchair custom-fitted with double barreled shotguns. There's a gleeful breaking of taboos, like the post-apocalypse roller vixen nuns who worship the Great Smiley Face (really) and take nude hot tubs together in *Roller Blade*. By necessity, it seems, no idea is too dumb, no explosion too big, and there is no such thing as gratuitous nudity.

In *Not Quite Hollywood*, Mark Hartley's hilarious documentary on Ozploitation, Quentin Tarantino identifies the appeal of outrageous cinema. "You live and breathe to wait for those weird moments that happen once in a while in genre cinema where it's like you can't believe you're seeing what you're seeing." This book is packed with WTF moments. As researched by Jeff Kirschner and Christopher Lombardo, it's the gift that keeps on giving. It offers chortles on every page, then hours of viewing fun if you care to follow in the authors' footsteps.

Brian Trenchard-Smith
Filmmaker/author

INTRODUCTION

The holy trinity of action films is hero, villain, and henchman. *Omne trium perfectum*.

Heroic exploits have dated back for millennia—long before the dynamic duo of Heracles and Odysseus, whose legendary adventures, like the action heroes of our age, would've generated countless needless sequels if epic poetry wasn't long enough already.

Heroes are awesome. They kick serious ass under the most trying of conditions. That every story needs a hero goes without saying. Not that much of anything is being said by the heroes themselves, as action heroes are notoriously abrupt and their dialogue notoriously sparse. Besides, who needs verbal gymnastics when so much more can be articulated with fists, feet, and gratuitous firepower? It's the monomyth with monosyllables.

Those that do get to open their yaps are the villains—oftentimes a little too much. For they are a notoriously grandiloquent bunch, prattling away about their nefarious plans when they really should be keeping things a little closer to their vests. They're the ones with the master plans: to hoard the world's water supply, create evil empires, coordinate heroin shipments to impoverished tenements. You know, all the stuff they don't teach you at Wharton but nonetheless requires some semblance of above-average intelligence.

Still, for the most part, their collective bark is much worse than their bite. They may be the brains of the operation, but a villain is no solo act. They need a backup band to carry out their dastardly deeds and aspirations of global domination. And that's where the henchmen come in. In *The Prince* (1513), Machiavelli pronounced that "the first method for estimating the intelligence of a ruler is to look at the men he has around him." And action film villains typically have plenty.

The likes of Chuck Norris, Charles Bronson, or Steven Seagal are lethal weapons, even in small doses. But unlike lead or asbestos, they are far more difficult to get out of abandoned warehouses (usually populated by dozens upon dozens of henchmen, typically little more than cannon fodder for our adroit avengers). Why action films so often favor shootouts in abandoned warehouses, and why derelict storage spaces are so prevalent in large, economically vibrant urban centers are questions unto themselves, but we'll leave those inquiries for another time.

But hero vs. henchman alone would not suffice. And that's not just because the latter typically has the personality of road signage, barely uttering enough dialogue to qualify for a SAG card. And even if they do, it may be quashed by someone else's voice in post-production (or worse, an off-screen Wilhelm scream accompanying them as they plummet to their inglorious demise). Besides, the talent pool of such men is shallow indeed: they barely know how to take cover in a shootout—and that's really all they need to know how to do.

Quite simply, henchmen need a leader. And even *with* a leader, they still find themselves woefully unable to defend themselves against the hero punting them into an iron smelter or shooting them through the chest with a crossbow. When armed, they attack in rows. When unarmed, they reach for billiard cues or other accoutrements at hand. Unfortunately, those instruments are often wrested away before being cracked against their respective noggins.

Nevertheless, action films need henchmen to carry out their leaders' plans, even if it's only to the best of their very limited abilities. If nothing else, they're there to up the body counts. They're the unheralded yet indispensable foot soldiers who are the canvases by which our heroes paint their masterpieces with blood.

In action films, when the triumvirate of hero, villain, and henchmen are set in motion, it's dynamic. It's exciting. There's a reason the phrase "action-packed" exists.

In *Mine's Bigger Than Yours: The 100 Wackiest Action Movies*, we look at films that have all the necessary components for greatness. They've got heroes. They've got villains. They've got henchmen. But something's typically amiss or missing. Usually, it's a budget or a line producer. Sometimes it's talent. But that doesn't mean these films aren't as fun and unabashedly entertaining as any mainstream fare.

In the pages that follow, we're going to round up some of the silliest, most fun, and yes, wackiest action movies around—from the mainstream to the independent; from our shores to far-off lands. Any time a bazooka is fired through a public square, a ninja emerges from the bushes, a goon is blown off a fire escape, or a truck is driven through a suburban mall—we're there. Keep low to the ground, pack some heat and a flak jacket, and of course, you know what to do when it comes to asking questions. Save them for later . . . there'll be plenty of time for inquiry once the shooting's done.

ONE

AIN'T THAT A KICK IN THE HEAD

PUNCH WHEN YOU HAVE TO PUNCH. KICK WHEN YOU HAVE TO KICK.

—BRUCE LEE

What *is* a martial arts movie, exactly? Aren't there lots of action movies where the heroes, who couldn't so much as fill up a voicemail with verbiage, let their fists and feet do most of the talking? Sure. And *Wikipedia* is of no use to us here: "Martial arts films contain many characters who are martial artists." (One would only hope.) We'll try and extend this definition further.

These films frequently have a) a dojo, b) ninjas, c) elaborate training montages wherein someone previously uninstructed soars to the summit of the field in a particular discipline in a matter of days, and d) spectacular ass-over- tea-kettle stunts and a whoosh of sounds. (You can hear a martial arts movie a mile away.) One could say the real stars of chopsocky are the Foley artists. It's those guys who make "the sound of violence larger than life," according to *Fists of Fury*, a fun documentary about Hong Kong Shaw Brothers' productions in the '70s.

Martial arts films have plots that are often so simple they can be pantomimed in charades. And some of the set pieces are truly unhinged. In the early nineteenth century, the "rotational chair" was one of the many bizarre ways of treating the mentally ill. It was thought that spinning people around at a high rate would increase circulation to the brain. Instead, it made the poor patients woozy. The wackiest martial arts movies can have a similar effect. They're frequently disorienting and defy physics and logic. But they're also super fun.

So, wear loose fitting clothing, remove your shoes and socks, and step into the dojo with us as we look at some nutty black-belt worthy flicks.

MIAMI CONNECTION (1987)

If you're looking to spread taekwondo awareness through song (and really, who isn't?), you've come to the right place.

We all know the entertainment business is tough. In *Miami Connection*, this point is driven home by this rickety premise: a crummy musical act, embittered at being replaced as the house band in an awful Florida nightclub, decide to war it out with their rivals by enlisting the help of a gang. Usually, gang warfare is precipitated by, oh, access to some lucrative drug or prostitution trade. But a performance slot? Is stage time in the Sunshine State so difficult to come by that an *8 Mile* squabble might break out at any moment?

Now this sounds like the stuff of any juvenile delinquent movie, except for these key points: one, the gang's target is a band of multicultural, orphaned taekwondo students; and two, they're plying their trade not for the money or the groupies, but to (wait for it) spread taekwondo awareness to their respective ethnic homelands in a tour itinerary that couldn't possibly be profitable unless Italy and Israel are seedbeds from which taekwondo-related enthusiasm will grow. Oh, and did we mention there are ninjas? Because once the plot gauntlet of martial arts musical ambassadorship is thrown down, where can you possibly go from there but to black-clad assassins?

The spurned gang in question look like meth heads with military surplus hand-me-downs, and their leader has a toupee that could be lifted off the dome of Al Pacino if it wasn't so tightly glued down.

Their target: the fervently positive band Dragon Sound, a Miami Sound Machine soundalike who won the gig with feel-good empowerment crooning such as "*We're on top 'cause we play to win/Friends through eternity, loyalty, honesty/We'll stay together through thick or thin.*" With sentiments like that, it's no wonder their rivals want to beat them down.

Rockers KISS wowed audiences with kabuki-style makeup and the avowal, "You wanted the best, you got the best." Dragon Sound wow nobody, but they do wear taekwondo *gis* on stage, which must be hell on laundry day. Their act also includes the sensei grabbing his students' noses between his toes with high kicks. We take back what was said earlier. Maybe there *is* a market for this.

Dragon Sound's hit "Against the Ninja" features the pre-chorus shout out, "Taekwon, Taekwon, Taekwondo!" You can definitely say that these guys love their taekwondo, yet they do take a strong stand against ninjas. But really, who doesn't?

Miami Connection has a plot hole so large you could drive a tour van right through it: the nightclub could have had the warring bands play on different nights! There. Done. No need for violence, people. Sure, Wednesday may be an off night, but is a prime Saturday slot really worth losing your life over?

Besides, Dragon Sound are about to embark on an international time-zone-crisscrossing-"spreading-taekwondo-awareness tour" anyway.

The movie features spectacular street brawls with nary a cop or gun in sight, ninjas (because nothing says Florida like black-clad, covert warriors of Asian descent), and a seemingly improvised script. An example: were a real-life dustup to go down, you would rarely hear someone say, "You don't scare me!" and have it followed by "Goodbye!" with everyone then going their merry way instead of brawling.

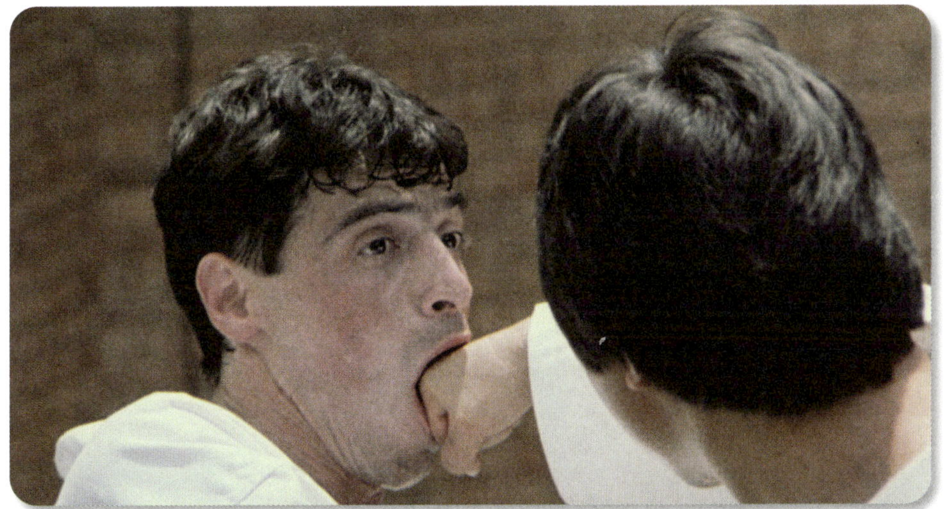

If the acting doesn't reach reverse roundhouse kicking heights, it's no surprise. Most of the cast were not actually actors, but rather students of Y. K. Kim, the movie's barely comprehensible producer and costar, who owned a chain of local taekwondo studios.

Kim is quoted on *CNN*: "When I finished the movie, I showed it to hundreds of different studios and distribution companies. They all said, 'This is trash. Don't waste your time.'" Luckily for all concerned, this treasure did find a distributor.

OF NOTE:

Before the closing credits, a message reads: "The elimination of violence is the key to creating world peace," and they might as well have added, "So please disregard the preceding 85 minutes of lead pipe fights, decapitations, sword gashes, knifings, beatings . . ."

Bad Action Movie signs, a.k.a. BAM! Attired of this

Camouflage doesn't equal tough. Tough comes from weapons, combat experience, scars, and muscles, and seldom from wardrobe choice (there are exceptions). Villainous '80s gangs always failed to give the same attention to bicep curls as they did to curling a can of Pabst Blue Ribbon, and you just can't compensate for the lack of any discernible muscle tone and protruding beer belly by the ability to blend into green surroundings. (Even more egregious when the film takes place in an urban milieu where the prevalence of any actual greenery is about as rare as a blonde European who's *not* an international terrorist mastermind.)

RAW FORCE

(1982)

Raw Force begins with a furor: a plane piloted by Adolf Hitler. But it's not the leader of the Third Reich—rather an undercutted, comb-overed 'stache-a-like. On board are a bunch of soldier of fortune types and an assortment of Asian beauties. The plane lands on an island in the Philippines, and the passengers are greeted by three men in hooded robes.

The monks (one of whom is played by the always fun, fat, and greasy Vic Diaz of *Too Hot to Handle*, a movie we review later that in no way is a reference to Diaz) order the women to strip naked, then imprison them in a bamboo cage. All but one, that is, who is deemed too skinny for whatever nefarious plot the monks have in mind. She begs the hooligans to take her back with them when a man dressed in a kimono steps out from the bush and slices her in two.

Cut to a car where three jokers are on their way to a cruise ship. One is reading a tourist brochure advertising Warrior's Island, a place where disgraced martial artists are buried and monks raise the dead to protect the island from outside forces. Forget boring old Disneyland. Take the family there!

The ship is captained by cantankerous Cameron Mitchell (*Deadly Prey*), and the three men are introduced as Taylor, Schwartz, and O'Malley (partners in law—actually, accountants). And they're martial arts students, too! Ass-kicking accountants . . . couldn't *Raw Force* have stayed away from occupational stereotypes?

On board is a motley crew, including the tour operator, sex-crazed alcoholic passenger Lloyd and his wife, and a group of bikinied beauties, one of whom just happens to be a member of the LAPD swat team.

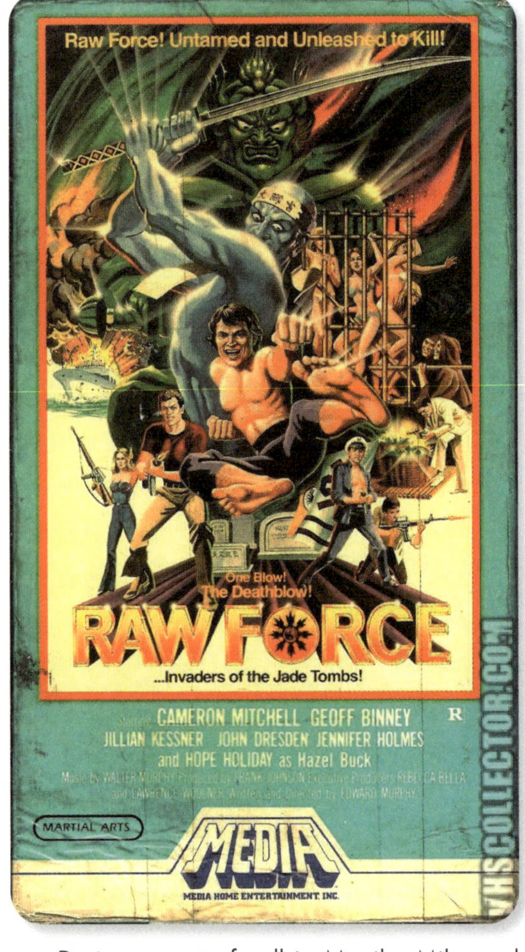

During a port of call in Manila, Mike and Lloyd sneak off to a "cathouse." The baddies from the opening, whose evil plot involves swapping kidnapped women for rare jade, pose as police and stage a fake raid to acquire more human cargo. Lloyd and Mike escape, but not before mentioning to Adolf that they're planning a visit to Warrior's Island. The bad guys, displeased that these buffoons may inadvertently disrupt their black market activities, make plans to thwart them. (Memo to villains: If you're using a remote island in the Philippines to conduct nebulous criminal activity, first make sure it's not publicized in a glossy travel brochure.)

At a bar later that night, the captain is kidnapped while draining the Carlsberg. Luckily the three stooges are there, as is the ship's cook, who also happens to be a kick-ass martial artist. Go figure. Finally, after a lengthy interlude where the film morphs into a T&A romp, the action returns as the baddies invade the ship, slaughter most of the crew and passengers, and set the boat aflame.

The principal cast members escape in a lifeboat, eventually washing up on Warrior's Island. The baddies are there, and Adolf mentions that the monks require the women, not for sex, but for food. Apparently eating barbecued human flesh gives one the power to raise the dead. Who says watching action flicks isn't elucidating as well as entertaining?

The heroes then have to battle their way off the island, fighting off not just the villains but also the monks and the undead disgraced martial artists.

Raw Force is certainly different. It's an exploitation Kung Fu/T&A/Zombie/Women in Prison/Cannibal hybrid that could only have been made on the cheap in the Philippines. A film such as this should and could be low-budget B-movie nirvana, but *Raw Force* just feels overstuffed, like the monks after snacking on a kidnapped nubile. The film ends with the line "To be continued." That's pretty optimistic to hope for a sequel. However, if a *Raw Force 2* ever *did* go into production, one wonders if there would have been any exploitation genres left for the screenwriter to shoehorn in.

GYMKATA

(1985)

In non-Euclidian geometry, two parallel lines meet at infinity. Do gymnastics parallel bars do so, as well? While we contemplate this Zen kōan, let's bow our heads and first examine the complexities of international diplomacy.

In whenever period *Gymkata* is set, the United States wields soft power. In fact, they use kid gloves when dealing with the tiny fictional country of Parmistan—which sounds like a grated cheese. The Special Intelligence Agency (SIA) has designated the region to be of strategic importance for satellite defense systems, but since military intervention has fallen out of favor, probably due to Cold War fatigue, they are trying a different approach. And what an approach. The country (which is supposed to border Pakistan yet has architecture that oddly resembles somewhere Eastern European where Steven Seagal would likely location scout to film another turd) has a longstanding tradition called "The Game."

The Game is a death match á la *The Running Man*, where contestants navigate a rugged natural and urban obstacle course demarcated with black flags. If only it were that simple. In addition to battling the elements, contestants have to keep an eye out for Ottoman-garbed ninja archers as they scramble across a gorge by rope, battling gravity and sapped core strength.

And the last man left standing? To the victor goes . . . not the spoils, but a wish. Instead of hoisting a gaudy trophy over their head and bagging a huge cash prize, the person still sentient at the conclusion of this fight-to-the-death tournament/race receives an actual wish. C'mon, is this a dirty genie-in-a-bottle joke or human cockfighting?

Ergo, the US Special Intelligence Agency figures that if one of their own can win said tournament, the victor can then *choose* to set up a satellite station in Parmistan as their wish. So, a few issues with this. You figure a foreign combatant could also win the tourney and use their wish to annex the territory or another could proclaim themselves Supreme Leader of Parmistan (or for that matter, wish for all the contents of the country's treasury to be deposited into his bank account). But we haven't examined the contest's fine print.

While these pages chronicle a Latin American– influenced taekwondo band that has to fight a gang and a group of undercover supermodels tasked to topple a third world dictator, *Gymkata* stands alongside the soon-to-be-mentioned *Ninja III* as the most ludicrous movie premise contained here. And as you proceed, you'll realize just how amazing that is.

The go-to guy for this certain death intelligence mission is Jonathan (real-life ex-Olympian Kurt Thomas who had ZERO martial arts experience going into this), a gymnast who incorporates floor routines, parallel bars, and pommel horses to pummel opponents in a unique and very hokey martial arts style of his own creation.

While he fights for his life, he also fights for the affection of Princess Rubali, played by former Filipina *Playboy* model and busy-to-this-day actress in her homeland, Tetchie Agbayani. (At least she's still fielding agent calls; *Gymkata* remains Thomas's only leading film credit.) A Parmi prince casually explains the princess away as "part Indonesian." She really stands out in crowd scenes where townsfolk don't look Filipino or Indonesian at all, but more like the toothless extras from *Borat* via a medieval renaissance fair.

Along The Game's route, gymnastics equipment seems to mysteriously appear out of thin air. In a narrow alleyway, a lone metal bar joins two apartment blocks, and Jonathan uses it to spin his mass 360 degrees around the rod, up and down-kicking whatever assailant is stupid enough to stumble into his path. Though he's not shown applying it to his hands, Jonathan must be carrying magnesium carbonate chalk on his person to account for his tremendous grip.

Later, he happens upon a pommel horse, conveniently set up in the town square, which enables him to spin his legs like blender blades, KO-ing the angry villagers-with-torches types screaming for blood. Either the fortuitously placed exercise equipment is a tremendous stroke of serendipity, or Parmistan is vying for the first completely outdoors summer Olympics.

Hilariously, not only is Jonathan trying to rescue his princess while competing in a to-the-death tournament, but he actually has the misfortune of being a second-generation Game competitor. His dad went through the obstacle course and is now MIA. Commander Zamir, who has designs on one day ruling Parmistan, is a moulded muscled traitor and the Princess's husband-via-arranged-marriage. He makes life especially rough for Jonathan, singling him out for abuse along The Game route by tasking his underlings to try and stick arrows in his back. And what's more, poor Jonathan also has to fight off a nasty German national competitor, Thorg, played by bulky former World Arm Wrestling Champion Bob Schott, who keeps coming despite having arrows—deadly projectiles meant for Johnny-Boy— embedded in his chest. As we'll continue to see in *Mine's Bigger Than Yours*, expert marksmanship isn't exactly a "must have" when it comes to crony personnel staffing.

Director Robert Clouse is no stranger to wacky or the martial arts. He directed *Enter the Dragon*, yet he's also the man responsible for *Deadly Eyes*, a Canadian horror film where dachshunds and Yorkshire terriers were dressed to look like giant killer rats. It was part of the so-called tax shelter era, where investors were given a tax deferral if they used a two-thirds Canadian talent. We're not sure if that applied to pets.

AMERICAN NINJA

(1985)

American Ninja is not to be confused with *American Ninja Warrior*, a game show that will have anthropologists wondering how viewers became so emotionally invested in the exploits of fully grown adults traversing jungle gyms.

While it's easy to look down on—or as the case may be, up—at these goofily perky parkour disciples swinging like chimps, don't look askance at the hilarious *American Ninja*. It's a Cannon production full of the kind of flag-waving brio and tone deafness we've come to expect, nay demand, from the Golan/Globus duo.

Michael Dudikoff is Joe, a guy with a personality as spellbinding as his name, whose face expresses not one but two degrees of scowl. We meet him in the first frames: an outwardly unexceptional GI ferrying an army convoy across Philippine dirt roads accompanied by a wheezing trumpet soundtrack so atonal it's as if Miles Davis were kicking his cat.

Suddenly, he and his fellow soldiers are ambushed, first by machine gunners, then by ninjas courting carpal tunnel with all the Foley fist-cracking. The bushwhackers massacre a slew of GIs and take the colonel's daughter hostage, pulling her deep into the jungle.

While ninjas are generally known for their stealth, skulking head-to-toe in black against a very green South Asian forest misses the key element of surprise. But who are we white belt nobodies to question their methods? That being said, movie ninjas generally follow this color schema: white for good; black for evil. Green is practically nonexistent, even if you need to blend in with the chlorophyll. (Mauve and sepia ninjas have yet to capture the public's imagination.)

Luckily for the US Army, Joe kicks as well as he squints. A reform schooler and former delinquent adopted by a Japanese martial arts expert dad, Joe is a force to be reckoned with—a man who can deftly deflect arrows shot from point-blank range with a shovel. Color the leader ninja impressed: "He possess great skills!" Screenwriting tip: subject-verb disagreement always makes things sound more Oriental.

Joe fights off the ninjas, rushes into the jungle, and saves the girl from certain peril, but not from

'80s sexism. She whinges about her broken pumps and subjects her handsome savior to that time-worn action cliché: "I can take care of myself!" Clearly not, if her idea of sensible footwear for tooling around in a military cavalcade is high heels.

Meanwhile, back at the base, the clichés are coming fast and furious. As army brass inquire about the deadly ambush, the meek response is, "We tried our best . . ." and then, "Well, your BEST WASN'T GOOD ENOUGH!"

Joe's courage doesn't win him many friends in the barracks, because heroism is actually *scorned* in this platoon. He runs afoul of his comrades, plus his tough-as-rail-spikes drill sergeant Jackson (Steve James), a guy so shredded he's probably packing a cheese grater along with a sidearm.

When called out by Jackson, Joe showcases his butt-kicking bona fides, beating up the sergeant in front of everybody, eventually earning Jackson's grudging respect by fighting him blind with a metal bucket over his head.

With so much backstory to fill in (such as why anyone would be brazen enough to make mincemeat out of their boss in such a conspicuous way) and only so little time to spare, we learn that Joe's memory has been erased. But not enough for him to forget his earth-shattering martial arts—just his mysterious upbringing.

Something else is missing, though. While the US army has had a lasting footprint in its former colony of the Philippines, who in heck were the guys ambushing them and what were their motivations? *American Ninja* never addresses that bit. No authorities when it came to geopolitics, anachronisms never stopped the Cannon boys from placing a platoon in a random Vietnam jungle years after they had any historical business being there (see *Missing in Action 2: The Beginning*).

To advance a plot sagging from the weight of its inanity, Joe is fingered in a weapon-smuggling ring, a scheme orchestrated by a supervillain who speaks French, the *lingua franca* of reactionary Reagan-era action movie treachery. The guy has a ninja training facility under his command that looks like an Al-Qaeda fat camp by way of, yes, *American Ninja Warrior*.

The martial arts guerrillas are being trained by Tadashi Yamashita, a genre actor billed on these shores as Bronson Lee, who even looks like Charles Bronson's pompadoured Japanese cousin.

Joe has to clear his name and foil the plot, all with the help of the granite-chiselled sergeant Jackson, Joe's new ally, as bygones will be bygones even if you beat the snuff out of your superior while donning a water pail.

OF NOTE:

American Ninja contains a preposterous motorcycle jump featuring a stunt driver whose hair color and build differ significantly enough from Dudikoff that after he sticks the landing, you're not sure whether to award a "9.5" to the stunt man or to the producers for being so brazen.

CITY NINJA, A.K.A. NINJA HOLOCAUST (1985)

In the early '80s, *Cannibal Holocaust* offended mainstream sensibilities. But horror folks are made of sterner stuff. Still, the word "holocaust" is box office poison, so it came as a surprise to us to see that ubiquitous '80s staple, ninjas—those cloaked, mysterious mercenaries with roots dating back to feudal Japan—associated with such an incendiary term.

Much like a horror film, *City Ninja* begins with an asinine period prologue, set back in World War II, where an American guy is attacked by Japanese ninjas and left for dead. In his possession is a clunky piece of jewelry that wouldn't pass muster on QVC but is imbued with meaning. So much so that his dying words to a kung fu warrior who intercedes on his behalf are "Keep this necklace for me, please."

This is the quickest introduction to a "MacGuffin" you'll ever see, coming in right at the one-minute mark. That's the infamous plot device that keeps coming up in every genre film. Alfred Hitchcock, describing the MacGuffin at a lecture at Columbia, said "It is the mechanical element that usually crops up in any story. In crook stories it is almost always the necklace."

While *City Ninja* is partly a crook story—especially if you count the movie stealing 90 minutes of your life—it is that very rarest of hybrids: a kung fu film spliced together with softcore porn. Made sometime between 1986 and 1987 (the details are murky), the smut-peddlers figured all this business about ninjas and a necklace would help, given the limited plot-forwarding capabilities of your average porno once the delivery man arrives.

After the kung fu guy warrior fends off the WWII ninja assault (when they're touched, the masked men explode like discount firecrackers), we flash forward to the 1980s. We're in a sleazy bar owned by that very same warrior's son, and wouldn't you know it, the promise has not been kept. Sadly, the deceased American's necklace is missing and in two halves, each in the possession of two rival gangs.

The bar owner, David Lo, confusingly played by . . . David Lo, is hosting a victory party for champion kickboxer Wang Lee, with lots of backslapping camaraderie and poorly dubbed "HA! HA! HA!" ADR laughter. Savvy David figures out that once the necklace's constituent parts are combined, its etchings will spell out a numerical sequence to a Swiss bank account. He needs to get that jewelry back.

Naturally, Wang Lee is the very tough customer conscripted for the mission. We witness Wang accidentally KO-ing his trainer during a sparring session, the trainer then losing consciousness to the strains of a Vaudeville spring ("DO-ING!"). He also beats the snot out of an opponent twice his size by spitting blood in his eye and dropkicking him. It's what Wang does because he has "no other qualifications." A bit like why the authors of this book write.

But wait. There's another kickboxer: Jimmy, a young up-and-comer working for sinister forces who's trying to procure the necklace, as well. He's played by taekwondo champ and genre legend Wong Ho (a.k.a. Casanova Wong, The Human Tornado[1]), who's hunting after the other half (or is it all?) of the necklace. It's pretty convoluted stuff.

All signs of the jewelry heist point to Red Head, a villain so named because of his red hair, and the Bald Headed Gang so named because . . . you get the gist. The gang is comprised of Korean toughs

so hard they do single-hand handstands on billiard tabletops *while still shooting pool*!

But they're still not tough enough. Wang tracks them down, infiltrates their pool hall hangout, and beats the holy tar out of them, batting billiard balls in their direction and pummelling them with cues. The leader gets it the worst: he has a 9-ball shoved down his gullet and is then drop kicked into a razor-sharp wall-mounted statue.

That's not all the movie has going for it. There are nude mud wrestling brawls, flying torpedo head-butts, and irate white foreigners shaking down businessmen while yelling "Yellow shithead." And naturally, Wang and Jimmy independently karate chop their way through much of the city's underworld before inevitably battling one another, even if technically neither one is a ninja. Otherwise, *City Ninja* doesn't disappoint with its ninja count.

All the while, Wang's attention is divided by other missions: continuing his training as a champion kickboxer and bedding all the eligible women of Hong Kong. At Winner Boxing Association, his hangers-on are blowing smoke rings up his ass to the strains of a synth polka, telling him "You're in excellent condition, better than Ali. Even Rocky can't compare to you." (Putting aside for a moment that one of those two is fictional.)

Also somewhat confusing: *City Ninja* is also called *Rocky's Love Affairs*, and there are affairs aplenty, as amidst all this ceaseless bickering and punch-ups over the necklace, Wang gives his wang quite a workout. He celebrates victories by *shtupping* women against ring posts, rubbing them down in the gym's showers, and fornicating on rowing machines. That's one way to have rock-hard abs.

When one of his many lovers catches him with another, she asks, "Who is this woman?" The mistress's reply: "I'll tell you the truth. I'm having his baby now!"

A ninja porno with Brazilian soap influences. It's too bad this hasn't birthed a sequel!

DRAGON HUNT (1990)

God bless vanity projects: those delusional, ego-driven pieces of "art" meant to showcase the creator's talents (or lack thereof). For without them, we wouldn't have misguided masterpieces like John De Hart's *Road to Revenge*, Y. K. Kim's *Miami Connection,* and Michael and Martin McNamara's exemplary *Dragon Hunt.*

The McNamaras are identical twins who grew up in Belfast, Ireland before immigrating to Canada. In 1972, they founded the first of many Twin Dragon Kung Fu Clubs, the first kick-boxing and kung fu club in Canada.[2] While there are still three clubs operating throughout Toronto to this day, it seems that the McNamaras were more interested in continuing their long-standing feud with former Ontario Athletics Commissioner Ken Hayashi[3] than teaching the martial arts.

A sequel to their previous film *Twin Dragon Encounters*, *Dragon Hunt* continues that story, with blond-mohawked baddie Jake (B. Bob) and his "People's Private Army" maintaining their vendetta against the brothers for shooting an arrow into his hand in the prior film (shown in hilarious flashback, with Jake emitting a ten-second long scream upon penetration). Now fitted with a metallic hand, Jake is shown buying enough ordnance to level a small city. The arms dealer demands to know whom he's buying the guns to use against. "The Twin Dragons, they did this to me," growls Jake as he holds up his laughably plastic-looking prosthetic.

Cut to a bunch of septuagenarians boarding a ferry for a leisurely midday cruise through Ontario's Thousand Islands. A helicopter hovers overhead and roughly a dozen camouflage-wearing heavies and two females get on board. They hold up the boat while Jake declares war on the Twin Dragons and recites their (unintelligible) manifesto for at least three minutes. It's understandable that a militia group would want to make their mission statement known, but why this audience? Seniors on a day trip from their retirement villa obviously couldn't care less about the designs of a group of whack-a-doodle minutemen who bear a grudge against two slightly built, mustachioed, Canadian martial arts instructors.

Ah, but killing the Twin Dragons would be too easy for a nutcase like Jake; he wants to make sport out of it. Hence, he hatches a scheme and places ads in all the mercenary, hunting, and martial arts magazines. He wants to attract only the best to his (evidently private) island to play the "ultimate survival game." The twins are headed to the island too, but it's not clear if they answered the ad or if Jake knew *a priori* they were heading there and then put his dastardly plan into motion. ("The twins think they are going on a summer vacation; some vacation!")

Among the out-of-shape meritorious assembled are The Beastmaster and his dog Apache, whose bite can exert 800 pounds of pressure per square inch; master poacher The Fatman; Vern, "A mindless mountain of a man; too stupid to be hurt, but he can hurt others;" your usual garden-variety assortment of ninjas; and the master ninja, the fearsomely named Red Skull of Death.

Michael, Martin, and their two female companions take a pontoon to the island. Unbeknownst to the twins, their girls are the same two who helped hold up the ferry earlier. They arrive at their cabin and see a Twin Dragon poster affixed to the door with a bloody arrow head stuck through it. "I think someone's expectin' us," says

one of the twins. (It really is impossible to tell them apart.) They immediately run off into the forest in unison, arrive at a cliff side, remove their tank tops in perfect synchronicity, and dive on in. That they enter the water wearing Adidas swim trunks and exit the other side wearing Speedos is just one of the many continuity errors marring the film (not to mention the shoddy editing and the repeated inserts of the same shots and snippets of dialogue). We also see ninjas running toward the shore, supposedly to meet them, and then . . . nothing . . . for in the very next scene, the twins are relaxing back at their cabin as if there was no reason whatsoever for them to take their frantic dip. (Because there really wasn't.) The girls spike their drinks and they fall into a deep, drugged slumber.

When the two awake, they find themselves locked in a tiger cage, Jake looming over them repeating "Tick Tock, time to rock" ad nauseam while the assembled ne'er-do-wells chortle dementedly. The rules of the game are then explained, and like the film, they're completely inane.

After being locked in the cage for two days, the twins will then be let out and given a two-hour head start before the mercenaries attempt to hunt them down. The mercs are to be divided into three teams, each team given shifts of eight hours to find and kill their prey. Any weapon *but* firearms are allowed, and whoever manages to kill the brothers will receive a cash bounty of $200,000. But lest you think killing the Dragons will be a cakewalk, as portly henchman Carl explains, "Although the twins are vastly outnumbered, they are masters of kung fu and kickboxing . . . They're also skilled woodsmen [who could] survive in the harshest of conditions."

The film proceeds in predictable fashion, with hunters going in alive and coming back dead. But the film's *raison d'être*, the fight scenes, frankly stink. They are poorly choreographed dances with painfully obvious pulled punches that are pretty much over before they begin. And the film's final third dispenses with martial arts and devolves into a standard Rambo-like shootout anyhow. (Lots of militiamen shooting at the brothers' feet and missing them by a country mile, yet the brothers can shoot down a chopper with just two bullets.) As a showcase for the McNamara's brand of martial arts, *Dragon Hunt* is a front face kick that misses its intended target.

With only a handful of lines of dialogue to utter, Michael and Matthew prove to be inert actors, unconvincing at playing even themselves. The same can't be said for B. Bob as Jake. He's a villain so over-the-top cartoony he may as well have been created by Tex Avery. Given to spouting nursery rhymes and non-sequiturs and singing "A hunting we will go" to the tune of "The Farmer in the Dell," Jake is so insane he makes Gary Busey look like the paragon of mental fitness.

The end credits proudly begin with the line "This film was in no way Assisted [sic] by TELEFILM CANADA or THE ONTARIO FILM DEVELOPMENT CORPORATION." Good on the McNamaras for going at it alone, but it's unlikely that those two government bodies would have wanted to have been associated with the dreck that is *Dragon Hunt* anyhow.

PSYCHO KICKBOXER (1997)

The world of professional wrestling has spawned a number of bankable action stars; glowering baldies like the capable "Stone Cold" Steve Austin, former Minnesota Governor and current conspiracy nut Jesse "The Body" Ventura, and bona fide A-lister Dwayne "The Rock" Johnson have all acquitted themselves well in at least one shoot-'em-up.

Professional kickboxing, however, has proven not as fertile but can likely get you more bang for your producer buck. The closest thing to a crossover superstar the sport has produced is French World Champion Olivier Gruner, but as evidenced by *Crackerjack 3*, Gruner isn't earning any kudos from the Academy anytime soon.

There is, of course, the Muscles from Brussels, but JCVD never competed for any championships during his brief full-contact career. That leaves us with five-time World Kickboxing Champion Curtis Bush. But any dreams Bush had for movie superstardom were back-fisted back into oblivion after the incapable $10,000 production *Psycho Kickboxer*.

Although released in 1997, *Psycho Kickboxer* took five years to complete. That goes a long way toward explaining the preponderance of mullets on every male character, minus Bush. Here he plays amateur kickboxer Alex Hunter and favors a more close-cropped 'do and a moustache (making him resemble a 'roided-up Freddie Mercury).

Alex has a loving girlfriend whom he proposes marriage to (thus sealing her doom) and a father whom he asks to be his best man (thus sealing his doom). Pop, who's a cop, is working on putting away the dastardly Hawthorne, a man ". . . responsible for about 80% of the drug trade. Racketeering, extortion, murder, prostitution . . . you name it, he's involved." In the valley of crime kingpins, Hawthorne is no Vincent D'Onofrio. He favors frilly shirts and speaks like Paul Lynde. Intimidating he is not, but he does have lots of henchmen. And when Alex, girlfriend, and pop are leaving a restaurant, it's those henchmen who descend.

The trio are kidnapped and brought to an abandoned warehouse.[4] Alex is chained up and forced to bear witness as his girlfriend is violated then murdered and daddy gets his head blown off, in a scene that calls to mind that famous Louis Del Grande head explosion in *Scanners* if that effect had been achieved for $25.00.

Alex is left for dead, but the warehouse wasn't completely abandoned after all, for it is where paraplegic, ex-combat medic Joshua Commons calls home. Joshua nurses Alex back to health and offers to train him in the art of getting revenge, both by Miyagi-ing him and barking lazy motivational clichés such as "You gotta walk before you can run!" Casual racism rears its ugly head when Alex remarks "Great, just what I need . . . A black man in a wheelchair. I might as well be dead." While it's understandable that one may not want a disabled man as a fighting mentor, there is absolutely no need to bring race into it.

But before Joshua can bellow "You can do it!," Alex is on the street, averting crimes. He's kitted out in a ridiculous day-after-Halloween, half-off ninja costume, and what follows are at least six scenes strung together depicting attempted misdeeds broken up by Alex, who leaps into the fray and uses his half-hooks, crescent kicks, and knee-strikes to knock the miscreants silly, then feebly asks the victim "Are you OK?" before awkwardly running away like a man who really needs to use the facilities.

The press dubs this kick-ass crusader "The Dark Angel" (hence the alternate title *The Dark Angel: Psycho Kickboxer*), and the cops place a $10,000 bounty (equal to the film's budget) on this dime-store vigilante's head. We know this because the film keeps cutting to two mustachioed DJs at a new country station who report the news of the day. They also sing a horribly off-key, doo-wop version of "Earth Angel," replacing the word "earth" with "dark."

The film culminates in a fight to the death between Alex and four of "the best fighters from all over the world," a group assembled by Hawthorne. Alex makes short work of the first three but has a little more difficulty with the final opponent—a balding, ponytailed fat guy in a *gi*. Can Alex's David chop down this Goliath? No spoilers here, but the climax does feature Joshua sliding out of his chair before shimmying on his stomach to deliver a blow or two of his own.

Psycho Kickboxer delivers the low-budget, lunkheaded goods. Curtis Bush, while not much of an actor, is a kick-ass fighter. Hence, the fight scenes are quick, efficient, and effective. The rest of the film, not so much, but with a title like *Psycho Kickboxer*, how can you leave this one laying in the ring?

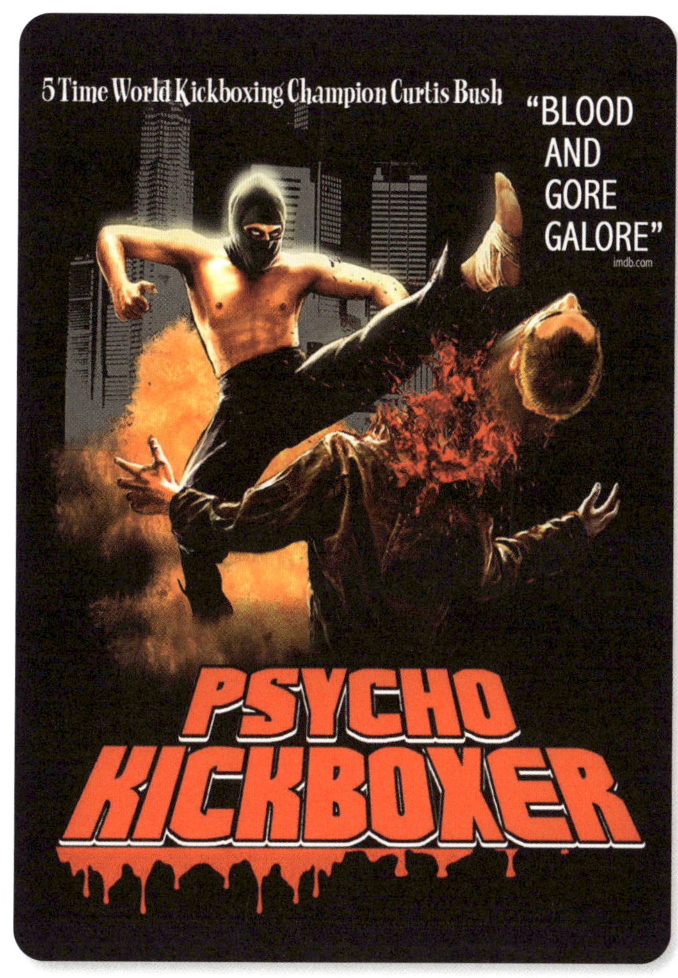

KILL SQUAD (1982)

To master kung fu is a rigorous pursuit, requiring years of extensive training and unwavering discipline. But if one were born in the whacked-out world that writer/director Patrick G. Donahue (*Parole Violators*) created for *Kill Squad*, they'd be delivering a flying front kick to the lip of the obstetrician. For this is a world where command of eagle strikes is as innate as respiration. Here everyone—from Vietnam vets to used car salesmen right through to construction workers and cowboys—is kung fu fighting, and it's more than just a little bit frightening.

Starring nobody-you've-ever-heard-of plus Cameron Mitchell (the man who handily wins the award for appearing in more films featured in this book than any other actor), *Kill Squad* is an extravaganza of more WTF moments than a Bollywood-version of *Eraserhead*. From the nonsensical tagline ("12 Hands . . . 12 Feet . . . 24 Reasons to die!") to the kindergarten Christmas recital acting, there is nothing right with *Kill Squad*.

Our hero: Vietnam vet Joseph Lawrence. At the outset, in a clear case of telling, not showing, Joe turns to his wife Joanne and exclaims "Things are looking so good for us." Hey Joe. Don't you know that in action movies, acknowledging contentment is second only to being a cop five days away from retirement as a sure-fire harbinger of doom? And just as beat-'em-up kismet would dictate, skulking outside Joe's window at that very moment is crime boss Dutch (Mitchell) and a cadre of louts, including bespoke cowboy-hat-wearing Jesse, who spies Joanne and expresses thoughts of a decidedly libidinous nature. On Dutch's cue, they bust in, and while Joseph is able to feebly roundhouse kick a couple into submission, the numbers prove to be too many. He takes a bullet and is paralyzed, unable to prevent his wife from being assaulted and killed.

Now granted, such emotional and physical trauma must take its toll on the victim, but unless Joe took one too many kicks to the throat, there's no reason to explain why, henceforth, his voice has dropped three octaves. For when next seen, Joseph is a paraplegic being wheeled out of the hospital, and actor Jeff Risk's natural voice is inexplicably dubbed over by the much huskier-sounding Russell Johnson (The Professor from *Gilligan's Island*). He gruffly (and much more sonorously) orders his former squadron second-in-command, current business partner/best friend Larry to take him home to ruminate in his garden. "Fragrance opens a man's mind to a lot of things," explains Joseph. He orders Larry to reassemble the squad and it's on!

What follows is lather, rinse, and repeat. Each member is approached after some wild altercation of poorly choreographed kung fu, and each is told the exact same thing: "Joseph needs you." They each then immediately drop everything that's germane to their respective lives at that moment, join without any hesitation, then move on to the next recruit.

Once the band is back together, Larry and the boys head out into the mean streets of whichever-generic-town-this-is-set-in, trying to triangulate the location of Dutch. It's never a warm welcome, and since every city resident holds some sort of degree in karate, there are casualties along the way.

And there's also that pesky masked sniper clad in black who's taking out squad members to contend with. It ends with Larry, the last of the squadron left standing, confronting the sniper, who in the best *Scooby-Doo* fashion, reveals himself to be (spoiler alert) Joseph! Seems Joe's meddlesome wife and business partner were preventing him from selling off the electronics company for a tidy profit, so Joseph orchestrated this whole *fakakta* scheme to off the opposition.

The final scenes of *Kill Squad* elevate the film from the ridiculous to the preposterous. To illustrate the physical wounds delivered by Larry's fists and feet, the makeup artist decided to paint Jeff Risk's face like some sort of Halloween ghoul cross between Donatella Versace and Chaney's *The Phantom of the Opera*. Two teeth are conspicuously painted over the lip in amateurish fashion, right above Risk's continually visible full set of chompers. Black pancake makeup surrounding the actor's lips and eyes completes the look. There is no way that anyone on set could have possibly seen Risk and thought "Yep, that oughta do it." Yet, evidently they did.

Kill Squad is recommended for Cameron Mitchell completists (they're also called masochists) and really, anyone who's up for a good, goofy old time.

THE OCTAGON (1980)

Young parents use a pram prop to smuggle machine guns and mow down some suits outside a gated mansion, an embassy we're guessing. In *The Octagon*, you'll have to excuse the frequent guesswork as it's more than a bit convoluted. In fact, if it weren't for that old standby, the newspaper-headline-as-plot-explanation and the vendor yelling a bunch of exposition to sell his wares, we would not have even known the vics were diplomats or that the massacre took place in France. Still, what this has to do with anything becomes clear as mud as things proceed. Not shedding much light on the situation, we meet Chuck Norris as Scott, too early in his career to fill his face out with facial hair, taking in a dance recital in full tuxedo. Impressed by one dancer, Nancy, he asks her out, and over Mexican food, her idea of raillery is something about how the salt lining her margarita prevents her from throwing up. This first-date red flag is put aside though when the twosome eventually bonds over martial arts and how the discipline infuses her dance routine, something which we don't actually get to see. We'll have to take the former karate champ Norris's word for it. It's one of the many things left unseen in *The Octagon*.

Meanwhile, back at the ranch—or in this case, a ninja training camp—a plot is being hatched, but there will be time for that. Let's get back to dinner, shall we?

After taking Nancy home to her parents' house, Scott and his plus-one are attacked by mysterious figures clad in black, and Norris destroys them all, likely tearing the pants of his rental tux with roundhouses but not before realizing that everyone in the household has been murdered. Why the director chose not to show this scene as well is anyone's guess. But the most incoherent and baffling aspect of *The Octagon* is Norris's weird echo whisper voiceovers throughout the film when he's trying to make sense of things (so in that sense he's an audience surrogate): "Ninjas . . . it had to be . . . but they don't exist anymore."

Maybe someone else can be of some help regarding what in hell is going on? There's a mysterious femme fatale (ex-Miss America contestant Karen Carlson), but she's too busy being cryptic and stealing Scott's keys, not to mention sporting a luxuriant fur coat in the middle of Los Angeles heat. So if not her, then associate and Scott's ex-mercenary buddy McCarn? Hey, it's genre legend Lee Van Cleef, uncharitably and accurately described in *Wikipedia* as "hatchet-faced," who lives out in a hunting lodge that's decked out in taxidermy chic, and seems vaguely interested in Scott's storyline: "Do you see these ninja often or only when it's a full moon?"

Well, there are ninja. Or ninjas. Ninja, like deer, is occasionally used as the plural form.

At the ninja training camp, a bunch of would-be mercenary westerners in khaki, that staple of martial arts instruction if you're studying American Eagle rather than Tiger Style, are told to "expect the unexpected." As part of their training regimen, a trap door opens in their barracks, sending one of the recruits hurtling into the basement, and a ninja stabs a cantaloupe through the clutched fingers of a frightened prospect. They share a "blood in, blood out" tenet common to prison gangs: to join you've gotta spill blood, and if you try to leave, your blood will spill.

They can't even leave the compound until their training is done or else they'll get a ninja star lodged in their noggin.

That dance troupe we mentioned earlier? Nancy was apparently an operative, working for a terrorist group. There's so much clunky exposition here with interchanges like "Remember that guy who adopted you?" No, but while we're on the subject, thanks for the background info. Every little bit helps.

Scott, whose karate skills are "good on the world market," spends the rest of the film tracking down his evil half-brother Seikura, who we get glimpses of through flashbacks, and who everyone wants dead because he's aiding and abetting terrorists by training them in the most enigmatic of martial arts.

We get fortune cookie speak like "What I like about the Oriental way of thinking is it's a double-edged sword." and "To take no action is an action." And you'd never accuse *The Octagon* of being action-deprived. You get to see Norris in his prime attacking a heavy bag like it's a Black Friday security guard, and destroying ninja. Or is that ninjas? And there are blow-darts. And bamboo cages. What more could you want, really?

NO RETREAT, NO SURRENDER (1986)

Geographical rivalries are nothing new. Consider New York's thin crust pizza versus Chicago's deep dish, Memphis BBQ versus Texas style, the Yankees versus the Red Sox. *No Retreat, No Surrender* introduces a rivalry heretofore unknown, since forgotten, but evidently no less contentious. Who can claim the better karate? LA or Seattle. And if that martial arts mix-it-up ain't enough, the film also gives us a kid, whose best friend is a breakdancing Michael Jackson impersonator, receiving martial arts tutelage from the ghost of Bruce Lee *and* it's the cinematic debut of Jean-Claude Van Damme, here in a largely mute role as the fearsome Russian, Ivan.[5]

No Retreat, No Surrender opens right where it should: inside a Los Angeles dojo. There, Sensei Tom Stillwell is putting the class through their paces but takes umbrage when his son, Jason, deviates from the usual front forward punch and kick routine and gets a little flashy. "This isn't Bruce Lee's Jeet Kune Do, it's Karate!" chastises Stillwell Sr. But his bravado soon fades when a trio of heavies enter: A cigar-chomping mafia type, a guy in a *gi* who looks like Kenny Loggins, and the Russian himself, one-upping Colonel Sanders in a snazzy white suit. Seems that the New York mob has targeted every dojo in the United States to become a front for organized crime, a plot device so improbable it requires a leap of logic wider than the Grand Canyon. Apparently, it's a better use of mob resources to crisscross the country to strongarm hundreds of people than it is to just open a spate of crap businesses in a derelict area in order to launder money.

When dojo dad refuses to capitulate, Kenny Loggins takes him to the Danger Zone. Dad barely holds his own, then the Russian leaps in with a flying dropkick and it's simply academic. The Russian brutally breaks Dad's leg in front of his stunned son and students.

Humiliated and broken, Stillwell Sr. shutters his dojo, packs the family up, and heads to Seattle. First retreat, first surrender. The move is illustrated quite literally by two separate establishing shots of the Space Needle and the family station wagon passing a "Welcome to Seattle" sign. Yet the filmmakers still saw fit to insert a subtitle reading "Seattle" to make sure that there was no confusion as to where we were now. Probably because of the clearly visible palm groves later.

Upon arrival, Jason immediately gets to turning the family garage into a training dojo. As he's working, a Jheri-curled kid rides by on his bike while simultaneously dribbling a basketball and blasting some tunes. That's the inimitable R.J., a kid so unflappable that even repeated beatdowns by obese neighborhood bully Scott can't destroy his good cheer. Jason and R.J. become fast friends, and R.J. helps Jason settle in while taking breaks for moonwalking, break dancing, and freestyling a rap about Bruce Lee. Bully Scott observes from across the street, taking a moment's break from subtly stuffing his face with a massive piece of cake to bemoan that a "Bruce Lee freak" is moving into the neighborhood. And that's a problem, how? Better a Bruce Lee freak than some high-school band camper keeping the neighborhood up by torturing a tuba.

Later, Scott and his buddies are at a fast food restaurant. As he's stuffing his face with a plate of burgers so large it would put Wimpy from *Popeye* to shame, he spies poor R.J. in the parking lot. This raises his ire, and mustard-stained Scott and his cronies run out to beat on the poor kid some more. Why the irrational hatred for poor R.J.? There must be some backstory left on the cutting-room floor somewhere. Anyhow, R.J. is surrounded, ready to take his beats, but Jason arrives in the nick of time. The two brave combatants stand back-to-back and R.J. utters "No retreat, no surrender." But before the brawl can commence, the proprietor of the establishment runs out, sending all involved scurrying. Second retreat, second surrender.

Wanting to continue their martial arts training, Jason and R.J. visit the local dojo. (Pops has since abandoned teaching karate, L.A. style or any other regional variation, in favor of pulling pints at a local watering hole while affecting a patently obvious fake limp.) Unfortunately for our dynamic duo, Scott is a student there and puts it in the ear of interim instructor Dean how Jason has been running around town denigrating Seattle Karate while boasting of the superior qualities of Los Angeles Karate. Like there's any discernible difference. Anyhow, this disparaging of the local ka-ra-tay infuriates Dean. He retaliates by pitting Jason against karate jumping bean Frank, who gives Jason a taste of Seattle by beating him down so bad, no Starbucks frappuccino could revive him. R.J. has to run in to stop the fight. And for those keeping track at home, that's the third retreat followed by the third surrender.

Jason suffers humiliation after humiliation, the breaking point being when pacifist dad forbids him from fighting and tears his Bruce Lee posters down. This sends Jason running in the night, to the grave of Master Lee himself. There, he gets down on his knees and implores Sensei Lee for help. He also runs to R.J.'s, who for some weird reason answers the call wearing a shower cap. He helps Jason set his dojo up anew in an abandoned house. That night, as Jason is sleeping, there's a flash of light and . . .TA-DA . . . the ghost of Bruce Lee appears! Now, to be fair, the actor playing Lee, Tae-jeong Kim, did double for the master himself on the set of *Game of Death*, but nonetheless looks about as close to Bruce Lee as Arnold Schwarzenegger does to Danny DeVito. The GOAT takes Jason on as a student, mutters some nonsense about *qi* and emptying the mind using a can of Diet Coke as realia, and overall proves far less demanding a teacher than Pat Morita.

So, where's this all leading too? Well, Jason's karate does improve considerably. (Chalk it up to the immediate training boost that comes from a protracted heavy-bag montage.) Meanwhile, the exact New York syndicate that tried to shake down LA Karate is now pulling the same shenanigans at Seattle Karate, and again they are rebuffed. So the Mob decides to settle their dispute with Seattle Karate in the place where all mafia disputes are settled: in the ring, at a karate tournament held in a high-school gymnasium. It's the Manhattan Ballers vs. the Seattle Sidekicks, three against three, but really, it's all about the Russian single-handedly destroying Seattle Karate. Without a word of hyperbole, the man is a monster. Ivan fights dirty and with such ferocity, it certainly appears that all hope is lost. But wait! In the stands are R.J. and Jason. "No Retreat, No Surrender!" says R.J. Jason hops into the ring, and you don't need the foresight of the Long Island Medium to see that Team NYC is going down.

No Retreat, No Surrender, followed by two sequels which have absolutely *bubkis* in common with the first film, is a bit of a weird bouillabaisse of *The Karate Kid* mixed with a dash of *Rocky IV* and an "airflare" of *Breakin' 2: Electronic Boogaloo*. Nowadays, its biggest selling feature is the inclusion of JCVD, but his Ivan character occupies no more than ten minutes screen time max, far removed from the *Rocky* fighting namesake. Nonetheless, it remains a nutty confection well worth watching. And as The Boss so triumphantly exclaimed lo those many years ago, "*Well, we made us a promise we swore we'd always remember/No retreat, baby, no surrender . . .*"

THE TRUE GAME OF DEATH (1979)

It's not unfair to say that action cinema of the 1970s and early '80s, especially at the grindhouse, was a collection of several types of 'sploitations. There was your Blacksploitation (*Shaft*), Hicksploitation (*Walking Tall*), Carsploitation (*Dirty Mary, Crazy Larry*), Ozsploitation (*Mad Max*), Vetsploitation (*The Exterminator*), and so on. But of all the 'sploitations, the most brazen has got to be Brucesploitation.

Bruce Lee was larger than life, eminently charismatic, exceptionally talented, and one-of-a-kind. Putting aside his obvious martial arts bona fides, Lee was, simply put, a star in the truest definition of the word. And because of his early and untimely death in 1973, on the cusp of his superstardom, he was a star that became a legend.

Trouble is, he passed away just as Lee-mania was taking hold, and with only three completed films and forty minutes of footage shot for the film that would ultimately became *Game of Death*, how could producers satiate the rabid desire for more Lee? Easy. If you're an unscrupulous producer looking to make a quick buck, you attack with the clones.

And hence came an entire subgenre of films tangentially related to Lee, with titles such as *Return of Bruce* and *Re-Enter the Dragon*, starring actors named Bruce Le, Bruce Li, Dragon Lee, and Lee Bruce, most of whom bore only the most superficial resemblance to the real McCoy. It's a practice that truly hadn't been done before nor has been replicated since. To understand just how audacious this was, imagine if Stallone had kicked the bucket while filming *First Blood*, but instead of shelving the picture, producers carried on with Frank Stallone completing the film, then churned out a cottage industry of films with titles such as *The Real Rocky* starring a bunch of interchangeable, no-name Italian-American actors.

The True Game of Death may very well be the most shameless Brucesploitation flick of them all; a film that is the veritable definition of the word chutzpah.[6] It's a bit by bit rip-off of Lee's posthumous *Game of Death*, which in itself is considered Brucesploitation due to its employment of doubles for both Lee and other actors from Lee's original footage, yet it is to *Game of Death* what the Gobots were to Transformers—a pathetically inferior imitation. And then to give it the adjective "true." That's some major *cojones* right there.

The film begins with a bunch of stock footage of the genuine article attending the wrap party for *Enter the Dragon*, followed by footage taken at Lee's funeral and a shot of Lee lying in his casket. It then abruptly cuts to a man working out as a wooden-sounding Ed Wood Criswell-like narrator intones "This film is about another Bruce, who looks rather like Bruce Lee." (Not very, that's for sure.) As pseudo-Bruce is doing squats, the camera zooms in on his crotch, and it's very evident that Bruce-lite's fly is about to bust wide open. Next, we're on a film set, where our Bruce analogue is filming a fight scene dressed in Lee's iconic *Enter the Dragon* black pants. Like Lee, he's a burgeoning star married to a Caucasian woman, here named Alice. He also looks suspiciously different than the Bruce-a-be we're introduced to at the beginning. (Reports indicate that the film employed two Bruce-a-likes, but neither one is credited.) And his name isn't even Bruce. It's Shao Long! Oy!

The plot bounces along like a Chinese knock-off discount store version of *Game of Death*. Shao Long is greeted on set by a stogie-chewing heavy in a white tuxedo that makes him look like a maître d' at a seafood restaurant housed in an actual boat. His name is George, and he's flanked by a couple of useless henchmen. He demands to represent Shao Long's career . . . or else! Now they say that entertainment industry agents are a slimy bunch, but this level of coercion would shame even Ari Gold. Shao Long refuses, and George figures that if he's not going to represent Shao Long, nobody else will.

When Alice returns home, she finds two of the henchmen waiting for her. They try and strongarm her to drug her husband, assuring her that all the substance will do is put him to sleep for three days, just enough time for him to miss the press junket for his latest film. She, of course, refuses. But when they return later—entering through the marital bedroom which a) is adorned with posters of the real Bruce Lee but are meant to be of Shao Long and b) has a curtain apparently covering absolutely nothing since the heavies enter by walking right through it—and threaten her at gunpoint, she has no choice but to acquiesce.

Shao Long is in the shower, giving Alice time enough to lace her husband's coffee with the poison. He takes a sip and lies back. As a Muzak version of "Don't Cry for Me Argentina" swells on the soundtrack, they make love. She's writhing atop him, fully nude, when the drugs kick in. He throws her off, clutches his head screaming in agony, and contorts himself all over the bed like Regan MacNeil in *The Exorcist*. (This is pretty sleazy since Lee died from an allergic reaction to the narcotic Equagesic, given to him to alleviate a severe headache.) And how can you trust a henchman? Three-day slumber, our patootie! Shao Long's slo-mo death throes continue while Alice stands over her husband, 100% in the buff, wailing out his name.

The grieving widow hires two servants to assist her after her husband's death, one of which is an elderly, bearded gentleman. Meanwhile, there are rumors coming from the States that Shao Long's coffin was empty. George's henchmen walk through another curtain, into Alice's home again (are they living in a tent?) and question her as to the veracity of Shao Long's demise. One is about to assault Alice, when a kung fu-kicking avenger wearing a mask not dissimilar to the one Lee wore when he played Kato on *The Green Hornet* series lays the smacketh down upon him. Oh, and that elderly servant? Soon to be revealed as Shao Long in disguise. "Don't be so surprised," he tells the incredulous Linda. "It takes more than poison to kill me!" And trying to figure out the logistics of how Shao Long managed to fake his death is a feat that would task even the mind of Elon Musk, so let's not even try, shall we?

As the film limps to its conclusion, Alice is kidnapped by George's goons and taken to—where else?—a pagoda. Shao Long races to her rescue, wearing a very familiar yellow jumpsuit, and must take on a gauntlet of assailants before getting to George, the ultimate one naturally being a large and rather overweight black man. Alas, no Kareem Abdul-Jabbar is he; this guy's physique is more akin to Boston Celtics-era Shaquille O' Neal.

That *The True Game of Death* is derivative—a rip-off of a film that itself has a dubious pedigree—is but the least of the film's sins. It's also sleazy, exploitative, non-sensical, slipshod, and rife with continuity errors. Oh, and in addition to the two nobodies playing Shao Long, the actress playing Alice is credited as "Alice" and the director is credited as "Steve." If a film can't even get the credits right, what hope is there for the rest of it?

AMERICAN KICKBOXER (1991)

American Kickboxer[7] features what may be *the* most unlikable, biggest asshole hero in the history of action cinema: champion kickboxer B. J. Quinn, as played by sixth-degree black belt and Chuck Norris protégé John Barrett.

The film begins with Quinn in the dressing room getting taped up for the main event. An unfortunate competitor on the undercard is stretchered in, beaten, bloody and out cold, having just gone toe-to-toe with brash upstart Jacques Denard. The decidedly "seasoned" looking Quinn (picture a less-bronzed but pompadoured George Hamilton) enters the ring for his title bout.

He vanquishes some ham-and-egger, but the fight isn't the fair contest of wits and technical ability you'd expect from a hero in a movie of this ilk. The fight is stopped midway when Quinn's spinning back fist turns into a spinning elbow.

Quinn is declared the winner nonetheless, as the blatantly illegal move is declared by the judges to be an "accidental butting." The crowd cheers as Quinn's arm is raised in victory; the only dissenter being reporter/photographer Wilson. He's employed by "States News" and is an Owen Wilson-esque smartass reporter on the kickboxing beat. Glad to know print media was still flourishing enough in the early '90s that a paper could employ an investigative reporter whose sole function was to cover bloodsports. Not exactly Watergate, is it Wilson?

Later that evening, an already well-soused Quinn and his girlfriend, Carol, attend a party at fight promoter Bob's estate. Bob is trying to woo a sponsor, and for some reason is dressed exactly like Colonel Harland Sanders, the white suit and black string tie looking particularly silly on the squat, avuncular promoter. Quinn gets into an altercation with Denard, and a partygoer steps in to break the two up. Quinn punches the Samaritan in the face, sending him flying backwards and through a glass table. The prick! Our supposed hero does run to his victim, and while Quinn is cradling the head of the man he just brutally assaulted, he bellows "Get a doctor for Christ's sake!" which is then repeated with echo a full six times over the soundtrack. It's too late anyhow; the man's a goner.

The incident makes the front page of the paper,[8] and soon the "Champion Killer" is on trial for murder! Denard[9] testifies for the prosecution while fellow kickboxer Chad Hunter (US National Karate Champion Keith Vitali) defends Quinn. Hunter's testimony is not enough, however, and the jury finds Quinn guilty on all counts. The judge deems that this "top performer in martial arts . . . used his skills recklessly and willfully" and sentences Quinn to a year in prison and bars him from participating "in any championship events" for a five-year period (remember those words).

Instead of giving us a white version of *Penitentiary*, *American Kickboxer* flashes forward ten months as Quinn is released from the hoosegow. Hunter is now ranked second in the world and is scheduled to take on new champion Denard. Quinn looks Hunter up to thank him for testifying on his behalf, and Hunter convinces the reluctant parolee to train him. But no Apollo Creed/Rocky Balboa relationship here. Quinn is bitter, resentful, and jealous. He drunkenly questions his girlfriend's fidelity during a dinner with Hunter and takes a few too many liberties at a sparring

session. Hunter walks off and Quinn is forced to watch his former charge's championship bout on television: a bout where the no-good, ne'er do well Denard punches Hunter right into the hospital. Quinn, ever the gentleman, does visit the convalescing Hunter, only to verbally beat the poor guy down some more for getting his ass kicked. What a jackass!

And the dickishness continues. Again pickled, Quinn gets into yet another altercation with Denard at Bob's. The current champ beats the snot out of the ex-champ, breaking a couple of chairs across his back for good measure. Fed up, Carol gets in their 'Vette and drives off, leading into yet another staple of the action film: the driving montage flashback. Only this one features Carol ruminating on what an utter schmuck her boyfriend is. Quinn is soon looking for new digs. Shoddy editing makes it look as if Carol was the one who wised up and sent the louse packing, but it was Quinn himself who left because he "need[ed] some time."

Some anger management would've been in order, if not a significant number of billable hours on a good therapist's couch, but in *American Kickboxer*, it's redemption through carpentry. The disgraced champ rents a dilapidated beach cottage and gets to work fixing it up. And of course it's in montage (set to a tepid pop-rock number entitled "He's a Man"). And there's Hunter, who just so happens to be running a kid's karate camp in the vicinity. He enlists Quinn to help him, and Carol even agrees to take the bum back. Things seem to be finally looking up for 'ol Quinn, but there's still a pesky fly swimming in the ointment named Denard.

See, all this time, Wilson has been stirring the pot, hoping to goad both Denard and Quinn to settle their differences in the ring. But Quinn can't fight in any "championship" bouts, right? Judge's decree. No worries. We'll make this one for the money. Denard puts up a $100,000 purse to face his nemesis, and after a vaguely homoerotic training sequence which features Quinn and Hunter kickboxing on the beach before frolicking in the surf, it's on!

The final fight is your fairly standard affair save for the fact that at least fifty senior citizens are in attendance, all going positively apeshit. Perhaps BINGO was cancelled so they were bussed in to fill the seats for this one. Denard is on offense for most of the bout, utilizing several underhanded tactics, and at one point, punches Quinn clean out of the ring. But it's the mighty Quinn who prevails, using the old rope-a-dope to exhaust Denard, then delivering a blow which results in a slow-motion knockout/pirouette/backflip that must be seen to be believed. It would have certainly earned a "9" from the Russian judge in an Olympics gymnastic floor routine.

As a pile of clichés masquerading as a movie, you could do worse than *American Kickboxer*. The fighting is legit, and the laughs (albeit unintentional) are plentiful. On the soundtrack to *Mad Max Beyond Thunderdome*, Tina Turner sang "We Don't Need Another Hero." Not if they're anything like B. J. Quinn, we don't. But thankfully, his next abject humiliation is just another scene away.

MISSION: KILLFAST
(1991)

Why is it that valuables are always kept in an aluminum suitcase? Top secret codes, wads of cash, blow, etc. should be stashed away as unobtrusively as possible, say, in a knapsack stuffed with soiled underwear. An aluminum suitcase is the "kick me" sign you'd slap on the back of someone in elementary school, except for mugging. It's one of those rare movie mysteries to go along with the inexplicable brand loyalty film characters always have to J&B whiskey.

In the opener to *Mission: Killfast*, there's a scuzzy bad guy carrying "the ultimate weapon" around in an aluminum suitcase, something that'd be easier to believe if said weapon didn't look like a bicycle bell crossed with an egg beater.

There are certain things in movies that are harbingers of doom. If it's a horror film, shining a flashlight down a dark hallway or stairwell while calling out someone's name means you have about two minutes to get your affairs in order. For action, blathering something about "by this time tomorrow, we'll be in ________" (insert tropical country of your choice) is a surefire predecessor to arrest or fatal double cross. The guy utters this very phrase to his lady friend, as if he's never heard of a femme fatale in his life—a life which she soon ends. But there's another double cross. A double-double cross? She ends up dead on a beach, minus the suitcase.

If an "ultimate weapon" falls into the wrong hands, and you're the feds, what should be done about it? Do you marshal the resources of a highly trained military tactical force? Use high-level diplomacy? A coalition of the willing? Why bother with that when you can enlist the services of a guy who "runs a chain of successful martial arts studios and just finished a world tour"? The feds have a clandestine meeting with dojo man in, where else, a parking garage, the place where all things secretive and bladder-emptying take place. The agent drives him around in circle after nauseating circle, probably to get him to sign on for the mission in exchange for a Gravol.™

Mission: Killfast is the brainchild of genre legend Ted V. Mikels, the director who brought us first date movies like *Apartheid Slave-Women's Justice* and *Blood Orgy of the She-Devils*, so expect the unexpected. Or, expect Artistic License to Kill.

The dojo man signed on for the undercover mission is none other than Cheng-Wu "Tiger" Yang, playing himself (something you'd expect of maybe, oh, someone you've heard of, rather than some obscure costar of *Game of Death II)*. And even though his command of the English language is barely enough to point him in the right direction on public transit, the feds think he's just the man to do the covert work required to retrieve the mystery suitcase and its nuclear weapon components. It doesn't matter that he's so high-profile, he's Grand Marshall of the City of Anaheim Parade (with his very own name, "Tiger Yang" inscribed on the side of the convertible) and the mob has even heard of him.

So feared is Tiger Yang that the evil criminal syndicate (whose front is a skin mag, so running time can be padded with poolside photoshoots) is tailing him and putting a contract on his head in an effort to take him out along the parade route. And as if to not be outdone, their ride of choice is a garish gold stretched Rolls Royce rather than something less obtrusive.

So it's up to Tiger Yang and some G-men to fight for what's right.

For all his shortcomings, Tiger Yang brings the goods, ever cool in his cherry red taekwondo *gi*, chopping gangsters and shooting antiaircraft artillery with aplomb.

Mission: Killfast is a delight. It contains two indispensable elements of what one could conceivably title an action film. And its debrief set pieces are legendary: FBI headquarters looks like a man cave that had a ski chalet fall on it, this as the Bureau touts Tiger's expertise with: "He's the best ever. And he's got the trophies to prove it!" One of the FBI agents lays out some intel at, of all places, a mini-putt course, where the waterfall drowns out some of the dialogue.

The local mob is wonderful too, with bon mots like, "We have a leak, but the plumber's on his way." Their poolside shindigs are joyous affairs too. One of the skin flick models shows off her work to a guy in a keffiyeh, cooing "I love foreign men," when he's as white as a trillium. The mob is connected to Latino guerrillas with richly rolling "el Presidente" accents. Best of all? The mysterious underworld hitman figure that is Cocoa Charlie, a swarthy Tom Jones with postage stamp eyebrows and blackface that would shame Kramer's tanning bed mishap on *Seinfeld*.

OF NOTE:

According to *Film Alchemy: The Independent Cinema of Ted V. Mikels*, *Mission: Killfast* took nine years between principal photography and release. Director Mikels reports, "it was said that any film available for the world market, and Rated R . . . had to contain nude scenes, or it probably would not be sold."

DYSTOPIAN HELL

THE FUTURE HAS A WAY OF ARRIVING UNANNOUNCED.

—GEORGE WILL

It's hard to get everyone to agree on what constitutes a utopia. Is it communism, capitalism, socialism, frotteurism (Look it up . . . yes, we're kidding!)? Hell, the literature goes back half a millennium and still nobody's figured it out. In Thomas More's *Utopia* (1516), he admitted as much: "It is only natural, of course, that each man should think his own opinions best: the crow loves his fledgling, and the ape his cub."

However, we can find common ground on what a dystopian world is—at least in the movies.

In urban backdrops of the future, crime is so rampant it makes the Chicago of today look like the Chicago of . . . uh . . . tomorrow. And humanity has all but given up on the "broken windows theory" of policing, policing of any sort whatsoever, and social programs. Instead, it's turned to either superhuman hybrid cops or machines—entities who won't drain municipal budgets with overtime—or worse, grizzled loners who take matters into their own hands.

Mad Max-type societies, meanwhile, lack the basics: food, water, freedom of speech, freedom of mobility, and good fashion sense. Is a fledgling desert culture wrecked by nuclear war worth protecting if the only sartorial choice is a jerkin? Is a sweltering-leather-vest human society one that's worth repopulating? As advocates of deodorant, we'd say probably not.

While many dystopian societies may be found wanting, the not-so-distant future has an abundance of one thing: the genre's copious employ of opening crawls. These are never as famous as *Star Wars*' "A long time ago in a galaxy far, far away." These descriptions are way more important. For without this plot device, we would not know that in the year 2081, what's left of Earth has one freshwater lake, or that a gang of ruthless tyrants entertains itself by pitting one group of rollerskaters against another in a velodrome roll-to-the-death.

Why are so many dystopian movies the same? Why do they all look like they're filmed on pillars of road salt or on the outskirts of a cement plant? And what about the dune buggy chicken-and-egg question: Did sand dunes necessitate dune buggies? Or were these vehicles so durable they withstood the nuclear holocaust?

In urban milieus, why does every future city look like a Dollar Tree *Blade Runner*? How is it that subways still run when every other essential service, like garbage collection or curbside recycling, has been cut to ribbons?

So many questions. What unites these movies, unfortunately, is a distinct lack of attention to personal hygiene in THE FUTURE.

Make sure the leather breathes, and join us in finding that dystopian action movie oasis.

R.O.T.O.R. (1987)

The technological singularity is a hypothetical event where machines become more intelligent than humans, and we "rush headlong into servitude," as Roman historian Tacitus put it—basically becoming slaves to machines. *R.O.T.O.R.* asks, "How do you stop a killing machine that goes berserk?"

Well, for starters, you could get its creator to help, a guy who blows up tree stumps on his ranch with improvised explosives, feeds his horse coffee from a "Texas Sized" mug, and spouts off one-liners such as "You want product, you got product!"

The "killing machine" in question is R.O.T.O.R., an engineered cop that's part of the secretive Dallas Robotic Officer Tactical Operation Research lab, whose scientists are "prognosticators for the future?" (Is there any other kind of prognosticator? Maybe in the immediate future, the dictionary definition of "prognosticator" has changed.) These are men of science who make portentous pronouncements about playing God yet change hotel room numbers because of superstition.

Their valiant leader is Captain Coldyron, a robotics engineer-slash-police captain who is pressed by a local corrupt politician to develop his super cop ahead of schedule. He protests by saying, "If you fire me, I'll make more noise than two skeletons making love in a tin coffin." The man may know robotics but he certainly has difficulty in forming similes that make any degree of logistical sense. And yet he can quote lengthy passages from *Paradise Lost* verbatim. Go figure.

The laboratory project was supposed to be a quarter-century in the making, but at the sixty-day mark, the super cop in question, who has a "combat chassis-issued prime directive" (we're not sure what that is either) escapes from the high-security lab by walking through a very flimsy plastic cover.

Suddenly the "first prototype of a battalion of the future" is hell-bent on:

a) Remorseless killing, and

b) Ripping off *Robocop* and *The Terminator* (the latter a vastly superior film they actually have the audacity to namecheck).

Robocop was undoubtedly ahead of its time: a sharp-shooting satirical prognostication of an unconstrained surveillance state. *R.O.T.O.R.*, on the other hand, features a super cop with the stout physicality of George Costanza and a Ned Flanders mustache. If modern robotics has become so details-obsessed that engineers are now applying fatuous facial hair, we must say, we're impressed.

One of R.O.T.O.R.'s numerous design flaws, putting aside the mustache and the shooting people indiscriminately for a moment, is that it's deactivated with a key and that car horns are its kryptonite.

Coldyron flies to Houston and enlists the help of R.O.T.O.R. co-creator, the very gabby Dr. Steele ("Oh god, the brain matrix. It's modelled after your lower brain function without the higher functions to control it!"), who doffs her clothing at the drop of a hat to reveal truly impressive, beefy delts that would shame Brock Lesnar.

All the while, the rogue super cop manhandles gas station attendants, shoots people for minor traffic violations, plants a hash slinger's face down on a barbecue grill, and takes out a few bar toughs, one of whom rips off his muscle tee Hulk Hogan-style and urges R.O.T.O.R. to try "taking on a real man." Bad move. In the battle of man versus machine, it's far safer to play chess against a supercomputer.

R.O.T.O.R. has it all. And by "all" we mean impenetrable sciencey jargon, dismal special effects, telegraphed fights, forced humor, and something that truly makes it a stand-out: a jive-talking Native American lab tech. Certainly a cinema first.

ROBO VAMPIRE (1988)

R.O.T.O.R. is undoubtedly one of the wackier of the innumerable *Robocop,* um, homages, but it's positively prosaic next to the mind-bogglingly ludicrous American/Hong Kong co-production *Robo Vampire.*

Directed by the indefatigable Godfrey Ho, a man of at least two dozen aliases and director of roughly thirty films with the word "Ninja" in the title, *Robo Vampire* tackles a question that has confounded thinkers from Diogenes of Sinope to Voltaire: Who would win in a battle between a cyborg super-warrior and a league of Chinese Hopping Vampires that are under the employ of an American drug lord operating "somewhere in the Golden Triangle"?

A Chinese Hopping Vampire, or *jiangshi,* is miles removed from the conventional image of a Bela Lugosi bloodsucker. Heck, they don't even suck blood. The *jiangshi* are reanimated corpses whose origins are rooted in ancient Chinese folklore and are typically shown wearing garments representative of the Qing dynasty. Due to rigor mortis, they can only move by hopping around, arms outstretched, so you'd naturally assume they'd be no match for a cyborg. But just to even the odds a bit, they're also quite adept at the martial arts. Their facial appearances range (as they do in *Robo Vampire*) from slathered in pancake makeup to horrifically decomposed. One of the hopping vampires in *Robo Vampire* even has a simian-like face—an obvious cheap Halloween gorilla mask.

The plot of *Robo Vampire* is nigh incomprehensible but revolves around a heroin cartel run by one Mr. Young, who, when his operations are threatened by the presence of American DEA agents, enlists hopping vampires for protection! One particular agent, Tom Wilde, proves to be a particularly pesky bee in Young's bonnet.

During a shootout with Boss Young's men, the vampires appear and suck Tom's "*qi*" right out of him. (Don't you hate when that happens?) Back at headquarters, Tom is hooked up to a machine which registers a "+" for alive and a "-" for no *qi*/lifeforce/dead. Unfortunately, it's minus for Tom. As the doctors exit the operating room, they pass two soldiers and this exchange occurs.

Soldier #1: So how's Tom?
Doctor: It was a fatal wound. He's dead.
Soldier #1 to Soldier #2: Since Tom is dead, I want to make use of his body to make an android-like robot . . . I would appreciate you approving my application.
Soldier #2: Are you assured of its success?
Soldier #1: Hmm-hmm
Soldier #2: Alright, your application is approved.

So much for bureaucratic red tape . . .

Tom is turned into ROBO WARRIOR! He's impervious to bullets and has superhuman strength and expert marksmanship. He's also wearing a costume which looks like something a parent would make if their child needed a Robocop costume the very next day, and all the parent had at hand were everyday household items and a surplus of silver lamé. (The two-foot-long radio antennae affixed to Robo Warrior's visor is a particularly nice touch. Perhaps they figured he'd like to pick up a little talk radio to listen to while he's doing his blasting.) Robo Warrior moves like the robot in Styx's "Mr. Roboto" video and announces his presence by heavy Foley footsteps which continue even while he's standing still.

Much of *Robo Vampire*'s impenetrability stems from the fact that it's obviously two separate films edited together to form a (barely) cohesive whole: One, the vampire/robot nonsense, and the other, a much more gritty and conventional tale of an Asian village battling drug smugglers. To wit: A female DEA agent is kidnapped and Robo Warrior is tasked with her rescue. However, she's obviously a character from the second film as she and Robo Warrior share nary a single scene together!

Instead, we get Robo Warrior standing still and shooting where he's not looking as vampires hop around him in a demented version of "Ring Around the Rosy," and Beast Vampire (the one with the monkey face) shoots fireworks at him.

Robo Vampire is audacious filmmaking at its most egregious. The poster art depicts the actual Peter Weller *Robocop*, and the title is a complete misnomer. Yes, the film contains a robot and vampires, but never once does a robot *become* a vampire or vice versa. Instead, we'll have to settle with the kung fu fighting female ghost who distracts her enemies by baring her breasts. Yep, it's that sort of film.

RUN LIKE HELL (1995)

Nineteen-ninety-five's *Run Like Hell*[10] takes place in the far-off future of 2008, minus the *Mad Max* interceptor vehicles and other tropes of the post-apocalyptic genre. Actually, there are hardly any vehicles at all—likely because vehicles cost money and this one looks like it was shot for a tenth of the gas budget of *Fury Road*. Goethe said, "There's nothing worse than aggressive stupidity," so we'd love to hear his thoughts from beyond the grave on this one, easily one of the most aggressively stupid action films of all time and glorious in its own "let's throw everything at a wall and see what sticks" sort of way.

War and disease have decimated the world. In order to keep the population in check, the "new, corrupt central government" has declared single women a threat to society. (This should be a sure-fire means of having your government toppled immediately, but here it makes zero sense whatsoever.) There are bounties on the heads of unattached women, and they are hunted down and imprisoned in a structure which looks like a sugar refinery. We know this because the exact same shot of the structure is shown repeatedly, again and again, before every scene that takes place in the "penitentiary."

The prison is run with an iron jaw . . . er, fist by an unscrupulous warden played by Robert Z'Dar—Yamashita himself from *Samurai Cop*. Z'Dar's character is never named, so he will henceforth be referred to as The Warden. He's first glimpsed while watching a Sapphic shower on his surveillance monitor. For the next approximate five minutes, the film cuts from scenes of the two topless women soaping each other up to reaction shots of Z'Dar looking either really horny or really confused, much like the viewer. He wants the prisoners in his office STAT, and they are immediately brought in, still topless yet completely dry from hair to toe.

The Warden shoos his guards away, then attempts to have his way sexually with one inmate, but she manages to beat him down with his own Billy club. Apparently, the Warden's lechery was well known among the prison populace, so this titillating ruse was hatched in order for some of the prisoners to break out of the facility. The inmates convene with two other topless, thong-clad women who are in the midst of distracting a guard through flirtation. A shootout ensues, complete with blood spatters on the walls that look like they came from a paintball gun, and our bare, buxom heroes manage to break free.

Upon exodus, the quartet hatches their plan—still topless, mind you. The de facto leader Elsa mentions, "The guard I was sleeping with told me there was a division point just beyond the ridge. They'll want us to sleep with them in trade for supplies." "So we'll have to fuck them for guns," says another. "Oh, we're gonna fuck them all right," responds Elsa. "Just not in the way they're expecting." Meanwhile, the duped Warden is calling for backup to bring the girls back dead or alive. This means summoning a cyborg bounty hunter (in shades and a trench coat, natch) and his droid partner (just a guy in combat fatigues and a motorcycle visor since budgetary constraints obviously precluded any sort of robot suit).

The girls manage to make off with clothes and supplies at the division point, though why two numbskulls in a Podunk shack in the middle of the desert would have a cache of mini skirts,

Daisy Dukes, and halter tops is never clarified. Of course, it's not an easy escape and the worst shootout ever ensues, featuring one of the girls stomping around as if she were crushing grapes for some homemade plonk.

That night, while sitting around a campfire, Elsa relays their destination. For in post-apocalyptic films, there must always be some legendary, quasi-mystical journey's end. "We're heading for Paradise City, where anyone can be themselves. Where dreams lie in wait for anyone that seeks them." At least no one can accuse the screenwriter of plagiarizing Guns N' Roses.

Before you can say gratuitous booby shots, the girls are attacked by a Country & Western-wear bandit incongruously wielding a sword, and things are not looking good until a lone black-clad figure is spotted in the distance. A NINJA!!! He saves their respective well-toned rumps, introduces himself as Jag, and although his destiny is elsewhere—namely to emerge victorious in The Arena—he'll follow the girls for a while and teach them how to fight. Which of course can only mean one thing. Training Montage![11]

There are just so many cul-de-sac subplots and non-sequiturs in the ADHD-fest that is *Run Like Hell,* it's hard to know where to begin. While following the girls to Paradise City, the film cuts away for a good 15 minutes to introduce John Steel, a bounty tracker taking a girl back to her parents. She gets offed pretty quickly by slave traders, but at least we get to see Steel, in a scene with zero context, kung fu fighting a random adversary on a flatbed parked in between two Wal-Mart trucks. (Civilization may be a shell of its former self, but the world's largest retailer still endures.) There's also talk of mutants that come out at night, but the only character with any mutation whatsoever is witnessed during the day and is just some guy with a face covered in silly string.

And lest we forget The Arena, which, as is par for the course for this film, is *not* a physical building but merely a small grove in the desert. There, Jag the Ninja must face a masked, chainsaw-wielding Leatherface-type. Throw in a prison-basement-naked-catfighting-league, and we're left with Spaghetti Theory filmmaking where the al dente pasta isn't exactly adhering to the wall.

Run Like Hell is a scant 80 minutes, but its poor pacing renders it a slog worthy of Bertolucci's *1900,* which tests the bladder at a whopping five hours plus and remains the longest film that these writers have ever watched in one protracted, interminable sitting. And the viewer hoping to witness the lustful Warden get his comeuppance is in for a bit of a letdown as the film ends ambiguously in anticipation of a sequel that never came. Still, a film that features cyborgs, ninjas, *and* mutants (of sorts), plus more eye-popping nudity than an Ibiza beach has got to be worth at least a rental.

ELIMINATORS (1986)

If ever a movie needed a definite article, it's definitely this. However, while we're on the subject of adding things, it's nigh impossible to improve upon a cyborg buddy revenge film that features Neanderthals getting beaten with nunchucks by a ninja who fishes telekinetically. (Even if you consider for a moment that if he's able to summon fish out of rivers using his mind, perhaps he could've used the same technique to control the nunchucks, thus avoiding placing himself in harm's way with the cavemen. But that's just one of many questions raised.)

We're introduced to *Eliminators* through an ocular prosthesis, a red-eye backdrop to a montage of breast-plated soldiers, and then a light aircraft pilot yelling "Mayday!" What these disparate elements could've meant to people watching this in a theatre in the '80s is anyone's guess, but we later find out it's a former pilot/ current cyborg's attempt to bring a centurion's shield back from Imperial Rome.

The ocular prosthesis belongs to a lab-created, time-traveling killing machine and the brainchild of an evil scientist criminal mastermind known as a Mandroid (Robocop essentially). And really, is there any better mastermind than a criminally inclined one? His reluctant assistant Takada, sensing much like Einstein did that the fruits of his labors would eventually lead to mass destruction, gives his own life to help the Mandroid escape, which it does, scuttling away on a kitted out ATV with tank treads. This prompts one of the many questions brought up in this discussion: If the creation has the ability to time travel over millennia, how is its main means of transport essentially a souped-up golf cart?

Mandroid tracks down one Colonel Nora Hunter, a blonde researcher visionary who doesn't envision the need to behave modestly around menfolk and whose research was pilfered by the evil genius. Hunter is played by Denise Crosby, Security Chief Tasha Yar on *Star Trek: The Next Generation*, who boldly goes without a bra here.

She agrees to help Mandroid thwart Dr. Very Evil's unspecific evil plans and brings along a mini floating helper robot which resembles a rice maker, crafted from spare droid parts and outfitted with a slide-out calculator (but no keyboard) as an interface.

Believing that the evil genius is hiding out somewhere in Mexico, Hunter hires a riverboat captain to track him down. Not by sourcing competing bids by independent contractors, mind you, but by having a bunch of them duke it out in a bar. After a barrel-shaped, plaid-shirted woman wipes the floor with the bulk of the "river rats," she's KO'd by a beer bottle and *voila*—lazy salvage man-cum-soldier-of-fortune Harry Fontana wins the bid.

Together, the threesome goes downriver—or is it up? It's hard to know which end is which in this baffling exercise—with aggrieved criminal boat captains in hot pursuit, threatening to "blow their top hats clear to Texas."

They're eventually kidnapped when their vessel runs aground. Not by bandits hiding in the hills, but by hairy spear-chucking Neanderthals who could easily pass for Donald Trump's security detail. Luckily our heroes manage to escape by throwing bullets into their fire, that all too common persistent movie myth that exposing cartridges to open flame causes an immediate explosion. The heroes then flee by raft, propelled by none other than the cyborg's outboard motor feet!

It's not too difficult to know where to go from here because really, if you already have a time-traveling, Segway-riding, laser-shooting, lesbian bar brawling, cutesy robot action film, you're still short one indispensable component: a ninja. (Man, did the '80s love their ninjas.) The kung fu man is the late lab assistant Takada's son, who just happens to be traipsing around Mexico in the very same vicinity as our intrepid stars.

There are so many reasons to laud *Eliminators*. Whether it's an attempt to conceal Mandroid's identity by draping a tarp over him and having him don an open crown hat sourced from wrestler The Undertaker's greenroom, or terrific lines like Hunter to the Mandroid: "You weren't given much memory storage." That's a considerable drawback for a killer cyborg tasked variously to explore ancient Rome and drive a tank. They gave him the capabilities of lassoing small arms away from antagonists and underwater self-propulsion but came up short in the Random-Access Memory department (but at least he wasn't given a mustache like poor, beefy R.O.T.O.R.).

There are also choice lines like "*Quo vadis*? That's Italian for we kick ass!" Hmmm. Certainly a unique spin on Apostle Peter's famous query of *quo vadis*? or "Where are you going?" to Jesus along the Appian Way. Especially since the Italian language hadn't yet materialized from Latin for another several hundred years.

Either way, it's really impossible to know where *Eliminators* will take you, but you'll definitely find wacky movie salvation along the way.

WIRED TO KILL (1986)

In a book with *Hard to Kill* and *Hired to Kill*, it was practically alphabetical elimination that we'd finally get to *Wired to Kill*.

It is 1998. The US Constitution has been amended and the contentious Second Amendment right to bear arms now includes . . . the right to detoxification. However, this has nothing to do with cleanses and bowel movements.

Crime is so entrenched that homeowners are booby-trapping their domiciles with motion-activated sprays known as antipersonnel devices. As Thomas Hobbes put it, "'THE RIGHT of Nature,'. . . *jus naturale*[12] . . . is the liberty each man hath to use his own power as he will himself for the preservation of his own nature."

A bunch of robbers in this dystopia learn a tough lesson about the brutish state of nature and also about one suburban home's elaborate defense capabilities. And it's not like they weren't warned. The sign did say "PREMISES PROTECTED BY CAUSTIC SOLUTION," a city-approved ordinance.

The thugs regroup after their spraying down and decide to head down to the barrios where the *casas* aren't as heavily fortified.

There, we're introduced to enterprising engineer Steve via "Yankee Doodle Dandy" Civil War pipe music. He's a surfer dude, budding EDM musician, and inventor of Winston, a personal android that looks like it'd be recycled parts in a *BattleBots* scrap. Steve, limbs perennially exposed in his wife beater tank top, controls the device remotely via a glove strapped to his forearm. The gizmo doesn't have the deftest touch, however. When it tries to pick up glasses, it shatters them like a glass at a Jewish wedding.

Winston is also attached to a closed-circuit television, so he can prank attractive women using robotic arms to hike up their skirts. Hey, it was the '80s!

But all is not well.

Steve's hood is burning, much like Detroit of old, and Detroit of new. Brigands, who operate by torchlight and don mining helmet floodlights, bust into Steve's home, viciously attack him and his family, and put Grandma in the morgue.

The thugs, one of whom is played by Hulk Hogan's antagonist in *No Holds Barred*, the strapping Tommy 'Tiny' Lister, are promptly arrested. However, they get off on a technicality. The gang, fearing they'll be fingered by the survivors, decide to intimidate, then run down Mom, putting her in the hospital with a broken back.

In one of the numerous infirmary motifs running through *Wired to Kill*, we see a future that is automated. You can sue your personal physician by dialing 1-800-MY-BODY. You can also call to get quick justice via 1-800-CIVIL-LIBERTY, an odd government service given that homes have the constitutional right to shoot toxins at unwanted intruders. Anyhow, someone in 1985 thought that toll-free 1-800 telecommunication lines were THE FUTURE!

Steve manages to survive the home invasion, but he's left with *Blade Runner* legs—not the movie but the South African murdering runner. Since he's wheelchair bound, the gang figures he's not much of a threat to their operations anymore.

How wrong could they have been? Steve is one wheel ahead of the goons, keeping himself busy by manufacturing IEDs and testing Winston to shoot off gunfire. He's also attached the bot to the underside of the gang's vehicle to listen in on their conversations. Luckily for the film's plot, the gang blather on incessantly about their criminal exploits, including admitting to "the old bitch they wiped out at the house," rather than keeping their conversations to less controversial topics like the weather or the fortunes of the local basketball team.

Steve and girlfriend Rebecca eavesdrop on a dope deal that will involve a hooker, so Steve's girlfriend goes undercover as a lady of the evening to sell the gang fake drugs and to get intel on the specific perps responsible for the attack. They could've just indiscriminately wasted hundreds of them, *Death Wish 3* style, but we digress. There's only one Bronson after all, and he ain't here.

With their new info, Steve and Rebecca are primed to hunt down the baddies. And while this may be a dystopian hellscape, military-grade binoculars, night-scopes, and tons of ammo are conveniently available at your better army surplus stores.

Dependable Winston is pimped out to shoot rounds and knives. Thinking the thugs will come back to finish off Mom, Steve surreptitiously places the remotely controlled-via-camera Winston underneath her hospital bed.

Sure enough, the assassin arrives on cue, and to the strains of some tub-thumping tuba music, and the bot grabs him by the balls and wheels him out into the hallway before flinging him down a flight of stairs.

What's extraordinary about *Wired to Kill* though isn't just the impossibly vast geographical range and capabilities of Winston, but that when Rebecca is eventually revenge-kidnapped by the gang, they don't have any designs on her sexually. Instead, they use her as the female lead in an impromptu production of *Romeo and Juliet*!

The head goon, likely a beneficiary of a well-rounded education in the humanities before he turned to a life of crime, even quotes passages at length: "O, then, dear saint, let lips do what hands do. They pray; grant thou, lest faith turn to despair."

Just when you thought you'd seen it all. . .

LAND OF DOOM (1986)

"The nuclear holocaust wiped all semblance of rhyme or reason. All that's left is a parched arid wasteland . . . And whoever controls the water, controls the world." Stop us if you've heard this before. No really, that's not an expression. Please stop us, we can't take it anymore.

Wait, wrong movie. The above is from *Stryker*. It's hard to keep these wasteland movies straight. Ah, close enough. That one's another *Road Warrior/Escape from New York* facsimile where all the evil guys shopped at the Goggle Depot and ransacked John Travolta's closet for leather jackets. At least *Stryker* offered an explanation as to why humanity is in the state it's in.

For *Land of Doom*, you have to guess. Global warming?

Land of Doom is not so much a *Mad Max* as a Mildly Miffed Maxine. It's also set in a post-apocalyptic desert wasteland where heroine Harmony, who has a penchant for groin kicking everything in sight, doesn't exactly live up to her amity name.

In a post-nuclear age, this warrior princess (Deborah Rennard, ex of *Dallas* and ex of *Million Dollar Baby* millionaire and ex-Scientologist Paul Haggis) sports a black thong worn outside her khaki ensemble and is basically a paragon of self-sufficiency. Reluctantly, she teams up with a suave soldier of fortune, Anderson, and they combine their efforts to battle against roaming and ominous Raiders.

The Raiders are kitted out much like their NFL namesake's fans, who themselves ape wrestling stalwarts, The Road Warriors, a.k.a. the Legion of Doom. *Land of Doom*, Legion of Doom . . . it all comes out in the wash when you're squaring the circle of who's ripped off whom.

The Raiders race souped-up vans and motorbikes across the landscape, much like *Mad Max Beyond Thunderdome* and Tupac and Dre's "California Love" video. Or at least it would be if the production values of those two were less than an average bachelor party and they were lensed in a Turkish desert.

In the course of their travels, Harmony and Anderson fight off a cannibal bearing a crossbow and speaking in an extremely unconvincing and highly incongruous French accent. There are also *Star Wars'* Jawa midget knock-offs who scurry in from offscreen, then scurry back again with nary a backstory's thought given to them. (Then again, the Jawas in *Star Wars* didn't have much of a backstory either, so we'll give them this one.)

The duo's mission: to "head south" while avoiding Raider gangs and the plague to find a land free from one, or ideally both. And not to quibble much, but for a land decimated by an undefined plague, no one on screen seems particularly ailing.

If only it were so easy! (It sort of is though, as nowhere in *Land of Doom* does anyone seem to avail themselves of any of the readily available water.)

Cheap and cheerful, the movie features sizzling interchanges like "We got jumped by surprise!" (Er, that's kind of the point), "Do you have an outhouse I can use? It's somewhere outside." (One would hope), and "There's food on the table" (see, previous). Harmony's discourse consists almost exclusively of different ways of saying she doesn't like being touched and repeating that she "can take care of herself" about a dozen times.

Along the way, our intrepid duo encounters a balding medieval buff ally who's traversing the arid desert by bicycle, puppy in tow and armed with a flame thrower and an instrument that looks like a bouzouki—because that's what you need to survive in post-plague civilization: a Greek stringed instrument. So much for packing light in this inhospitable milieu.

There's also the sadistic Raider leader who looks like he wandered in off the set of *Phantom of the Paradise*. He's a puffy-maned blonde named Slater, a moniker better suited to the captain of a high school lacrosse team than a warlord who favors chains and torture. He does sport a luxurious blonde bouffant hairdo which looks like it's been conditioned nicely, so maybe someone is using that water after all.

Director Peter Maris is also responsible for the lurid vigilante Vietnam vet video nasty *Delirium* and the abysmal alien-invasion flick *Alien Species*. So his range is not in question, only his talent.

Land of Doom's explosive cave shoot 'em up finale is gleefully corny, with a peppy major key score, a flamethrower-wielding character running in to save the day, and gas mask-wearing gang members sent flying.

In the realm of rip-offs, it's impossible not to be charmed . . . well . . . to the *Max*.

FUTURE FORCE (1989)

The man in me will hide sometimes
To keep from being seen.
But that's just because he doesn't want
To turn into some machine.

"The Man in Me,"
Bob Dylan

Announcing itself by way of the awesome-sounding Action International Pictures, we find ourselves in a future where "You are presumed guilty 'til you are proven innocent and have a right to die." So much for *habeas corpus* in the looming abyss that is "THE YEAR 1991."

Oddly, *Future Force* was filmed in 1988. Maybe director David A. Prior (*Deadly Prey*) thought we were only a few years, um . . . prior to being overrun by a savage police state, populated by private, unaccountable rent-a-cops. George Zimmermans, but a hint more stylish and not nearly as plump or immoral.

Usually, movies which spotlight some dystopian hellscape are set well into some far-flung future, but when a budget is this miniscule, the future is now. As such, 1991 looks remarkably similar to 1988. Who would've thought?

And it's an ugly, um, "future." Crime in America is out of control, running rampant in fact, with overloaded prison populations, cities turned into war zones, and neighborhoods with nary a locally sourced gluten-free mason jar of organic tea to be had.

And it doesn't help matters that justice, such as it is, is meted out to suspects if they're "in the computer," the be-all, end-all authority that cannot be questioned. Did *Future Force* forecast the era of DNA databases? In a word, no.

The man taking down all the criminal riffraff? A groin-punching David Carradine, who we're introduced to laughably from the ground up; the camera panning from his sturdy boots as they step out of his police vehicle, zooming past his paunch, then up to his hula-hoop thin arms.

He's John Tucker, a denim-resplendent member of C.O.P.S., the Civilian Operated Police Systems. If this is the future of law enforcement—a ripened David Carradine who spins his revolver around his hip before returning it to its holster like he's dueling in Tombstone—we're all in trouble.

He's basically a bounty hunter and "top gun in his precinct." Faint praise indeed, as the precinct is populated by on-the-take mustachioed layabouts who frequent strip clubs, get into bar brawls, and guzzle beer.

When things get out of hand at the local "gentlemen's club," the aproned barman fires a shotgun into the air, Moe Szyslak style, as a call for calm. At least he's not engaged in that time-honored movie cliché of cleaning the glasses. Movie bartenders, regardless of whether their establishments are the kinds of places that would even bother cleaning their glasses, seem to never be taxed by drink lineups and are free to passively polish away while all the action goes on in front of them. (And do the glasses in some of these decidedly down-market watering holes really *need* to be that clean?)

Tucker basically sits around in these kinds of establishments, waiting for an assignment. His bosses urge him to "bring one in alive for once!" but when you consider the urban scum he's responsible for tracking down, you can understand why this isn't a hard and fast rule.

Carradine's Tucker, way too elder a statesman to be taking on young bucks, compensates for his lack of physical gifts by sporting a comically oversized prosthetic arm that shoots lasers. Why? This is the future, remember! It was some government science experiment or something, perhaps the same kind that's affected our short-term memory.

The device, when fitted to Carradine's pipe cleaner arm, looks like an oversized novelty hand you'd wave at a football game. Still, it's powerful enough that, when activated, can stop vehicles driven by ponytailed trash-talkers dead in their tracks.

Even without the hand, Tucker is the quickest draw in the land, shooting out a strip club television Elvis-style from his perch in perv row[13] while relaxing between bounty hunting gigs.

A reporter tasked to "smile and read the copy," becomes the Woodward and Bernstein of B-movies when she finds herself in possession of a surveillance tape exposing the C.O.P.S. higher-ups for who they really are—venal law and order sadists.

Of course, the lady journalist soon finds herself "in the computer" and marked for termination. Tucker gets the assignment, and while he's trying to take the scribe alive, his authority is questioned by C.O.P.S. brass who insist she be killed outright. Soon he's battling mulleted hoodlums who cackle like morons. He's then involved in a breakneck car chase through an industrial wasteland (where everyone in future dystopias invariably live). Tucker lobs a tear gas canister at his pursuers, blinding them before sneaking around their ride and nudging them off a rock face with his bumper.

Ultimately, Tucker is forced to follow his conscience. He must battle evil colleagues who also run a protection racket on the side and flatten double-crossers into waffles using industrial car crushers, all the while musing optimistically about the niceness of the next day. And the corrupt C.O.P.S. *capo* is in cahoots with, of all people, an underworld figure who's also a man of the cloth.

"I want some more of your ass," is one bald goon's goading line to Tucker. Is that a threat or a come on? Either way, he gets a straight punch right to the family jewels to erase all doubt.

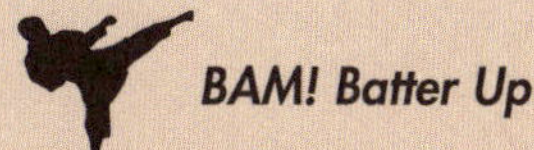

BAM! Batter Up

If you're a budding henchman (and this really should be covered in any *Introductory Henchman 101* textbook), a bat is intended for causing blunt force trauma to the cranium and not for strangulation (a handy length of rope would work just fine for that purpose). So please resist the urge to sneak up behind a hero and throttle them since it's inevitable they will use the force of a nearby wall to kick themselves backward, thereby breaking your grip.

ROLLER BLADE (1986)

Roller Blade begins pretty much the same as every post-apocalyptic film: on-screen text elucidating what caused humanity to regress to such a pre-civilized state. Only this crawl is so vague, *Green Eggs and Ham* has more exposition. We are in "The City of Los Angeles" during the "Second Dark Age." That's it; that's all we learn. Luckily, for non-readers or those with short-term amnesia, *Roller Blade* also features two scantily clad women rolling toward the camera brandishing blades. Literalism at its finest in a movie which never misses an opportunity to depict scores of women stripping down to their thongs, be it to fight, to train, to pray, or to participate in nude Sapphic hot tub cleansing rituals.

"Write what you know" might also apply to directing, and if there's one thing that can be said about Donald G. Jackson (helmer of the Roddy Piper vehicle *Hell Comes to Frogtown)*, he really knows his roller blades as he's responsible for directing seven (!) further films with either the words "Roller" or "Blade" in the title.

The "Second Dark Age" is a time when batteries are precious commodities and everyone tools around in leotards and on roller skates. It's also a callback to the first since all spout *thee, thou, thy,* and *verily* like they're roller-refugees from a Renaissance Faire. We learn that there was a time when people skated for fun; now they either "skate or die."

There are two groups locked in dire conflict. The first, evil Doctor Saticoy and his minions. The second, the Cosmic Order of Roller Blade, a convent comprised of women who look like they walked off the set of a Mötley Crüe video, led by the sage, Teutonic Mother Speed. Although confined to a wheelchair, she still wears her skates!

The Order, kitted out in what looks like a cross between a nun's habit and a red Ku Klux Klan hood, are the guardians of the Power Crystal, a talisman which has the power to mend the broken world. They also have the ability to use their knives to heal, waving them over a wound as psychedelic happy faces flash on screen. ("With this blade, thy shall be healed.") This prompts the question of why they don't actually *use* their stupid crystal and healing powers rather than sitting on it and letting everyone else suffer?

They're also "the only force on Earth where weapons and tools of combat are converted into tools of love." Like a marital aid? It's not specified. While the sisters are all proficient in various fighting styles and weaponry, they're really all about love. But these are dark times (the second!) and the sisters must put away the hippy-drippy gobbledegook and get out there to kick some heinie!

Their stronghold has enough smiley face emoji décor to trigger an acid flashback, and this contrasts nicely with the surreal milieu of Doctor Saticoy's lair, which boasts as its most prominent design feature suspended, upside down revolving shopping carts.

Although Saticoy is the heavy, he's not fully shown until a good hour into the film. Before that, all of Saticoy's communiques are mediated through a rubber-monster sort of thing that has the face of a shrunken-head Billy Barty. When the camera finally pulls back from the creature, it's revealed that the monster is indeed a puppet that's actually part of Saticoy, its rubberized, wrinkly face plopped onto a cheap silver spray-painted baby doll. Saticoy, for his part, is a disappointing generic big guy in a red jumpsuit and gimp mask. This implies that anyone wearing a gimp mask could be described as generic, but with dreams of Lord Humungus dancing in our heads, Saticoy can't help but disappoint.

The Order gives sanctuary to a she-wolf named Hunter. She is initiated into the Order's ways, ordained, and given the name Sister Fortune. Good fortune for her perhaps, but bad for the Order, as Hunter is really a traitorous mole working for Saticoy and makes off with the crystal. Mother Speed sends out Sister Sharon and her Bod Sisters (more excellent literalism) to both retrieve the Power Crystal and rescue Little Chris, the kidnapped son of the local chief of the Roller Police.

Will the Bod Sisters manage to recover the Power Crystal and return it to its rightful place? Will Little Chris be rescued? Will the evil Saticoy be vanquished? Will cosmic skating order be restored to the galaxy? Is the rubber hand puppet an organic part of Saticoy's body á la Kuato in *Total Recall*, or is Saticoy some sort of demented ventriloquist? Is the Pope Catholic? We're just testing to see if you're paying attention. To answer all these pertinent questions, glide your way over to this post-apocalyptic piece of puerility called *Roller Blade*.

22 ROBOT HOLOCAUST (1986)

It's the future. Humans coexist with robots. These robots grow crops and perform all manual labor, and humanity is buffeted from shifting economic headwinds that previously plagued us. People are free to roam about in unprecedented safety, to explore hobbies and self-actualize, realize untapped potential, get to know their neighbors in a new era of peace, love, and . . . ah, who are we kidding? Robots are mean, vindictive, they hate being anthropomorphized (we're guessing, it's hard to know how they feel) and in this movie, they "brought the world to its knees" in a "robot holocaust." The world, thusly genuflected, is forced to live in absolute servility.

Here's a handy reference for knowing when a movie is bad: when the title is mentioned somewhere in the dialogue. This of course excludes biopics where it'd be near-impossible for someone not to utter, "Malcolm X!" or "Ray!" And here's another handy reference: a movie is really bad when its title is said in a voiceover. Hell, voiceovers themselves are a sure sign of bad.

Robot Holocaust is a dystopia. You might've guessed from the title that it's not about a large suburban family who decides to adopt a loveable Belgian sheepdog. In this society, "free-bots," brazen C-3PO rip-offs but with less lustre and more bulk, commit petty crime to pay for their own mechanical upkeep, a strange conceit in a world with no visibly functioning economy or currency.

And what's left of humanity is a hardscrabble group of survivors of the "robot rebellion of 33." Kudos to the director for leaving the chronology open-ended rather than the usual nonsense we've come to expect from dystopian hellscapes like "In the year 2020, human beings have gills and swim in giant vats of gin martinis."

Apparently, the human-robot rebellion of 33 battle left radiation residue, "poisoning the air," and creating a subservient class of "airslaves" controlled by the Dark One, an evil being who controls the atmosphere through a power station and an army of evil robots. He keeps the facility running at full tilt, and as soon as there's any kind of uprising, alters the balance to choke dissident forces.

He has indentured servants bring fuel to the station, causing one of them to remark, "If we stop bringing fuel to the power station, the Dark One will have no power to control us." With this pathetic an opposition, it's no wonder the Dark One's reign of terror has been so long-lasting.

However, one thing stands in the Dark One's way; two if you count the help—his second-in-charge is Valeria, a boa-and-heels vamp who looks like a Dodge City prostitute. She delivers flattened lines as if she were in an English instructional video and operates the Room of Questions, a chamber which forces people to answer questions truthfully. We've got quite a few questions. Can we visit?

Dark One is opposed by rebel forces, some of whom have built up an immunity to nasty atmospheres. Like Los Angelinos. Their leader is Neo à la *The Matrix*, an anagram even the most bored-out-of-their-mind armchair critic would recognize as the "One." He's a central casting Mad Max type, except for constrictive armbands to give him muscle tone. He posits that the Dark One may not know that there are people immune to the toxic environs, and therein lies their advantage.

He and the rebels martial their forces in post-apocalyptic New York City, in what looks like Van Cortland Park in the Bronx. This area is

"The She Zone," where men dare not pass, populated by women "from the wasteland" who deem men "useless and crazy" (hard to argue). However, they keep a male warrior slave on hand to supply. . .um. . .the stuff of life.

The ladies put aside gender differences and join the gents in the fight against the Dark One and to rescue a scientist being held captive at the Power Station, one who can apparently run the whole shebang should that be required.

But really, like most villains, the Dark One has all the cool stuff. This includes the Pleasure Machine, a reward for fealty to him. It's a cage attached to what looks like a glorified Van de Graaff generator, that electron collator that creates hilarious static hair. When users step inside the Pleasure Machine and activate the ball, it removes their clothes. This thing must be a blast at parties. And when it's engaged, nude dancers emerge out of the blue to gyrate around it. Then again, dancing in a circle is ancient and cross-cultural. Old habits aren't as easy to shake as a booty.

But there's more. The Dark One also has a green pulsating panopticon that looks like a party store orb. It's through this he can (mostly) see what his subjects are up to, which it should be said, is not a hell of a lot. The rebel forces are among the least active we've ever seen.

The authors of *Mine's Bigger Than Yours* are usually sticklers for exhaustive research. However, when it comes to *Robot Holocaust's* director Tim Kincaid's oeuvre, we've decided to depend on *Wikipedia* exclusively. Under the pen name "Joe Cage" Kincaid directed "landmark American gay pornography" from the '70s. Who knows? Maybe his *El Paso Wrecking Corp*, *L.A. Tool & Die*, and *Kansas City Trucking Co.* were the *Star Wars* trilogy of gay porn. Kincaid is the first recipient of a GAYVN Award we've covered in these pages, accolades given out annually, most recently (and appropriately) at Vegas's Hard Rock, an easy word-switcheroo the least creative event organizer could run with.

Boasting perhaps the single lowest *IMDb* viewer rating of any film in this book, *Robot Holocaust* can't be faulted for living up to (or down to depending on your frame of reference) its title.

Elon Musk once warned that artificial intelligence is "potentially more dangerous than nukes." Luckily, *Robot Holocaust* features very little in the way of intelligence, artificial or otherwise.

SPACE MUTINY (1988)

These days, ports around the globe have been automated, and the loading and offloading of cargo ships now involve robotics and sophisticated logistical networks. That's what makes the vision of "the future" as depicted in *Space Mutiny* so hilarious.

When a small spacecraft is about to dock at the colossus known as the *Southern Sun*, the crew still use roger/over breaker-breaker trucking language to guide it into port. And the *Southern Sun* still has boiler rooms and catwalks, and worse, land lines.

Isn't the future amazing?

In terms of size and amenities the *Southern Sun* puts the Imperial-class Star Destroyer to shame, even if every single minute of *Star Wars'* screen time puts *Space Mutiny* to shame.

The *Southern Sun* may sound like an ocean cruise liner, but it's a massive exploration vessel housing several thousand Earth expats. In humanity's future, Earth is overpopulated. Therefore, these intrepid explorers adorned in inverted triangle unis (the favored couture in multiple universes) are traveling far afield in hopes of colonizing a new home.

This might sound like a bit of needless backstory when they could've just gone with the time-honored "our planet was blown up while we were away" storyline, but it's been the source of a lot of discussion online. After all, if you have the technology to build such an awesome multigenerational spacecraft, how hard would it be to follow and perfect China's one-child policy? And there's a case to be made that, to borrow a wonderful phrase from the Roman statesman Seneca, "If you don't know to which port one is sailing, no wind is favorable." Just tooling around in a giant spaceship, hoping one day to eventually find somewhere to live, isn't a very sound plan. Space is big. Like giant Costco Toblerone big. For example, it'd take 25,000 years to get to the Canis Major Dwarf Galaxy, and who the hell knows if there's anything there. Doesn't sound very impressive.

And really, when a movie lifts battle scenes wholesale out of *Battlestar Galactica*, it would seem there are bigger planetary fish to fry. If you're going to shoot a film that's set in space (for future reference) ideally lift footage from other genres where it's less likely to get noticed, if that's possible, and maybe not a hugely popular sci-fi series.

Things are going smoothly on board, to the best of our knowledge, and that's assuming our future selves are protected from the harmful carcinogenic radiation of space. The good ship even has a giant nightclub, where denizens dance with plastic hula hoops and favor very fashion forward wife-beaters.

There's a compelling subplot, introduced to pad the running time then largely abandoned, involving a beautiful race of telepathic dancing witch women on board who gaze at crystal balls. They're known as the Bellerians, and we're introduced to them at the beginning. They're welcomed aboard pretty early on, and then nearly written out of the final script entirely. (Probably for the best, as lines like "You're much more attractive with your mouth shut," means *Space Mutiny* isn't Bechdel-ready, a bevy of seductive necromancers be damned.)

But all is not well on the ship.

"It is cruel fate to be born in space!"

Some of the ship natives are getting restless,

including evil Kalgan, head of the vessel's security detail. He wants to hijack the craft and take it to the Corona Borealis, a constellation which was known to medieval Arab astronomers as al-Fakkah. Fitting for a film that's *fakakta*.

Kalgan commandeers some explosives, and in a cynical act of space terrorism, blows up the docking hatch's guider beam technology. In sci-fi movies, just putting "space" in front of something is enough to confer linguistic legitimacy, as Kalgan's co-conspirators threaten to turn the Southern Sun's crew into "space dust." As opposed to just, you know, dust.

The explosion kills one of the occupants of the landing vessel, but luckily, not the captain, Ryder, played by the relentlessly positive, ever-smiling beacon of naiveté, Reb Brown.

The ship's commander is Alex Jansen (Cameron Mitchell, with a glued-on beard that makes him resemble an Orson Welles mall Santa), sporting a polyethylene blue necktie that would make you Glad® you're not him. He welcomes Ryder aboard and tries to get to the bottom of what happened. The ship's crew chalk the mishap up to a malfunction and things carry on as they did before, with much boogieing down at the hula bar while zooming through the empty void.

Eventually, Ryder, with the help of Jansen's daughter Lea (Reb's real-life wife Cisse) get wind of the plot and must battle Kalgan loyalists determined to steer the vessel into pirate territory. All the while viewers are treated to run-on hissing-villain dialogue like, "The survival of that viper pilot Ryder and the winning ways of Alex Jansen and his meddling daughter have caused us nothing but grief!" and "It's obvious I underestimated them."

Kalgan is one ruthless bastard, with a henchman who looks like a Roman centurion figure skater. They kidnap Lea, strap her down to a gurney, and Kalgan threatens her with a laser like in *Goldfinger*, all the while cackling, "I'm going to use this laser on one of your teeth. It works not unlike ancient dental equipment, not that you'd know anything about that." (Who would?) When she escapes, he tries to run the "space bitch" over. As opposed to just, you know, a bitch.

But really, it's all up to Reb Brown in his shimmering silver Sheena Easton disco pants to save the day. Or disco space pants, that is.

The hallway shoot-'em-ups are the stuff of Stormtrooper target practice (seriously, those guys charge headlong only to be picked off one by one), and things naturally move to the venue of so many shootouts, space or otherwise, the boiler room—the home of oh-so-many catwalks for shot henchman to tumble forward over.

It's said that in space nobody can hear you scream. But with all the indiscriminate yelling when people are shot up aboard the *Southern Sun*, it's more like in space, everyone can hear you Wilhelm scream. Plus, Reb Brown's in this. He's good for a solid shriek or two.

Space Mutiny was a notorious flop. And deservedly so. Despite being able to teleport astronauts a short distance, the old-school denouement features that all-time classic standby of action films—knocking someone out and putting on their clothing to avoid detection.

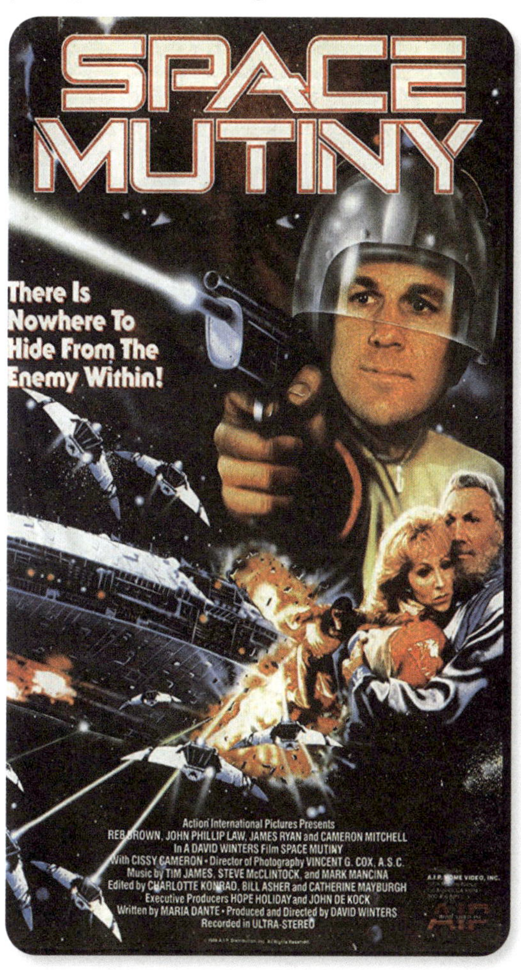

three

KICK-ASS WOMEN

IN USING WOMEN IN COMBAT, BECAUSE FEMALES ARE TOO FIERCE.

—MARGARET MEAD

In 2016, "The Beast" Eddie Hall deadlifted an astounding 500kg (1,102 lbs.), about twice what the sturdiest woman can lift. You can watch it on YouTube, but it's not particularly dignified. Sure, men are genetically far stronger than women, but really, cunning, guile, and ability are way more interesting attributes than brute strength. If you don't believe us, see if Arnold could mumble his way through a Bond movie.

A book with a title and topic like this, by guys like us, is perhaps not the first place you'd expect to see a vigorous, spirited celebration of the "fairer sex." But you'd be spectacularly wrong. Ergo, Kick-Ass Women.

Why not female action heroes? After all, childbirth is the sole argument required to know they're made of sterner stuff, not to mention how they power through common colds that leave men incapacitated. And that's not just conjecture—see *Time*'s "Why Men are Much Worse at Being Sick than Women."[14]

While we're far removed from action movie equality, in the genre, women have proven themselves to be just as capable of being badly attired, under-written, and under-plotted as the menfolk. They're also expert marksmen (sorry, markswomen . . . uh, markspeople?) and deadly martial artists, often with minimal training. Someone with those kinds of uber-perfect attributes is known colloquially as a "Mary Sue," but really, there's no shortage of those on the other side of the gender aisle, either. Women just get saddled with the unfair label. It's nothing a few well-timed training montages can't fix.

In 1941, Princess Diana of Themyscira, Daughter of Hippolyta, a.k.a. *Wonder Woman* (no wonder they shortened the name) was unleashed upon the world. DC Comics birthed a butt-kicking Amazon, capable of standing up to, then beating down, men. And as these following films demonstrate, Diana is not the only woman of wonder: far from it. So guys, put aside the testosterone and desire to hog the remote for a moment or two, and bask in the butt-kicking glory of the fairer, but no less deadlier, sex.

HIRED TO KILL (1990)

A *Zoolander* action caper that's pretty bananas. Or is it *Bananas*? When you add the rebels from the Woody Allen comedy and run it through a fashion model filter, you get this baffling counterrevolutionary lark. It's set in the fictional Mediterranean country of Cypra (actually a genus of the moth), which sounds more like an erectile dysfunction drug, not to mention the very real Republic of Cyprus. This was actually lensed in nearby Greece, and you'd figure this would've come up in conversation, unless this was co-director Nico Mastorakis's elaborate satire on the Cyprus Dispute. If so, that went over our heads since we don't follow the UN on *Twitter*.

We're introduced to head mercenary Ryan (*Cobra's* Brian Thompson) via a wakeup call, which calls to mind comedian Rodney Dangerfield's lament about a crappy hotel that missed his by a day and a half. Ryan doesn't answer it. In fact, he's so agitated he blows the phone away with a high-caliber pistol. Bit of an over-reaction, perhaps? You'd have to figure the inevitable ear ringing from an early morning gunshot would be far worse than the call.

He's tasked to lead a group of mercs into Cypra to oust Bartos, a tin-pot dictator whose mustache would give a Mexican sports bar logo envy, even if it weren't sported by the drunken legend master himself, noted souse Oliver Reed.[15] What Reed is doing in this piece of poo is a question that unfortunately can't be asked of him from beyond the grave without the aid of a reputable psychic.

The mercs' version of a Trojan horse: A fashion shoot with female model assassins descending on Bartos' sprawling island hacienda, led by a

noted American designer (Ryan, reluctant and very flamboyant when undercover). The ruse is that the girls are there to generate tourism, giving a jolt to both the island's economy and its menfolk. That this 6'3" beefcake and his crew are given free rein to an island run by a tyrannical dictator is a plot device that's a little hard to swallow; not having the Internet in 1990 is still no excuse for higher-ups not asking around to find out if this random American "fashion designer" really *is* a global leader in haute couture.

Lest you think Ryan is some kind of James Bond sophisticate—singlehandedly plowing through a gauntlet of women, shortening the lifespan of every villain by half and setting the baccarat tables ablaze—Ryan is fairly chaste and actually leans very heavily on his "models," who are all trained killers, to do the heavy lifting.

And given that this is a mercenary film, even if these mercs walk runways and lounge about in bikinis in their downtime, business is business. Each model killer comes equipped with a different look and specialty. A belligerent Aussie is the explosives expert (we're no expert, but constantly chewing on a cigar doesn't seem safe), and another is a dark-haired leggy Italian sharpshooter. And some have even done time at San Quentin. This is what you'd call a bit of inartistic license as the prison historically only held a handful of death row women. And you can bet none were this beautiful.

Anyhow, Ryan is an odd figure, the recipient of $350,000 upfront to do the job and that sum again if he completes the mission. Not bad, but also not great considering the substantial overhead that he's not even involving himself with sexually, not to mention risking his life and limb.

And speaking of body parts, while he's only undercover as a fashion designer, you could still call Ryan "Prada Face," as his lips are in a permanent purse with only a tiny hole as an opening. He's a perma-blowfish, even if he has no Blofeld as foil. It's a bit distracting. As is his casual resemblance to a gym rat Willem Dafoe with Matt Damon's melon head DNA spliced in.

You get the sense right off the bat that this banana republic—the state, not the fashion retailer—won't last too long, as Ryan's inside contact is Bartos's vixen lover. She's got the goods on how to connect with rebel allies hiding in the hills and how best to storm the dictator's compound and free weathered revolutionary Rallis. (Played by José Ferrer of *Lawrence of Arabia* fame, who bears an uncanny resemblance to an aging Fidel Castro, even if this film is about as political as an episode of *The Bachelorette*.)

Hired to Kill features everything you'd want in an action film: steely sunglass reflection gazes, workout montages where someone doing sit-ups goes in and out of the frame, henchman going ass over teakettle when grenades explode behind them, and of course, the all-time favorite genre staple: goons falling from balconies when they're shot instead of crumpling in a heap like the laws of physics dictate. And for the grand prize: An entirely extraneous Turkish prison/lesbian warden scene as well as a poolside catfight. And what film with fashion models would be complete without a photo-snapping costume-change montage? However, in *Hired to Kill*, even gazing at gorgeous women becomes exhausting.

The action though, brings the goods. We're no tactical doyens, but mercenaries under our command would probably spread out sneakily rather than approaching a target in single file and being visible from the naked eye from miles away. Luckily though, nobody's lives are in our hands.

HUSTLER SQUAD (1976)

There's a failed raid on a Japanese-occupied island and one lone survivor, Paco, a jovial fellow, is lucky to be alive after the spastic St Vitus' dance mow-down of all his Filipino rebel colleagues. He's summoned to Australia to help Allied troops get a sense of what they can expect should the Japanese try the stunt again, perhaps in another movie—one that looks like it could've conceivably taken place in World War II.

Major Stony Stonewell is the hard-bitten soldier plotting a sequel in order to roust the Japanese from their island stronghold. He's a hard-drinking gambler and hot head, and probably not the savviest man for the job, but hey, it's an "unorthodox mission for a guy with a devious mind." He hits the town with Paco to see if, over drinks, the two of them can hash out a way of besting the equally devious Japanese (they're particularly savvy in that they all appear to be ethnic Filipinos.)

After witnessing a prostitute clean "crikey"-accented army Aussie clocks in a bar brawl, a lightbulb goes off in Paco's good-natured noggin; maybe the fairer sex could do the island job? Or as they put it, "We can train 'em to kill the Jap brass!"

But who can they track down for such a mission? There's not exactly a deep talent pool of dead-eyed female assassins to draw from, even if they're dead-eyed when it comes to, oh, reading their lines. One unlikely conscript: a terminally ill volunteer Swedish nurse at a refugee camp! So far so good. Besides, she's got nothing to lose and wants to save lives fighting Imperial Japan with her few remaining days on the planet. But the rest of the pickings are pretty slim. In fact, the major bemoans, "What the world needs is a few more nymphomaniacs with killer instincts." Truer words have never been spoken.

Luckily, there's more where that came from in the form of a Filipina national whose family was wiped out/raped by the marauding army. She's understandably eager to join the mission regardless of the risk. Then there's the roughest, toughest inmate of the nearby women's prison, a sultry brunette who can't stop talking about how she needs a man and can't live without a man. To round out the crew, Stony strongarms a pimp to add a sweet blonde babe to his melange, for something "she's never done before." Nudge nudge, wink wink. She won't even utter the word "man" as it gets her so excited.

The girls are brought over to the base and given a debriefing that goes thusly: "You'll be mixed in with a group of prostitutes."

These "expendables" are put through their paces in basic training: rappelling down high walls, jogging in short shorts, crawling in dirt under barbed wire, and zip-lining to some bizarre ragtime piano.

This is so the motley crew can be parachuted in behind enemy lines, mixed in with the ladies of the evening rounded up for the amusement of the Japanese commissioned officers, then "decommission" them as it were.

As expected, the all-female mission plot isn't going over as smoothly as expected with the top brass. Colonels and other higher-ups checking in on their training doubt whether the crack team can act as a strike force unit—"What are you trying to do, turn this into an orgy?" They're a bunch of frustrated broads in hot pants!"

The girls show their mettle by stealthily breaching the officers' barracks and tying them up. No doubters now. On with the show.

Hustler Squad is produced by Cirio Santiago, though his directorial flourishes could've been used here as well. The cast? A bunch of drive-in regulars called upon to regularly drop their tops like the vehicles of choice for those types of movie venues.

FIRECRACKER (1981)

You have to admire the tireless dedication of action film pit fighters. The gate receipts for their fights aren't enough to sustain much of a career. After all, it's usually a hundred or so yelling underworld figures and their prostitute girlfriends. And you can't put a price on honor either. Or maybe you can? Zero dollars?

In *Firecracker*, we see a rippled fighter in immaculate silk robes with a gold lion embroidered onto it. He's either ready to hang from the wall of an Ethiopian restaurant or fight for his honor in a pit fighting contest to the death.

He kebabs his assailant with the guy's own spear, then deposits him in the corner. (Probably should have considered doing the same to his agent. After all, who cajoles their charge to sign on the dotted line to fight unarmed against some dude with a spear?)

The crowd erupts, and because this is a pit fighting movie, there's a cutaway shot to a couple of wizened fellows in the audience nodding appreciatively. Also, in true pit fighter form, the victor grabs a token (a dog tag) from the vanquished and hoists it into the air with a raised fist in an awesome display of valor and foreshadowing.

The no-holds-barred fighting matches are held in what looks like a down-market supper club with a salad bar. But it's really a front for an international drug trafficking ring. Don't know if they quite understand the purpose of a front. A front is a legitimate business designed to hide an illegitimate one. Not two illegal businesses conjoined that would draw attention to one another! C'mon folks, this was covered in Basic Criminality 101!

A missing American girl was last seen at the crappy club, and her sister Susanne, who as it happens is a kick-ass martial arts instructor, has come all the way to the Philippines from the USA to find out what happened. And what better place to look than a sleazy bar, the action movie equivalent of a local library when it comes to a repository of pertinent information.

Her presence there is not appreciated, but Susanne, in her purple jumpsuit, takes care of business, swinging a billiard cue into the face and midsections of a bunch of goons clad in a panoply of polyester.

The trail eventually leads to the supper club, the front for the heroin distribution ring. (Drug cartels are a great business. They're recession-proof and the largest single employer of henchmen/goons.)

At the club, someone throws down the vaguely sexual-sounding wager that she "can't go three minutes with Bruno," the greying heavyset champ of the Manilla dinner theater UFC. Susanne shows off her chops and pummels Bruno to show she's indeed *numero uno*.

That's when Susanne gets the attention of the Man in Silk, Chuck, a kind of not-so-great Wayne Gretzky, who probably sat down in the stylist chair and said, "I'd like the Ben Stiller in *Dodgeball*, please."

Chuck is so wooden you could lay flooring with him, but it seems he's the go-to source for all things pit fighting for blonde hot chick fighters "just looking to pay the rent." When she broaches the subject of fighting in the tournament, Chuck actually says, "Don't call us, we'll call you." Don't worry. Later, a top drug kingpin says, "We made him an offer he couldn't refuse." If this film had a script doctor, he was probably sued for malpractice.

Susanne remains unbowed. And that's saying something in a film with lots of obsequious and unnecessary bowing. Who knew no-holds-barred fighting was a place to find such solemn decorum? Her road to glean info about her missing sister is a winding one, as she includes a pilgrimage to learn about Filipino *arnis* stick fighting, the country's national sport. Her teacher dispenses some *Pinterest* meme-worthy insights such as, "The fruits of wisdom fall on different lands at different times." If you have a clue what this bit of malarkey means, don't hesitate to email us.

This Roger Corman production was advertised as "the screen's first erotic kung fu classic," prompting the obvious question, was there a glut of "erotic kung fu" movies and this one stood head and shoulders above the rest? Is this *the* erotic kung fu film that will be saved for posterity in the Smithsonian? *Firecracker* also goes by the cheeky title *Naked Fist* (for the love of all things holy, don't Google that) and was directed by none other than Cirio Santiago. The flick also has Cirio regular Vic Diaz waddling his way into the proceedings as a hood who threatens Susanne with a snake. And speaking of fauna, he grills her with, "What is your 'porpoise' here in Olongapo?" What Diaz lacks in English enunciation, he more than makes up for in menace.

Firecracker delivers the action Real McCoys with several swinging nunchucks and pool cues probed groin-ward, buckling dozens of unimpressive henchmen. Jillian Kesner as Susanne is a dynamo, swinging from ropes and using every possible horizontal surface, from billiard to tabletops, to swing kicks at her hapless opponents.

And as promised, there is some erotica—some tatas to go with those katas. Kesner sheds some clothing to extricate herself from a fence, battles some thugs in her hotel room wearing bra and panties, and takes on a thug with a sickle in the same getup. He swings and misses her goodies but slices clean through her bra to reveal her wonderful assets. It should be noted that this is the SECOND time someone slices through the bridge of her bra, the first being a protracted knife foreplay scene between her and Chuck. She masterfully cuts around his family jewels during some danger-fueled lovemaking.

Highly entertaining, with a climax in the ominous Arena of Death, and a blaring Casio rip-off of Henry Mancini's Grammy winning *Peter Gunn*.

TNT JACKSON (1974)

"I never made it with a chink before" is not exactly the kind of "Here's lookin' at you, kid"/"I'm the King of the World" line that'll make it onto AFI's list of 100 Movie Quotes.

But *TNT Jackson* is all about unity, beating down every race in the name of equality. Half kung fu, half Blaxploitation, and 100% crazy, *TNT Jackson* is billed as a "Spine shattering, bone blasting one mama massacre squad," if you believe the poster. Then again, this is the same artwork that puts the lead character in white bikini, matching furs, and holding a shotgun in front of a bank vault. *TNT Jackson* has nothing whatsoever to do with a bank heist. Nor does TNT wield a shotgun or sport any of that getup anywhere in the movie. A little artistic license is one thing, even if the promise she'll "put you in traction" would mean having said license revoked when you see the shoddy martial arts depicted here.

TNT Jackson formed the basis for the previous Corman-produced entry, *Firecracker*. It features the usual tale of a family member missing in an exotic locale, a loved one looking for them, and some underworld figures draped in polyester—a really unbreathable fabric, especially unsuited for the tropical climes of South Asia.

Jeannie Bell is Diana "TNT" Jackson. Bell, *Playboy* playmate of the month, October 1969, also stars in the fun exploitation curiosity *Disco 9000*, where muscle moves in on a record label and shakes down its mogul, Fass Black. *Disco 9000* has more disco than you can shake your rump at, and it's great viewing for those of you left unsatisfied by *Miami Connection*'s music business verisimilitude.

Bell's *TNT Jackson* has an incredible and ridiculous backstory: Harlem-born, at age thirteen she was locked up in New York State Prison (sic) for knifing a sailor. Given that the legal age for being put in the state pen is eighteen, she must've been a real badass. Now all grown up and back on the streets, her brother has gone missing. So, sis TNT sleuths her way through "Hong Kong's No Man's Land" to get to the bottom of it.

As a cabbie informs her, "even police are afraid to go there." Undeterred, she forges ahead and is met by thugs in Wing Chun silk shirts with white cuffs, the most formally attired backstreet brutes you'll ever see. But she's game and gives a couple of 'em a thorough valise beat-down.

Along the way, TNT gets help from kindly Joe, who acts as a local fixer and who can help her out with more than simple directions. After all, he runs the local dojo.

The trail grows hot and leads to a gang of heroin traffickers who quite ingeniously distribute narcotics using fake funerals and empty coffins as their delivery system.

The martial arts babe, dubbed "too fine to be fightin'," doesn't let that stop her as she lays out the usual incompetently overzealous unibrow goons. This includes an aggressor who juggles a butterfly knife right in front of her rather than just stabbing her post-haste. Ostentatious zeal like that will only get you killed, sir.

TNT then meets and brawls with a "lousy stinking pig" lady government agent. The flick also features the drug deal double-cross, where a rat tips off a drug shipment to be intercepted, resulting in the tragic loss of fifteen expendable goons.

Her path crosses Charlie's (Stan Shaw), a drug-runner who also trains at a dojo (like everyone, apparently). Charlie is a standout in that Shaw is an actual black belt. (*Rocky* fans will also recognize Dipper Brown, "a climber" not a "tomat-ah" as coach Mickey puts it.) That being said, having only one guy in a martial arts' movie with actual martial arts bona fides can only take you so far. It's like throwing John Coltrane in a junior high marching band. He might elevate the proceedings slightly, but not enough to make a difference. Charlie is connected to an evil whitey drug dealer, the guy ultimately responsible for TNT's brother going missing.

TNT has the scowl of someone whose steak was overcooked, and the soundtrack has enough flute to sate a half-dozen Ron Burgundys. There's loads of wacka-wacka wah-wah-pedal and sass like, "Listen, honey, and you get it straight. I'm not in your league. I work standing up, not on my back."

Not nearly as glute-kicking as *Cleopatra Jones*, the action sequences are north of ludicrous. There are Amish socials with more physical contact than Bell has with her opponents. Bell's body doubles are double in size, and the film looks like it was edited with a hedge trimmer.

In *I Hated, Hated, Hated This Movie*, Roger Ebert said of kung fu films, "Nobody can have a gun. If they had a gun they would just shoot you and you wouldn't get to go through the whole 'aaaaiiiiieeee' number and leap about with your fists flashing, your foot cocked, and your elbow of death savagely bent." True enough. But what fun would it be, especially when there's a lineup of henchmen with inferior martial arts so eager to test their mettle?

TNT Jackson is infamous for its nude karate, and not that we'd be a stickler for such things, but there's panty color continuity errors when TNT's battling topless. But, as Michael Jackson sang, *"If you're thinkin' about my baby/It don't matter if you're black or white."*

BAM! Shake it off

After you've emptied the chamber, shaking the gun (especially in the direction of your target) is not going to magically produce more bullets. Yet it's the last gambit before the useless gun trope sets in. That's when the perp (or sometimes the hero) surmises that his weapon is one-time-use only and tosses it aside. Why not keep it? You're throwing away hundreds if not thousands of dollars' worth of steel! Not to mention the ramifications of callously tossing aside a deadly weapon on a city street for anyone to find.

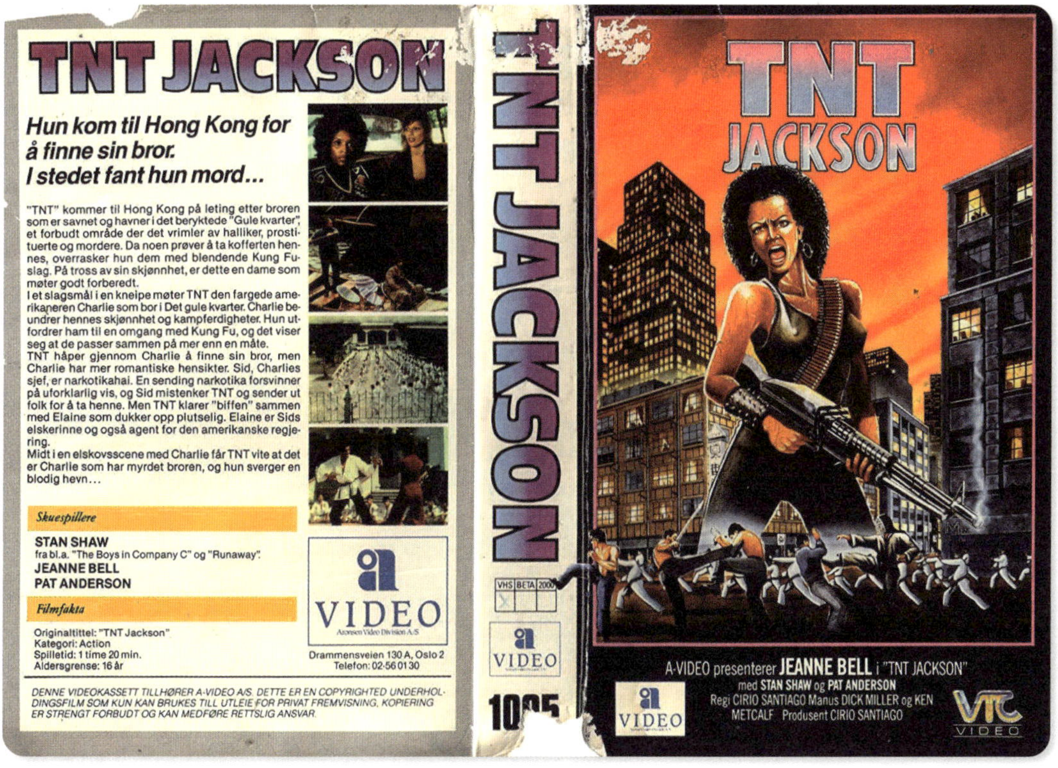

NINJA III: THE DOMINATION (1984)

In 1981, Cannon Films released *Enter the Ninja*. This was quickly followed with *Revenge of the Ninja*, and again in 1984 with *Ninja III: The Domination*. Each film in the *Ninja* trilogy had zilch in common with the one that preceded it save for the fact that they each featured a (different) character played by Sho Kosugi. In *Ninja III*, Kosugi plays . . . a ninja. (Were you expecting anything else? Sho does hold a bachelor's degree in economics from Cal State but it's hard to picture the face of Cannon ninja-badassery in the early '80s wearing pinstripes and standing next to Michael Douglas in *Wall Street*.) However, in this third installment in the franchise, Sho barely even shows up until the final third of the runtime. Until then, it's all about Christie, an aerobics instructor possessed by the spirit of a dead ninja. Oh that old yarn.

Ninja III begins with what may very well be the greatest opening in cinema history—ten straight minutes of over-the-top unadulterated chop socky carnage on a golf course which houses a mysterious cave in addition to its back nine. An enigmatic, white-suited man enters the hollow and finds a cache of hidden ninja weapons, including *de rigueur* throwing stars and a sword. He emerges outfitted in full ninja gear and bedazzled in black eyeliner.

The Ninja (who we later find out is an evil "Black Ninja") assassinates a man for seemingly no other reason than tying a yellow sweater daintily around his neck (the universal cinematic sign for he-had-it-coming smug insouciance). Black Ninja then cuts a swath of destruction through Sweaterman's (actually a prominent scientist in some unexplained discipline) numerous burly bodyguards, as well as the cops on the scene. He uses his elongated Ginsu to slice and dice his way through what appears to be an entire squadron, bringing them all down whether they're in car, on motorcycle, or in chopper. Yup. This ninja is so badass, he manages to take down a police helicopter with his bare hands!

He finally meets his end in a massive hail of bullets, but not before sending at least three dozen people to henchman heaven (we stopped counting after his perfectly aimed blow dart caused a pistol to explode.) As he's stumbling about in his death throes, he runs into Christie, the attractive aerobics instructor who also installs telephones, played by Lucinda Dickey of the Cannon produced *Breakin'* series. He mumbles something in Japanese and hands her his sword, a gift Christie happily accepts despite the fact that it's coming from a bloody, bullet-riddled ninja who doesn't speak a lick of English.

But everything free has a catch, doesn't it? For Christie, this means continually flashing back to being gunned down whenever she spots one of the cops who shot the Black Ninja. She also falls into nocturnal blackouts where she becomes her benefactor's avenging spirit.

One of the lawmen who was there that day is Billy, a guy in serious need of some manscaping, who pursues Christie and ultimately becomes her very hairy lover. They're in bed post-coitus when a thunderstorm that only she can hear wakes her. She opens her closet and her sword magically removes itself from its sheath. When her beau wakens, Christie acts dumbfounded, as if mystical swords free-floating around her bedroom were an every night experience.

We're then in an airport, and a man wearing what appears to be a giant Japanese coin as an eye-patch deplanes—that's our Sho arriving in America—but that doesn't really matter for now. What *does* matter now is Christie playing the arcade machine in her apartment. Suddenly, the game starts spinning, and Christie is bathed in a Pink Floyd planetarium light show. And here comes that darn sword again! Christie grabs it and begins smoldering like The Ultimate Warrior, then is led somnambulistically to the geological weapons cache. She emerges dolled up in her finest ninja finery plus eyeliner, locked and loaded for a little vengeance, Black Ninja style!

Next morning, Christie wakes unwell and unaware of the previous night's events. She sees a doctor who tells her that she's perfectly fine save for her "exceptional extraordinary sensory perception and her preoccupation with Japanese culture." Huh? Wouldn't E.S.P. alone warrant at least a follow-up, ideally with a physician who doesn't believe in mumbo jumbo? And up to that point, the only things that preoccupied Christie were leg warmers and leotards.

After another night of nocturnal butchering, Billy takes the ailing Christie to a Japanese medicine man, played by the wonderful James Hong (*Big Trouble in Little China*). She's chained and given something to smoke. Must have been a particularly good strain because suddenly she's spinning like a dreidel Regan MacNeil. She breaks her shackles and passes out, yet in the very next scene, is seen sitting on Billy's desk eating yogurt, blissfully oblivious to the fact that she went full *Exorcist* mere moments ago.

The rest of the film involves Sho and Billy teaming up to free Christie from the demonic curse and defeating the evil Black Ninja once and for all.

Ninja III: The Domination is 90 minutes of delirious sword slicing, *shuriken* throwing, arrow shooting, kung fu fighting fun. It's impossible not to love, especially if you're fond of gratuitous '80s aerobics, badass martial arts, and consenting adults using V8 juice as an aphrodisiac. Besides, any film where the opening credits are written in "Generic Chinese Restaurant Font" is aces in our books.

TOO HOT TO HANDLE (1978)

Forget Pussy Galore. *Too Hot to Handle* has accents galore—Dutch, Tagalog, Israeli, and indecipherable. But it's also got other James Bond staples, including cackling villain laughter, insta-courtship, and Fox . . . Samantha Fox, said in the same cadence as 007.

And that's Samantha Fox, not to be confused with the East London glamour girl and '80s dance-diva responsible for "Touch Me (I Want Your Body)." And you'll want to touch this Samantha too, as she's played by Cheri Caffaro, best known for the sleazy white slavery/sexploitation *Ginger* trilogy.

She's a bikini-clad *Dexter*, a hitwoman who only dispatches gangsters, pimps, and slavetraders. She lives on a yacht where she lies about topless on the bow, getting info about contract hits on a giant red phone.

Her assignment? One hundred and fifty large, hard-to-knock-off South Asian underworld figures, thus allowing her to showcase her various disguises and getups to get up close and personal with her victims. This includes S&M bondage regalia when she turns the whip on her target, ties him to his bed, and watches him asphyxiate by bag as she puffs her cigarette. (When she claims this, her first victim, a high-ranking official in Manilla "indulging his sexual perversions," even the lead detective concedes "I'll bet a month's pay, she is an absolute knockout.")

Her preparations are so extensive, she can wax poetic on "pre-dynastic Tahitian sand sculptures" while undercover as an arts journalist. She also pretends to be a beautician in order to knock off a brothel Madame who looks like Martha Stewart. She does this by attaching electrodes to the Madame's lathered-up face and zapping her to death (this probably really opens your pores). Finally, Fox cuts a very tall figure as the least convincing Filipina nanny in yellowface ever, part of a masquerade to sneak into the mansion of a drug lord so as to drug him and drown him in his own hot tub. (It doesn't help the ruse that she doesn't speak a word of Tagalog.)

In best film noir tradition, the lead detective falls for her, although this is not Otto Preminger's *Laura* (*Too Hot to Handle* Director Don Schain went on to produce *High School Musical*, of all things). That's detective Domingo de la Torres, who has enough chest hair to shame a bearskin rug. He's hot for her, and hot on her tail, aided by detective Sanchez, played by the omnipresent Vic Diaz, mopping his ever-sweating brow in the Manilla heat.

Fox and Domingo bond over that time-honored, girl-meets-boy, boy-meets-girl, boy-falls-in-love-with-girl-while-shooting-avocados-on-horseback-with-high-powered-rifles. Domingo woos her with the incomparably sexy, "I doubt our wild boar would prove much of a challenge for you," to which she responds, "No animal ever does. It's more of a turn on to watch something die slowly."

The two of them hit the sack to the torch song strains of the very literal "Samantha, he fell in love with you," as Caffaro's pendulous breasts sway to and fro.

Despite Domingo's suspicions, he's of course reluctant to bust the blonde Batman, who is ever the sophisticate, great in the sack and turned on by cockfighting! Seriously. There's an elaborate scene where Fox flashes back to a cockfighting tournament while lolling about on silk red sheets in the throes of ecstasy. What can we say? She likes cock (fighting)!

The poster promises that "her deadliest weapon is her body." Hard to argue. That's why we get to see so much of it, whether it's lovemaking, strip teases, or simply absorbing the sun's rays on a yacht.

There's glorious mangled badinage like, "Whether you like it or not, my men are going to stay close enough to smell what you had for breakfast."

This 1977 Roger Corman production is a whirlwind of wah-wah guitar, and lapels wide enough to double as clown bowties. There are weird directorial flourishes, including barndoor wipe transitions as well as pointless split screens as if this were *Annie Hall*. And there's a peppy brass score propelled by tuba, which is really at odds with the tropical setting.

THE CHALLENGE OF THE LADY NINJA (1983)

The "Linda problem" in psychology is fascinating. Study participants are given a description of a woman, told she's thirty-one and that she majored in philosophy and is concerned with social justice. They are then asked, "What is more probable? That she's a) a bank teller, or b) that she's a bank teller *and* a feminist?" Most people pick the latter even though the probability of two events occurring together is always less than or equal to the probability of either one happening alone. What does this example of how our minds deceive us have to do with a schlocky chop socky? *The Challenge of the Lady Ninja* features a protagonist, Wu Shiau-kuei, who's both a) a female ninja (rare) and b) (rarer still), a Chinese female ninja. Is that a problem? The guy she has to fight in order to attain "ninja" status grouses about it repeatedly, so don't take our word for it that it *is* a problem.

Then again, a movie set during World War II that features the Japanese training the Chinese (not to mention '80s Cadillacs and headbands) can't be held up as a barometer of cultural exactness.

Wu is one determined lady martial artist. She says, "I must satisfy myself. I want to become a ninja" as if these were mutually exclusive. Wu may have broken through the ninja glass ceiling along with Christie from *Ninja III*, but that doesn't mean she's not demeaned. Among her many talents: sword-play, dead-eye *shuriken* flinging (of course, nobody misses wildly with ninja stars in movies, even as the very best major league baseball pitchers occasionally leave a fastball in the dirt), and disrobing.

When she's accosted by evil ninjas, she magically metamorphoses into a pink silk bikini and shawl and sways her hips about. This causes her assailants to drop their weapons in wide-eyed amazement and rush in to fornicate with her. When they're thusly exposed, so to speak, Wu transforms back into her *shinobi shozoku* getup and tosses deadly explosives at them. This prompts the obvious question: If she was just going to blow them up anyway when they got in close, why the strip tease? Also, if you're able to go full Penn & Teller with such trickery, why not just disappear altogether when in danger? So many questions, so little to be gleaned from this plot.

After suffering the slings and arrows of outrageous ninja training, it's great that Wu is able to put such a formidable skillset to good use.

Lee Chun is a Chinese turncoat on the payroll of the Japanese, and stupidly, Wu's former betrothed. When Wu sees Lee's betrayed her as well as the revolution, she decides to take him out.

However, this poses a problem. Lee is living in a heavily fortified walled compound, defended by webbed doorways with cotton mesh that shoots out like it's right from the wrists of Spiderman.

After one failed solo siege attempt, Wu scales back over the wall for a tactical reassessment.

She then seeks advice from her fellow Chinese revolutionaries. And the question, "what in heck were you doing in Japan training with our sworn enemies, lady?" does not come up at any point in the conversation.

Wherever you are looking to find your bearings on an action movie map, one thing's for sure: everyone can use a kickass group of mercs to carry the freight. Wu assembles a crack team, even asking in true feminist fashion, "Can you find me girls to fight kung fu?"

Unfortunately, the equality goodwill goes out the window when her all-girl team is put through a training montage of up-crotch bendy rope calisthenics. And it also doesn't help the cause that her recruits come from the local brothel.

When pressed if they're willing to "give up their life and virginity" to fight the Japanese (strange given they're hookers, so the second one is already taken care of), the girls affirm yes.

They devise plans as to how they're going to eliminate Lee Chen's Top 4 Bodyguards, one of whom has a purple scorpion tattooed on his bald head, no eyebrows, and leather short shorts.

Each bodyguard is an "individual with their own habit!" and one is "So strong he can kill a bull barehanded . . . one to avoid in close combat." You don't say. His Achilles' Heel, though, is that "He loves going to the brothels and can't have enough girls!"

The plan of attack in part includes elaborate ways to convince the lead guard to abandon his favorite hooker in favor of a merc as well as means of concealing poison on one's person, easier said than done when naked.

There are many lessons to be learned from *The Challenge of the Lady Ninja*. One is that "Kung fu knows no borders." True. Another, "The test of wisdom is that of the mind," is a phrase which wouldn't even pass muster as a hot yoga homily. Also, apparently you don't think anyone in the audience will notice if you purloin what is perhaps the most famous music in movie history, Darth Vader's "Imperial March," which this movie does in the first ten minutes.

The best part of *The Challenge*, though, is the tendency for battles to devolve into elaborate mud wrestling contests. Maybe something was lost in martial arts translation when the ninja techniques crossed the Sea of Japan.

CROCODILE FURY (1988)

In the NFL, there's something called "concussion protocol," a series of medical procedures a player must undergo if he's sustained a serious blow to the head. Some kind of brain injury is the only way to explain how human creativity could possibly come up with *Crocodile Fury*, a movie woozy in its wackiness, a copyright and plot-oblivious foray into some of the weirder fringes of cinema you'll see anywhere.

A killer crocodile is wreaking havoc in Indonesia. For protection, villagers turn to a fourth-generation crocodile hunter, a guy who speaks to them via a ventriloquist skeleton that communicates in a high-pitched squeal while rattling its bones.

This alone requires a spinoff.

Crocodile Fury, at its heart though, is a love story between Jack and Maria. What's keeping the town's swamp-crossed lovers apart is that she's a reincarnated human-crocodile hybrid. When it comes to irreconcilable differences, bridging the human/reptile divide has gotta be up there.

And Jack's future family/in-laws are causing problems too. They're hybrid crocodiles as well and are treating his village like it's a buffet table. Maria implores, "If you really cared about me, you'd be a crocodile too!" But he's wracked with self-doubt and probably the thought that he's next on the menu. He expresses concerns that in the next life, she won't be reborn wholly human if she keeps eating the way she's eating.

But that's a tall order. Maria is a member of a shapeshifting croc coven and "humans are their natural enemies."

The coven is part of a movement of global conquest (with the assistance of hopping vampires) to take over the world and make this new Sea World (yes) their own.

They do this mainly by eating every Indonesian villager in sight, chomping them underwater, above water, in the forests, and in their boats. In fact, much of the film's running time is devoted to screaming rustics in silk robes variously knocked out of thatch huts or wooden boats by reptilian tails or rubber jaws thrust from below the plane of the screen.

But the true star of the show is witch-psychic Monica. When a film is called "episodic," this is fancy jargon for saying that the narrative makes not a lick of sense whatsoever. And Monica, in true Ed Wood-style, loosely holds together whatever semblance of a plot this has as the film's narrator. And an unreliable one at that.

Monica has the "power to invade with vampires" (whatever that means). And these are *jiangshi*, those reanimated vampire corpses of Chinese legend. She is a toothless soothsayer periodically and very haphazardly plunked into the proceedings, wearing what looks like a U-shaped memory foam travel pillow and a fez and speaking in frenzied "hubba hubba hubba" exclamations, summoning evil spells from her crystal ball. What this has to do with the crocodile/reincarnation plot is difficult to determine without a doctorate in Javanese folklore.

Her cutaway incantations are an endless source of amusement, even in a film that has levitation, attacking skulls, projectile vomiting onto a pile of maggots, and practical effect crocs being obviously dragged behind a boat. It's the vessel's wake, not to mention the utter fakeness of the rendered reptile, which give it away.

Crocodile Fury features a first—it uses stock footage of itself. So, it's hard to accuse the many-aliased director Godfrey Ho of plagiarism. In minute ten, one villager can be seen scaling a bamboo post to avoid predation and kicking at the open rubber maw of the croc. He appears forty-five minutes later to reprise the exact same scenario.

Crocodile Fury's effects are mesmeric, including toy rubber, papier mâché, and plastic inflatable crocs (the latter used when the beast is seen soaring over a canoe). One of the "crocs" is obviously just some dude swimming underneath a rubber reptile suit, kinda like James Bond's "submarine" disguise in *Octopussy*.

Finally, to add to the confusion, there are hopping vampires hot on the trail of a white missionary, who fends them off with a giant gold cross. We meet him in the first scene, fleeing machine gun–wielding men. Who they are or who he is is anyone's guess, but one thing's for certain, he's been dumped in from another film entirely. That being said, his martial arts skill against a group of marauding zombies is quite formidable.

Even the production credits are tough to keep straight. The film's a Tomas Tang production directed by Ted Kingsbrook (who are one in the same—Godfrey Ho).

But to his credit, pardon the pun, Ho stepped out of his comfort zone for this feature; out of his 150 *IMDb* director movies listed, a whopping 53 contain the words "kickboxer," or "ninja," so props to him. There are no ninjas in *Crocodile Fury*, though it's probably not for lack of trying.

32

LADY TERMINATOR (1989)

You'd think anything called *Lady Terminator* would reek of rip-off, a blatant cash-in by unscrupulous producers in countries with extremely lax copyright laws taking a smash hit concept and shamelessly replicating it wholesale but with local actors and settings. And to some extent you'd be right. After all, over the years, we've enjoyed films as deliriously entertaining as 1975's *Cellat* (a.k.a. Turkish *Death Wish*), *Aatank* (India's *Jaws*), and *Os Trapelhões na Guerra dos Planetos* (Brazilian *Star Wars*). What makes *Lady Terminator* so baffling, though, is that it didn't have to be a time travel robot retread at all. It begins as a straight updating of the Indonesian folktale *Nyai Roro Kidul* ("The Legend of the South Sea Queen") before morphing into a lurid, estrogen-fueled version of you-know-what, but with a lady in it.

We begin in the bedchamber of the South Sea Queen. She's a rapacious, polyandrous ruler, unable to find a single lover capable of sublimating her limitless lust. The first dude certainly isn't cutting it, but perhaps that's because he's still wearing his boxer-briefs as they make love! The frustrated queen clenches something down below as her lover's pangs of ecstasy transform into howls of agony. A clap of her hands brings her handmaidens scurrying in to take the poor bastard's lifeless, blood-soaked body away. "Is there any man who can satisfy me?" bemoans the queen. Jeez. Maybe if she'd allow the poor sap to show her his royal sceptre, he'd have had more of a sporting chance.

Another contender immediately enters (as it were), and it looks as if things are going pretty well. He doesn't even flinch when a black snake wiggles out of the queen's crotch. Instead, he grabs the creature and suggestively massages it, transforming it into a twisted sort of dagger. The queen demands he return it but is rebuffed. Outraged, she vehemently declares, "In one hundred years, I'll have my revenge on your great-granddaughter!" She then retreats to the bottom of the sea where she vows to "join forces with the power of evil!" Like she was such a saint before.

Flash forward however many years. Young Tania (Barbara Anne Constable, doing double duty as lead actress and makeup artist) is a student completing her doctorate on the South Sea Queen. She enters a library seeking a book and asks the elderly librarian if he has it. Naturally, he warns her of the dangers of meddling with forces she may not understand, and naturally she ignores him by responding in the most quizzical way: "In this day and age you speak of legends! I'm an anthropologist, huh!" And she's evidently very proud of her vocation too. When the boatman taking her to the purported locale of the queen's

sunken castle refuses to stop referring to her as "lady," she responds with the indignant retort "I'm not a lady! I'm an anthropologist!" As if the two were mutually exclusive.

The bikini-clad Tania, who's an anthropologist, refuses to heed any warnings nor harbingers of doom as she dives down into the deep blue sea. Except when we next see her, she's somehow found herself in the queen's lair, bound and spread-eagle on a flower petal-covered bed. A snake enters her hoo-ha, lightning strikes, and she emerges from the water naked as the day she was born. And very mean. And apparently some sort of indestructible robot too. Guess snakes entering one's nether regions does that to people. And they say you don't learn anything from action films. She encounters two hooligans drinking on the beach (one of whom is urinating straight up into the air), has her way with both, kills them, and bites off their manhoods, making sure to abscond with one of their leather jackets, presumably to affect some degree of modesty (but really just to ape *The Terminator*).

Soon she's breaking into a hotel room for a little nude meditation and electrical destruction (she's able to summon the stuff now). A security guard brandishing an Uzi (standard issue?) investigates, because if the excess noise wasn't suspicious enough to warrant inquiry, the abundance of dry ice rolling out from under the door certainly is. Unfortunately, he's toast and she now has a deadly weapon. Goodbye Tania, hello Lady Terminator. . .and goodbye interest in anthropology!

Where Arnie sought to terminate Sarah Connor, Lady Terminator's target is aspiring pop singer Erica, the great-granddaughter that the Sea Queen promised revenge on lo those many years ago. And like Sarah Connor, Erica has a protector from her unstoppable and impervious-to-all-ordnance assailant. But rather than Michael Biehn's capable soldier Kyle Reese, poor Erica is saddled with transplanted NYC cop Max McNeil, a blonde himbo with a shoehorned (and very much glossed over) backstory about losing his wife to a vengeful ex-con. ("Could've happened to anybody.") But hey, in desperate times, you take protection wherever you can get it. And when you're being hunted down by a cyborg leather-fetishist who sees the world through a red hue and goes around biting off men's penises, even a twerp like Max McNeil will do.

As Lady Terminator stalks her way through shopping malls and city streets, blowing away all she encounters in her single-minded determination to get to Erica, the similarities to *The Terminator* pile up higher than the film's impressive body count. These include:

- A firefight in a disco where Max rescues Erica from Lady Terminator's onslaught, then utters T's trademark "Come with me if you want to live."
- Lady Terminator driving a car through the front window of police headquarters followed by an intensely gory shootout where she lays waste to hundreds of Indonesia's finest.
- Lady Terminator in a hotel room bathroom using a scalpel to remove her eye for no apparent reason other then to plagiarize yet another scene from *The Terminator*.
- Plus scores of people being blown backwards through plate glass windows.

The climax of *Lady Terminator* is one for the ages. Because she's nigh unstoppable, Max joins forces with a quartet of cop buddies to take her out using all the weapons. And we mean *all* the weapons. "Get the Panzer," commands one of the four as they head to the beach for the final showdown. The Panzer! She's driving an Oldsmobile and they still can't take her out. They deploy choppers, missiles, and M16s, all to no avail. By the time Lady Terminator emerges from being hit dead-on by a bazooka looking like an ashen version of Michael Jackson in the "Thriller" video and shooting out lasers from her eyes, you'll realize they just don't make 'em like they do in Indonesia!

OF NOTE:

No discussion of *Lady Terminator* is complete without mention of the character Snake. Picture a cop who speaks like Keanu Reeves in *Bill & Ted's Excellent Adventure* and is a dead-ringer for *NeverEnding Story* theme song singer Limahl (go ahead and Google him if you must; the resemblance is uncanny, right down to the dual-hued Kentucky waterfall hairdo), and you've got an impression of the film's most entertaining character. And in a film as *loca* as *Lady Terminator*, that designation is *muy* impressive. Snake, just by uttering interjections such as "Fuckin' 'A,'" "Yeah!" and "Allright!," damn near runs away with every scene. And the fact that he's played by an actor named Adam Stardust makes it all the better.

33

ALIENATOR (1989)

A portmanteau of *Terminator* and *Alien*, this mixed-up piece of space junk deserves its own mashup adjective: craptacular.

We're in another galaxy. And it doesn't just FEEL like we are because this is directed by Fred Olen Ray, the shlock master-cum-professional wrestler we (briefly) considered to write the foreword of this book and who's graced us (well not us personally, though that'd be nice) with such work as *Invisible Mom 2* and *13 Erotic Ghosts*. We haven't seen it, but ghost sex has to be a pretty safe form of sex. And what do you get the mom who has everything for Invisible Mother's Day?

In this galaxy, there's a prison spaceship floating through the endless emptiness of space. On board, a felon who looks like a linebacker Fred Flintstone in a silver life preserver, blinking neck brace, and body armor. He's being held captive, awaiting death row, and because this is a sci-fi film, superior alien space races have dispensed with syllables. So the con's name is . . . Kol. Not to be a spoilsport here, but how is there a "death row" in space? Don't you just open the hatch and let the vast cold vacuum do the rest?

The ship's commander is played by the man who's always on warped drive, Jan-Michael Vincent, the man whose personal life impeded his professional one, derailing his career in a miasma of cocaine and booze. He's a sneering Thin White Duke of a captain who hits on his underling in her fetching pectoral-less crop top,[16] all the while soliciting advice from his very own knock-off Scotty. Captain's log rip-off, star date 1989.

Kol frees himself from his constraints and hightails it to the nearby escape pod (worst prison spacecraft EVER?) and high gears it into the cosmos. And it just so happens, conveniently enough for plot development, that they were floating right by our planet. Yes, things come crashing down to Earth, literally, as Fred Olen Ray didn't have the funds to do anything more in terms of space-plotting. So Kol's pod lands somewhere in the woods outside Los Angeles, although you'd never guess this was California, as later on some backwoods bumpkin right off the set of *Hee Haw* and armed with a "raff-le" happens by like he's prospectin' fer gold in these here parts.

Kol crawls out of the smoldering wreckage and onto a nearby highway. Before he has a chance to adjust to our gravity, a drunk-driven RV smacks him straight into the ditch.

To their credit, the vehicle's occupants pull over and haul the space traveller onto their ride, taking him to the local warden's cabin to get help, all the while examining their cargo. "Look at those eyes. He looks like he's strung out on PCP." While Kol convalesces, they pepper him with unfunny queries about *E.T.* and *War of the Worlds*. The crew also ask him about his home planet. ("It had no name; it was a penal colony.") In keeping with a fairly strict rule in sci-fi, aliens speak halting English.

But this isn't *Alf* redux or an episode of *The X-Files*. There is a bounty on Kol's head, and with that bounty, a bounty hunter. Enter the Terminator, um, the Alienator. Kol's blinking neckband is not only semi-asphyxiating the poor bastard by pressing down on his windpipe–worse, it's sending out a GPS signal to an interplanetary assassin, out to hunt him down and finish the job a clearly incapable Jan-Michael Vincent couldn't.

The Alienator is a towering force.[17] She's broad-shouldered, with *Labyrinth* hair, breast plates that look like saucepans, metal undergarments, and a giant laser gun bigger than your arm. (Isn't it nice to see a reference like that that isn't about genitalia?).

The attending physician, who's making a "house call" to Kol, complete with a leather overnight bag like he stepped out of the 1920s, is quickly the victim of the green laser fired from Alienator's big ordnance. But lest we forget, it's not the size of the ordnance, it's how you use it.

"To alienate," *Merriam-Webster* tells us, has a lesser-known meaning in addition to the more common usage, i.e. what this film does to 98 percent of its viewership. And that is, "to convey or transfer (something, such as property or a right) usually by a specific act rather than the due course of law." So that's what this Alienator is doing to Kol. It's all beginning to make sense now.

The strapping female bodybuilder sporting an unflattering bikini bottom fires lasers at everything in sight, but not in sights—she has terrible aim for such a fine-tuned piece of space engineering. Yet for some reason, her breastplates are impervious to puny earth-bullets.

The humans, despite not having any reason to do so, defend Kol's life from his assailant, a real dog of a bounty hunter. Risking their lives to protect this outer space shmoe, when for all they know, Kol could be some intergalactic sex offender. The human rescuers call in an army colonel whose home just happens to be in an adjacent wood. His character is there just to plan and strategize. Maybe he could've helped out on the production, as *Alienator* has the look and feel of something which was banged out in a couple of weeks.

In the book, *Wild Beyond Belief!: Interviews with Exploitation Filmmakers of the 1960s and 1970s,* Ross Hagen, who portrayed Kol, said that he and Fred Olen Ray used puffs from their cigars as effects for the crashed space pod! That's about as DIY as you get in filmmaking.

FOUR

ENLISTED MEN

PITY THE WARRIOR WHO IS CONTENTED TO CRAWL ABOUT IN THE BEGGARDOM OF RULES.

—CARL VON CLAUSEWITZ

Many of us are familiar with Sun Tzu's pronouncement that "The supreme art of war is to subdue the enemy without fighting." If this were the case, our book would run some 30 pages. Good thing we're not paid by the word.

When it comes to combat, some people will go to great lengths to avoid being drafted. Certain orange sherbet-faced presidents, for example. And we can understand why. After all, who would willingly face a hail of bullets, not to mention get up at zero four hundred hours?

Soldiers in exploitation films usually fall into one of two camps: they return to an urban jungle to deal contraband, or they're fighting in an actual jungle, usually 'Nam (as played by the Philippines), but often some island stronghold of a South American drug dealer.

Martial arts heroes might be the least verbose of any in this book, but a very close second are the army guys we cover here. After all, their mouths are perpetually stuffed with stogies, they're in perma-scowl mode, and lugging around M-60 machine guns in subtropical jungle rot milieus with no sunscreen nor womenfolk for miles is enough to make anyone hushed and ill-tempered.

Hacking through jungles with a machete, ready for poisonous snakes to drop out of the canopy while white-hot lead screams past your ears is one thing—but knowing that you probably have a superior back in Washington with a repurposed *National Geographic* map taped haphazardly to a wall leading you into a near and certain suicide mission is another. Stand up straight, speak only when spoken to, and be sure to avoid any major malfunctions as we give these fightin' men a three-volley salute.

STRIKE COMMANDO (1987)

Strike commandos are maneuvering behind enemy lines, and to erase all doubt as to whether this is a military movie, the title is referenced in dialogue barely two minutes in: "Where your air force has failed, my strike commandos won't."

Meet Mike Ransom, the commando honcho, and imagine the Abbott and Costello hilarity we missed out on. "Soldier, get me Ransom." "How much, sir?" "No, MIKE Ransom." "What about the hostage?" "You mean Bob Hostage? He's right here . . ."

The exceptionally idiotically named Ransom is played with surfer verve by golden boy Reb Brown, who was bursting out of his suit in *Captain America II*, not because he was that ripped but because it looked like cheap (and not very patriotic) two-sizes-too-small polyester.

He and his team are prowling around a Vietnamese base defended by a chintzy chain-link fence that can be breached with small pliers. The strike force includes a really dumb black guy with a Jimi Hendrix headband who makes racist jokes at his own expense about watermelons in Alabama and is a one-man argument against the draft.

The brains behind the assault, ruthless Colonel Radek, proclaims "The depot must be taken at all cost!" and demands that the IEDs are set off, blowing up Ransom's men before they've had a chance to escape, let alone mow down a bunch of Filipino extras for their troubles.

The whole shebang goes BANG, sending Mike Ransom headlong into a nearby muddy river.

A small boy who's fishing downstream pulls in a real live one: the befuddled Ransom. He takes the worse-for-wear Ransom to his village to recuperate. When Ransom comes to, he screams loudly, which for some reason, the filmmakers decide to juxtapose with a monkey screaming. And the whole village is there to greet him outside his bamboo hut, chanting "Amer-eee-can!, Amer-eee-can!" while pumping their fists, their faces painted like they staggered off the set of an Italian cannibal movie.

They haul a captured "devil" Viet Cong soldier before him and want Ransom to off the cowering sap. But our brawny blond hero is an ardent defender of the Third Geneva Convention: "He's the enemy, FINE! But why should I shoot an unarmed man in cold blood?" It's Reb Brown's foot-stomping kid delivery of the word "fine" that has made him such a genre folk hero.

Ransom's interpreter, a ripened hard-drinking Frenchman, Francois Le Due,[18] explains with a Pepé Le Pew accent, "You disappointed them. They were hoping you'd be their savior." The villagers voice their displeasure by getting up off their knees to trudge off into the jungle and find a new savior.

Ransom is eventually saved by helicopter but not before sending not-very-elite Viet Cong troops airborne with his machine fire.

He later returns to the village, whose occupants have since been massacred. The boy who pulled him out of the river is clinging to life, so Ransom cradles him in his husky arms and tearfully explains the wonders of Disneyland while the child is succumbing to his injuries in what is undoubtedly one of the most dazzlingly inept scenes in movie history.

Village Boy: American, will you take me to America with you?

Ransom: This country's at war now, I can't leave 'til it's over.

Village Boy: Mr. Francois told me about a wonderful place where Mickey Mouse and Donald Duck live. Tell me about Disneyland . . .

Ransom: Disneyland . . . they got tons of popcorn there. And all you have to do is climb a tree . . . to go eat it.

It is indeed a Magic Kingdom.

Turns out the mastermind behind the village extermination was—drumroll please—a Russian (this was the '80s, remember). The Slav uber-baddie Jakoda was also responsible for throttling the old Frenchman and later calls out Ransom in garbled "Russian," A-mer-reee-kan-ski! (because adding a "ski" suffix is instant-noodle Russian).

A Streetcar Named Desire had audiences yelling "Stella!" for decades. Then they bellowed "Adrian" after *Rocky*. Hurtling way down the list: "JAKODA!" bawled in Cali style by Reb Brown. Americanski/Jakoda is almost the Marco/Polo of *Strike Commando*.

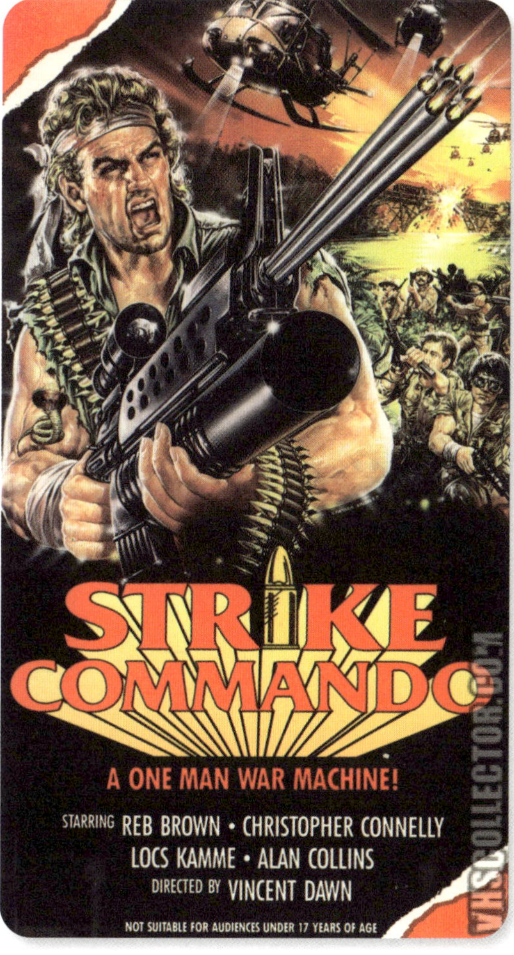

Now, regarding Jakoda's presence during the war: Russia *did* lend logistical support to the North Vietnamese, but if you're expecting historical exactitude from a cheap Italian production shot in the Philippines, with an obviously non-Russian, Italian American actor speaking faux Russian, you've likely wandered down the wrong booby-trapped jungle path.

Bald menacing Jakoda isn't there for his military expertise so much as he is to cut an imposing figure while doing lots of push-ups.

Naturally, after a very high body count and a protagonist, Ransom, ("One of our best!" according to a high-ranking official) who cannot be taken out even with shoulder-fired anti-tank weaponry and wave after wave of expendable infantrymen, when the dust settles all we're left with is Ransom vs. Jakoda.

What about the corrupt colonel, you ask? Ransom, out for retribution, does track Radek to—as the budget demanded it—Manila.

Strike Commando is one of the worst war movies of all time, by arguably the worst director of all time, the incomparable Bruno Mattei (credited by his anglicized *nom de plume* Vincent Dawn), the notorious, ahem, recycler behind this mind-boggling knock-off. You're known by the company you keep and Mattei's frequent collaborator and cowriter of this stinker was Claudio Fragasso, best known for directing (and defending) the all-time-worst horror contender, *Troll 2*.

We're not trolling when we say *Strike Commando* is so inept it makes the film it so desperately aspires to be, *Rambo: First Blood Part II*, look like *All Quiet on the Western Front*. Except it's not too quiet. Seriously, what's with all the yelling? "Is that you, A-mer-ree-kan-ski?!!!?"

STRIKE COMMANDO 2 (1988)

In a film where even the extras can't keep a straight face, it's impossible to demand the same suspension of disbelief from an audience.

Mike Ransom is back, though Reb Brown isn't (we get the buff Brent Huff in his stead). What we do get this time around is an actual ransom.

Ransom's heretofore unmentioned savior, Major Jenkins, who saved his life in 'Nam but not in *Strike Commando* as one might expect, is abducted and held for ten million bucks. And here, Major Jenkins is high-priced talent, portrayed by none other than Richard Harris! (*Harry Potter*'s Dumbledore and he of the beguiling '60s hit, "MacArthur Park"—sample lyrics: "*Someone left the cake out in the rain, I don't think that I can take it, 'Cause it took so long to bake it . . .*" Jeez, drugs really messed up the Beat Generation.)

We do get the luxury of a Ransom Vietnam flashback showing Jenkins saving Ransom's life. During the scene, where Ransom's sitting in his Manila apartment smoking, the constant ADR taxicab horn blowing is almost too much to bear. Ransom, not surprisingly, doesn't require much arm twisting to go save his buddy, if only to escape the damnable noise.

The abduction is all organized by Peter Roeg (pronounced "Rogue") who is a CIA rogue agent (makes sense) who may or may not have staged Jenkins' death and whose office is an exercise in more-is-less staging—his desk consists of two landline phones sitting side by side, an ashtray, and behind him, a histogram graph demonstrating exactly nothing.

Roeg baits Ransom, who beats him spectacularly with his own framed family portrait! We find out that Jenkins is being held captive in a heroin

lab, deep deep in the Filipino jungles, overseen by the ubiquitous Vic Diaz, a man without whom no movie set in the Philippines is complete.

As Ransom is trying to get a lay of the land and see how he can spring Jenkins, he wanders into the Moulin Rouge saloon run by blonde Rosanna (Mary Stävin, Miss World 1977 and recurring Bond babe). She's taking on a fat Filipino tough in a belching contest, sitting across a long table, lining up and then knocking back beer after beer while punters place bets on the outcome. It's basically a note-for-note *Raiders of the Lost Ark* bar shots scene, but with beer instead of shots, plus belching. The belching is director Bruno Mattei's unmistakable influence.

Despite the Buddha girth of her antagonist, the svelte blonde pulls through and Ransom's instantly smitten. They agree to partner up to free Jenkins and make off with the reward money.

But it won't be easy.

The chief villain, Kramet, sports crisp white suits and a Panama hat, and favors a garrotte as his MO. He's also a KGB agent, a callback to the inane Russian villain in *Strike Commando*, one of the tenuous ties that bind parts 1 and 2.

He cuts an imposing figure, even if extras laugh at his scenes, and comes equipped with a collection of useless ninjas who do his bidding, backflipping themselves into fists and getting their asses handed to them. Good thing they're masked to allay the embarrassment.

His powers of villainy are showcased when Ransom tries to pawn fake diamonds off on him in a bar—he crushes them with a bare hand.

Luckily, Rosanna is resourceful and, *Romancing the Stone*-style, the duo is able to bust Jenkins out of his confines, as she's also a capable helicopter pilot. She's able to match Ransom step for step and cigarillo for cigarillo.

There's an excellent slo-mo henchman machine gun massacre, and guard towers are no match for good old American firepower. The showstopper is the machine gunning of every available extra in the Philippines, bounced through the air, gravity be damned, as Ransom proves his undeniable heroism.

DEADLY PREY (1986)

If *Rambo: First Blood Part II* mated with *The Most Dangerous Game* and was then given a lobotomy, the result would be *Deadly Prey*, a ham-fisted '80s action flick that's as entertaining as it is inept.

In a forest somewhere just outside of Los Angeles, a large group of mercenaries are training "to be the best," under the tutelage of Vietnam vet Colonel Hogan. Of course, this being peacetime, in order to train, the mercs (each interchangeable, each without an ounce of muscle tone—seriously, did anybody work out in the '80s?) naturally kidnap average Joes off the street and chase them through the California forests before killing them. When the last portly "runner" proves little challenge, Hogan orders his men to get someone nasty this time. Big Mistake! (Best read in your finest Stallone lower register.)

Enter Mike Danton, your average former military killing machine now living a peaceful, domesticated life in the 'burbs. Danton (Ted Prior, brother of director David, who also directed Pam Anderson in *Raw Justice*) is taking out the trash in a pair of exceedingly short shorts when the mercenaries pull up and abduct him to be their next runner, unaware that they're picking up deadly prey. Ha!

The mercenaries strip down the jacked Danton and oil him up before turning him lose. Almost immediately Mike springs into action, taking out the mercenaries like a one-man army regiment. He grabs one unfortunate recruit for this awesome exchange:

Danton: How long has this been going on?
Recruit: I don't know! I just joined today!
Danton: BAD TIMING!

He then stabs the poor guy in the stomach.

Meanwhile, Danton's wife, who behaves like a wide-eyed fourth-grader, calls her retired policeman father for assistance. Pops, played by Hollywood journeyman Cameron Mitchell (great to see you again, Mr. Mitchell), goes off on a lone crusade to find his son-in-law. Why he didn't call any of his cop buddies for assistance remains a mystery, but to his credit, the old guy fights pretty well for someone who looks like he should be playing shuffleboard in Del Boca Vista.

Upon seeing the corpses of his mercenaries, Hogan—a poor man's Martin Kove but with no Karate Kid to bully—exclaims "I know his style, it's my style . . . Know him, I TRAINED him!" Danton then reaches out of the bush, grabs Hogan, turns him around, and growls, "You trained me to be the best. Well, I still am. . .I STILL AM!!!!"

Danton then lets his prey go, ostensibly just long enough for Hogan to bellow to the heavens "DAAAAAAAAANTON!!!!!"

Later, Danton, who to this point has been fighting with just his bare hands and the occasional dropped weapon of his fallen foes, discovers a weapons cache and shit gets super serious (and super ridiculous). Danton levels up huge. He surfaces armed to the gills and looking like a thrift-store *Rambo*, then booby-traps the entire forest to take out each remaining mercenary. All, that is, save for the one whose life Danton saved in 'Nam. How serendipitous! He changes sides and becomes Danton's ally.

At this point, many questions arise. For instance, why when Danton throws one knife, do two people fall down and die? Was there some sort of ricochet? And just how does machine gun fire cause a helicopter to explode as if a nuclear missile just hit it? Furthermore, we know that Danton is good, but is he from the planet Krypton? The man has grenades thrown at him and is shot point-blank yet emerges without so much as a scratch. And finally, why is that when a man shoots a machine gun in an action film, he makes the same face Eddie Van Halen does when ripping out a guitar solo?

It's impossible not to love *Deadly Prey*. The film is uber-goofy and outrageous, with an entertainment factor that is off the charts. Compounding the lunacy, for a film that features so much carnage, there is a complete lack of squirting plasma. Since they saved big-time on Danton's wardrobe budget, couldn't they have at least ponied up for a squib or two?

By the time Danton bludgeons one of the few remaining mercenaries to death with the merc's own severed arm, you too will be bellowing "DAAAAAAAANTON!!!!!!!"

BAM! Get to the Choppa!

As urban transit commuters, we appreciate that timing is everything on the way to work. Unfortunately, in the action realm, transport isn't nearly as reliable as catching a city bus or a subway. Case in point: choppers. Heroes are continually scrambling to catch that helicopter, and chopper pilots are a notoriously impatient bunch, not even stopping long enough for the hero to hop aboard. As a result, heroes must have the ability to hang from the sides of choppers as they take off. And if this feat wasn't difficult enough, they need the grip strength of a coconut crab as they usually have the benefit of only one arm.

COMMANDO

(1985)

Going commando means no underwear, which makes sense here as there's no fabric that can contain this movie's massive *cojones*. *Commando* is a movie which doesn't waste any time wasting superfluous civilians. In fact, just four minutes in and a suburban dad is used for target practice by assassins, a Cadillac car dealer is driven through his work's front window by a customer with designs on getting the vehicle for free rather than getting a deal on its undercoating, and a trawler is blown up in the harbor too. Ouch.

Up in the mountains of California (c'mon, you know you want to say that word in the Governator's Teutonic growl), Ah-nold struts out onto the screen as John Matrix. His sinews are undulating and he's doing the manliest thing anyone should ever consider doing while credits are rolling: lugging a log on his shoulder while casually hauling a chainsaw. If only he'd been gnawing a cigar *en route* to a hot tub as the Pied Piper of bikini models. Then the picture would've really been complete.

He catches fish and eats ice cream with his daughter, Jenny (Alyssa Milano), and you just know this bucolic bliss is going to be instantly shattered. And like clockwork, a visit from ex-boss Major General Kirby warning him that since he's made enemies all over the globe, intelligence rumblings suggest he's soon going to be targeted. No matter. Kirby assigns two guards—two of his best men in fact—to keep watch over Matrix, guys who you know will be lunch meat in a matter of minutes.

True to form, goons storm the place and shred the sentries. They make off with Jenny, kidnap Matrix, and hope to make him an offer he can't refuse: go down to some fictional banana republic and oust its El Presidente or he'll never see his daughter grow up to star in forgettable sitcoms like *Who's the Boss*? He's hustled on a plane, accompanied by a towering black henchman nattily attired in a pith helmet who looks like he's set to blow away gazelle on the Serengeti. Surely he'll be able to hold Matrix. But no one and nothing can. Not even a passenger jet in mid-ascent, as Matrix bolts from his seat, descends into the wheel well, and launches himself into a nearby swamp.

To the strains of chirpy steel drums, he makes his way back to the airport and goes after pithhead's mate Sully, played by genre icon David Patrick Kelly—he who cries out in the movie of the same name, "Warriors, come out and play-eee-ay!"

In the interim, Sully's been busying himself with hitting on flight attendant Cindy (Rae Dawn Chong) instead of doing what he should've been doing: focusing on his regularly assigned henchman duties. And you know what that means as far as his future is concerned. Matrix tracks him to a shopping mall, where he's picked up and body slammed inside a food court phone booth, which for the benefit of those born after this movie was released, is a structure you had to pay to stand inside to make a call. Luckily for the goon, he manages to escape the mall and its parking lot with his life. However, his Porsche getaway vehicle is no match for Arnold in hot pursuit, now joined by the reluctant civvy Cindy in her ride. They run Sully off the road, then Arnold drags him out of his vehicle and dangles/drops him over a gorge before making off with his fine piece of German engineering.

Forget pimps: it's hard out there for a henchman.

Eventually, new partner Cindy, a plot-convenient amateur pilot, is helping Matrix track down his daughter's captors, airlifting him to their island compound, and busting into an army surplus store that carries enough weaponry to arm half a breakaway Soviet republic. This gives Cindy the flight attendant a chance to showcase her impromptu bazooka-launching skills. If random civilians can fire lethal high-powered weaponry like that, maybe it's high time the US Army boosted its entrance standards and redesigned their munitions.

But really, this is all in preparation for a *massive* assault on the remote island compound where the daughter is being held. And we're not exaggerating about that. It's "like World War III," as one of the fringe characters puts it.

The fortress is defended not by Green Beret toughs or some other cold-blooded professional killers, but by foreign hired sentry so unremarkable they aren't even given subtitles. Co-leader Bennett is in charge, a giant Down Under Freddie Mercury in chainmail lacking upper body muscle tone (or maybe just in comparison to the Austrian colossus, everyone does) with whom Matrix had had a falling out with when they worked together in Delta Force.

Matrix rows ashore in bikini briefs, then applies war paint to himself as the camera leers at his junk like it's gay porn. This is all for storming the island, which he does without any hearing protection as he wastes several hundred jobber nobodies with a Beretta, an Uzi, other submachine guns, M16s, Rugers, machine guns, shotguns, throwing knives, hand grenades, rocket launchers, and (whew) a pitchfork. If there was a kitchen sink, it would've been uprooted from the plumbing and used to pummel a generic hoodlum into submission.

What's amazing about this carnage and all the other killings above is just how casual Matrix is in his approach, dispensing one-liners like this one: "My friend—he's dead tired," in reference to the thug whose neck he'd snapped on the plane and whose corpse he concealed with an in-flight blanket. One of the many indignities of having to fly coach.

OF NOTE:

Speaking of *Warriors*, its director Walter Hill was originally approached to tackle this material. How different that would've been.

THE ANNIHILATORS (1985)

Another in a long line of Vietnam vet returns home from war only to wage a bigger war on the mean streets of whichever city they chose to settle in, 1985's *The Annihilators*[19] distinguishes itself in that it's not a single vet wiping the streets clean of urban scum but rather an entire squadron.

The film starts promisingly with the title formed from machine gun blasts and five minutes of Vietnam War stock footage. Suddenly, the film stock changes entirely and a tank is rolling through what is supposed to be 'Nam but which looks more like an American national park.

The Annihilators, consisting of Sergeant Bill and his men Joe, Garret (Lawrence-Hilton Jacobs, Freddie "Boom Boom" Washington in *Welcome Back, Kotter*), and Ray (the ineffable Gerrit Graham of *Phantom of the Paradise*) are hunkered in their bunker when they get a nebulous order from Intelligence Officer Popeye to invade Red Zone Sector 2. "That's fine by me," says Ray, "I haven't been shot at in two days."

Red Zone Sector 2 is a cakewalk for a crack squadron such as The Annihilators, but the scene is notable for three reasons. First, jokester Ray almost gets impaled by a giant swinging log studded with spikes when he touches a trip wire. Second, this crackerjack bit of dialogue/unintentional sexual innuendo—Sarge: "I'll be the backdoor." Garret: "Oh c'mon Sarge . . . I want some of the fun." And third, Joe takes what appears to be a bullet to the shoulder. (It's hard to tell as no squibs were employed, thus no blood.)

Apparently, ambiguous shoulder injuries cause paraplegia as we flash forward to Joe tooling around the mean streets of Atlanta in a wheelchair, whiling away the days in his father Louie's general store. Unfortunately, it's not just PTSD and lower body immobility that Joe must contend with as a number of gangs are terrorizing the neighborhood, demanding protection money from local businesses and even raising the fee for said services from $25 to $50 a month!

Joe sends his aged father uptown to procure a shotgun. Before Pa leaves, Joe says two things which ensure he'll never see the old coot again. First, he reiterates just how much he loves him. Second, he tearfully implores Pa to "Sit next to a pretty girl on the bus for me, OK?" That's it, Joe; you're a goner.

And right on schedule, seconds after Daddy leaves, the chief gang, Roy Boy and the Rollers,[20] crosses the threshold. They terrorize the lone female customer by stripping her nude then stabbing her in the abdomen. Roy Boy, who looks like Kurt Russell's less-dashing cousin, then takes a meat mallet and bashes Joe's brains in.

Sergeant Bill is in attendance at the funeral. After poor Joe is laid to rest, Poppa Louie approaches his son's erstwhile comrade-in-arms and implores, "If you want to do something about Joe, teach us how to fight." Sarge puts a call in to Popeye and the band of brothers is soon back together.

This leads to a hilarious scene depicting The Annihilators teaching a bunch of neighborhood septuagenarians how to defend themselves using sundry at-hand items such as baseball bats, golf clubs, and No. 2 pencils (we assume for stabbing and not for poisoning, as "lead pencil" is just a name).

When Ray is killed in a shootout[21] with the gang, The Annihilators now need "to see it through for both of them." Oh, and did we mention that the neighborhood is also a thoroughfare for "a big drug operator in Colombia," who strangely smuggles heroin rather than his nation's chief export, cocaine?

When The Annihilators intercept a drug shipment, this doesn't sit well with Roy Boy. He summons his and a number of other interchangeable henchmen. (Obviously, in action movie-land, there's a Henchmen 'R Us that any gang leader can call at a moment's notice to place an order.) This culminates in Roy Boy stalking the streets with a flamethrower, immolating a car before ultimately getting dropkicked off a rooftop by Sarge and onto the very same conflagrant vehicle he set alight earlier.

The Annihilators is doltish fun and semi-plausible although the revelation of Popeye's identity is about as dumb as it gets. It's a treat to see Gerrit Graham in anything, and if Paul Koslo (*Vanishing Point*) is in on the joke as the over-the-top Roy Boy, he's certainly a better actor than we give him credit for. A fitting end to the directorial career of Charles E. Sellier Jr., whose first feature, the seminal Santa Claus slasher *Silent Night, Deadly Night*, was released only one year earlier.[22]

ONE TOUGH BASTARD, A.K.A. ONE MAN'S JUSTICE (1995)

Forget Hans Gruber in *Die Hard*. Who needs that angry Teuton when you've got the bastard, um, offspring of Triple H and the Vampire Lestat? Savak is a corrupt FBI man in the Brian Bosworth gonzo action pic *One Tough Bastard*, a.k.a. *One Man's Justice* (is another man's treasure? The latter sounds like Jason Statham should be in it).

Well, this trash is treasure. With the lowest expectations comes the greatest rewards.

Ex-Seahawks linebacker Brian Bosworth, known in some circles as The Boz, is Marine Corp drill sergeant and military combat expert John North (that's one syllable per name baby, the way God and action heroism intended).

His wife and daughter are murdered in a stickup hostage situation, and the film goes on to gloriously fail the Bechdel Test unless you count the kid screaming for her mommy.

North arrives on the scene but is pumped full of lead as he tries to save his loved ones.

Like Seagal, (or the famously pumped full of real-life lead 50 Cent) North is *Hard to Kill*, and as soon as he recuperates, he's off to lay down some very serious ass-whoopings.

His memories of the twin fatal shootings slowly start flooding back to him, particularly a greasy gunman with a bat tattoo on his neck who DNA testing cannot confirm nor deny is Willem Dafoe's meth-addled son.

North, in a great montage showing just how dangerous and scary tattoo parlors are, visits each and every one in Venice Beach while sporting a brown blazer with elbow patches. He eventually tracks down the tattoo artist who did the batty and, from an aesthetic standpoint, questionable artwork. When the man gives him attitude and threatens North for asking to divulge those particulars, the tools of his trade are rammed through his hand and the parlor goons get a fantastic thumping. With the tattoo needle still quivering through his tendons, the tattoo artist begrudgingly offers details about how North can pursue his quest.

Boz is in fine form here. His spinning back heels are frankly awesome, his elbows are sharp as diamonds, and he throws bad guys through glass and to turf with aplomb.

The true star of *One Tough Bastard*, though, is corrupt FBI man Savak. He's the brains behind high-tech military ordnances (hilariously marked as such on the carrying case) being stolen from North's base to be used on the mean streets of Los Angeles. Among the folks involved, a heroin-dealing gang headed by undistinguished floppy-pant rapper Hammer! Can't touch him. He's Kane, a badass with a pocket square folded into a crown.

But truth be told, this is all about Savak, whose nose ring and flowing locks set him apart from other action hero villains. And none of these villains would be worth their salt without a boatload of Earth-shaking catchphrases.

Savak's are terse yet lyrical and invariably involve "pony." ("You're gonna be in the dog-and-pony show until the pony dies!" and "You tryin' to fuck me again, Pony?")

His greatest offering though is, in between puffs of an ever-present smoke, "You packin' heat? No? Then what good are you?" Words to live by in an off-the-charts high body count action movie that packs a lot of heat into a dealer revenge framework.

Във филма се преплитат двесъдби: на Норт, тръгнал да отмъщава за безсмисленото убийство на жена си и дъщеря си, и на десетгодишния Мики, станал свидетел на нелепото убийство на своя приятел заради 2 сникера. Норт научава, че човекът, убил жена му и дъщеря му, е под закрила на федералните власти и поема собствено разследване. Така той попада на следи, водещи към престъпления от съвсем друг сорт: търговия с оръжие, наркотрафик, продажност в армията... Той ще открие убиеца, но отмъщението му ще бъде много по-различно от очакването.

Участват: БРАЯН БОСУЪРД,
БРУС ПЕЙН, ЕМ СИ ХАМЪР и др.
Оператор: ДЖОН ХЪНЕК, ЮРГЕН БАУМ
Музика: ЕНТЪНИ МАРИНЕЛИ
Сценарист: СТИВЪН СЕЛИНГ
Режисьор: КЪРТ УИМЪР

ТОП ВИДЕО РЕКЪРДС
Адрес: София, ж.к. "Красно село"
бл. 189, вх. В, ет. 3, ап. 10
тел.: 02/556 029, тел./факс: 02/560 963

LIVE INTERNATIONAL

ЕКШЪН

One Tough Bastard

Един Луд Кучи Син

ТОП ВИДЕО РЕКЪРДС

Кат. №: 0243

САЩ 97 мин. ©1995г. TBP

(Дистрибуция и оформление)

ТОП ВИДЕО РЕКЪРДС ПРЕДСТАВЯ

Браян Босуърд

Един Луд Кучи Син

LIVE ENTERTAINMENT Presents A WESTWIND PRODUCTION
A KURT WIMMER FILM BRIAN BOSWORTH "ONE TOUGH BASTARD"
BRUCE PAYNE JEFF KOBER DeJUAN GUY and HAMMER
Directors of Photography JOHN HUNECK JURGEN BAUM
Editor MICHAEL TRIBAULT Music By ANTHONY MARINELLI
Line Producer LANSING PARKER Executive Producer GARY WICHARD
Written By STEVEN SELLING Produced By WILLIAM WEBB
Directed by KURT WIMMER

LIVE INTERNATIONAL

COMBAT.
IT'S ABOUT TIMING. IT'S ABOUT DISTANCE. IT'S ABOUT WINNING!

John North (BRIAN BOSWORTH) wakes up in hospital to discover that the man who killed his wife and child is under federal protection.

Savak, the agent assigned to the case, is after a ruthless drug-lord named Dexter Kane but North doesn't trust the sly Fed and embarks on his own investigation!

His passion for revenge is extreme and in a spectacular twist ending, North manages to not only get revenge, but also round up a lethal gang of cop-killers and find a new happiness.

9 317731 496813

WESTWIND

APPROX. 96 MINS

LIVE

VIDEO BOX OFFICE

ONE TOUGH BASTARD

VHS STEREO ON LINEAR TRACKS MONO COMPATIBLE Hi-Fi

VBV 24968

BRIAN BOSWORTH

LIVE INTERNATIONAL

ONE TOUGH BASTARD

REVENGE IS EVERYTHING

VIDEO BOX OFFICE

RESTRICTED 18

Restricted to persons 18 Years and over

NOTE: Contains violence and offensive language.

BLIND FURY (1989)

After a mortar shell blinds him in the 'Nam jungle, villagers train US soldier Nick Parker in the deadly art of sword fighting, just like what would happen in real life. Priorities. It's a lesson in letting bygones be bygones, overlooking the fact that his company might've wiped out half the village.

They cover his peepers with banana leaves and heighten his undamaged senses by exposing them to various stimuli, including a snake. Maybe cucumber pads and a rubdown would've been a better transition after such a harrowing ordeal? But don't ask us, we've never served in combat, and by the looks of it, neither did anyone associated with this movie, as the battle scenes wouldn't pass muster as *Platoon* B-roll.

Soon, Nick is chopping through fresh fruit like he's ready to get girl-drink drunk, as cantaloupes and coconuts are lobbed at him from all directions. For all the budding botanists out there, a coconut is not a nut, but actually an indehiscent fruit. But that's ok, there's enough nuttiness to go around.

While he can certainly chop, Nick, played by Rutger Hauer, lacks the comedy chops of his twin, Conan O'Brien. Their close physical similarity, apart from the gingerness, is actually a bit distracting. Still, *Blind Fury's* fun can, um, be spotted a mile away.

Back home, Nick is navigating his way through sweltering Florida, stepping over gators with his bamboo walking stick, actually a scabbard made to look like one, containing one seriously sharp carbon steel sword.

When a bunch of Latino bar goofs play keep away with a woman's purse—the same ne'er-do-wells who earlier played a trick on Nick by replacing his burrito sauce with dollops of hot sauce—the blind man calls their bluff and makes quick work of all of them, disability (and reasonability) be damned.

His first mission back on US soil is to track down one of his army buddies, Frank, now a chemist and in hock to the Nevada mob who want him to use his lab talents to cook meth or whatever designer drugs the kids were into at the time. Frank's been kidnapped, and now neither his estranged wife nor their son are safe. (Why they have to go through this rigmarole of kidnapping the son is anyone's guess when they could've just as easily threatened to kill Frank.) While Nick is making an inquiry as to his old pal's whereabouts, baddies burst into his Florida home, put a hole through the woman's chest even larger than the one for the plot, and make off with Billy.

Now it's up to blind Nick to save little Billy, find out where Frank is being held, and save the day (not to mention do everything that sighted people can do, but at a far superior level, with proprioception better than the top half of all the batting orders in Major League Baseball).

After cutting a swath of destruction through able-bodied, sighted henchmen, tales of Nick's exploits reach the mob boss who opines, "I don't wanna hear about this blind man!" But by then it's too late. Nick tracks the operations to Reno, dazzles at the roulette table while making James Bond look like an amateur, and is lucky enough to overhear the mobsters plotting in the casino. Good thing they were within earshot.

The slashes are sharp, and Nick's lines are tight. After he slices one mobster's thick eyebrows off, he casually mentions he also "does circumcisions." There are chase scenes with Nick driving. And because gangsters are such lousy shots, they put Nick's hands in the fate of another swordsman to finish him off: a ninja assassin played by Sho Kosugi, for a battle to the death atop a hot tub situated perilously close to some electric wires.

SHOCKING DARK, A.K.A. TERMINATOR 2 (1989) [TIE FOR 40TH PLACE]

Not the Arnie *Terminator 2*! This one, *Shocking Dark*, sits at 23% on *Rotten Tomatoes*, and that's actually a rating as generous as Bill and Melinda Gates.

The film features a military tactical team known as Megaforce who dress in "business casual" versions of Michael Jackson's "Thriller" get-up. They are named Kowalski, Franzini, et al, and make horrible ethnic jokes at one another's expense.

Megaforce is given a debriefing in a room that looks like the waiting area to renew driver's licences, and the intrepid crew teams up with a member of Tubular Corporation, a company that is contracted to help remediate Venice, Italy's water supply.

They're sent into the bowels of Venice to investigate what turns out later to be the evil corporation's attempt to poison the city's inhabitants gone horribly awry . . . or something. It's legitimately difficult to make sense of this. And speaking of making sense, if any city's going to have "bowels," Venice certainly ain't it. Why set a film that's predominantly underground in Venice, the City of Bridges? You might as well recreate a 42nd Street peepshow on the front lawn of a Long Island bungalow.

In future Venice they've circumvented the engineering problem of what is essentially a city sinking atop a highly unstable mud lagoon by building a vast network of catacombs. Highly

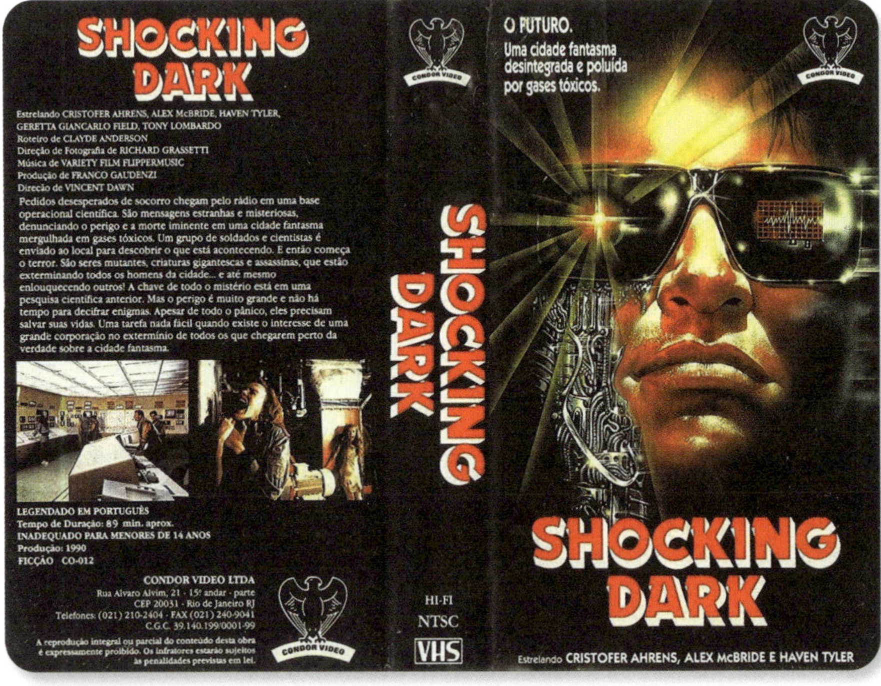

un-foreboding and extremely cheap-looking *Alien*-like creatures lurk below, complete with fangs, goo, and a lousy temperament. Megaforce battles them with ample firepower and an array of action film dialogue clichés. ("What does he wanna do, get himself killed?", "We're gonna get you outta here, I promise.")

And also from the typewriter of Claudio Fragasso (*Troll 2, Women's Prison Massacre*) come equally uninspiring gems like:

You either come with us, or I'll blow your head off.
Do I have a choice?
No!

(We don't mean to quibble, but isn't that a choice?)

We've encountered movies with far worse dialogue (hard to believe given the above), worse special effects (again, not many), and worse acting (a few dozen), but *Terminator 2 Shocking Dark* can plant its flag as the most appalling cinematography we've ever encountered.

Poorly lit, muddy, and uber-cheap (it was "shocking" to find out this "dark" movie was lensed in '89), it has the aesthetic shared by Bruno Mattei's other glorious rip-off, *Strike Commando* (though that one had the benefit of being shot during daylight to make sense of what was going on). At the end of the day, *Shocking Dark* stinks worse than any Venetian canal.

We'd love to ask Mattei why, if you're going to do a scene-for-scene remake of *Aliens* underground, would you title it *Terminator 2* when you've waited until the final frame to parachute in a time-travelling cyborg. (At roughly the same time you've decided to finally showcase the non-subterranean side of arguably the world's most picturesque city.)

MERCENARY FIGHTERS (1988)

B. B. King had a signature guitar sound, identifiable in one note. Reb Brown is identifiably one-note too, a husky ever-effervescent Californian with "golly-gee" permanently etched into his mug. Yet somehow this naïf with a high-tenor and barely enough acting chops to replace a maître d' became a staple of action cinema. Sure, other, more high-profile names have been battle-tested in this space, but nobody . . . nobody can touch Reb when it comes to indiscriminate yelling while unloading round after round of muscle-rippling belt-loaded machine gun fire.

In *Mercenary Fighters*, Reb is a cutthroat making bank for an African dictator, taking out tribal rebels to make way for a large power dam project outside fictional Shinkasa. If that name sounds familiar, it's a near-anagram of Kinshasha, the Congolese city where Ali fought Foreman and the backdrop for one of the greatest documentaries of all time, *When We Were Kings*.

Why the silly "Shinkasa," a linguistic slight of hand that's as effective a disguise as Clark Kent's spectacles? Why is a guy with an eternally sunny mien who looks like he'd empty his pockets for the wallet inspector playing a stone cold killer-for-hire?

Because this is a Cannon production! As a result, *Mercenary Fighters* brings with it the atonal strangeness and alien lunacy that showcased Israeli cousins Menahem Golan and Yoram Globus's giant Cannon balls. Case in point: when the mercenaries are assembling, a soldier-of-fortune buddy joins their crew by hopping out of a biplane that lands on top of a moving bus! This dangerous stunt makes absolutely zero sense. And somehow, bus passengers Reb Brown (as T.J. Christian) and fellow merc Ron O'Neal (playing Cliff, and whose name is misspelled "O'Neil" in the credits) don't seem the slightest bit surprised as their comrade shoves his way through an open window into the seat beside them. It's just another day at the office. They all just whoop it up on their way to their mission debrief with a limping, long-haired Peter Fonda (portraying their "goombah" Captain Virelli).

And for a film with a bunch of hookers brought in to ease the stress of filling tribal villagers with hot lead to make way for modernity, strangely it's the male nudity that is most memorable. In one scene, the ladies of the evening mock the tiny manhood of one of the mercenaries, who is frolicking in a nearby river. With the crews' big guns, they're clearly overcompensating.

But at least there are some serious "merc perks" here for action fans.

First off, that is some cast. Superfly, Mike Ransom, and two Captain Americas! (In *Easy Rider*, Fonda played "Captain America" and as discussed in this book, Brown squeezed himself into the tights for a made-for-TV dud of the same name.)

After seeing the government's corruption and bloodthirstiness with his very own deer-in-the-headlights eyes (and with a little sweet-talking from a do-gooder nurse), Brown switches sides. The rebels gather around him and belt out a tribal chorus to him in the bowels of a cave.

Yes, much like Mike Ransom was in *Strike Commando*, so too is Reb Brown's T.J. Christian practically worshipped here. That is one amazin' Caucasian!

As a tribal warlord in his dying breath pleads for help, Brown exclaims, "You speak English!"

before protesting that he "cannot be their leader," either because he has already mowed down hundreds of their ranks before the change of heart or because he feels he's not quite ready for a role in senior management. Finally, viewers get to see a clearly bored Peter Fonda calling Brown "dick brain" and "dick brains" as the captain starts to get a sense his young charge is going rogue. Will our muscled hero stop the dam and save the villagers? Damned if we care.

Also, in another bit of casting that could've only been the product of, well, minutes of Cannon Group brainstorming, Bond giant Richard Kiel was initially pegged for the Peter Fonda role. That's not only incredibly odd, but somewhat embarrassing for Pete as the Fondas are second only to the Barrymores as Hollywood family royalty, and being a backup after Richard Kiel turns down a role is a heaping helping of humble pie.

Mercenary Fighters has nowhere close to the name recognition of other Cannons such as *Missing in Action, Death Wish II, Masters of the Universe*, etc. Perhaps this is because the year it was released, Cannon Film Group executives bowed to pressure from anti-apartheid activists and agreed to stop using South Africa as a filming location (three *American Ninja* films were among the nearly two dozen features that either filmed there or used a South African crew.)

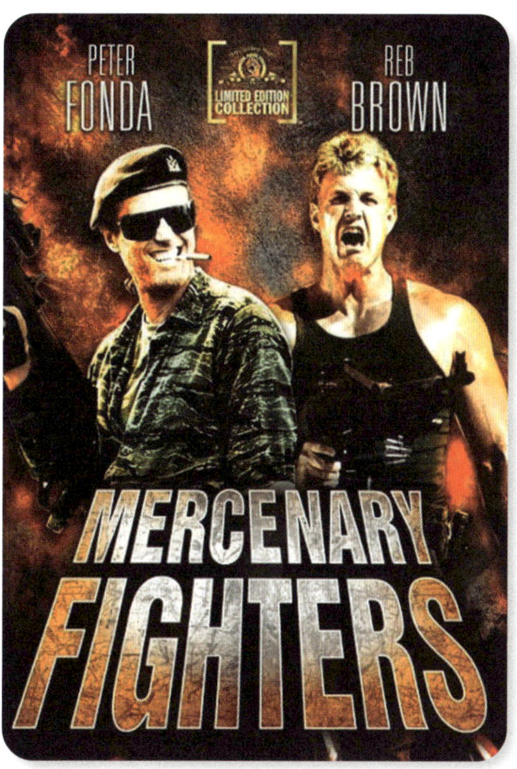

42

DOUBLE TARGET (1987)

Most people know Bob Ross as the PBS landscape painter who made viewers comatose even before the pledge drive snack breaks, his meme afro making a near-eclipse of TV screens.

But there's a much less well-known Bob Ross, the fictional muscle head of *Double Target*, a badass Vietnam vet who in true action movie fashion, *is* the movie's title. He's played by "Worst New Star" Razzie nominee for *Tarzan, the Ape Man*, Miles O'Keeffe. And this IS a Bruno Mattei (Vincent Dawn) directorial production, a man who couldn't light a cigarette, and as a result, most of *Double Target* is shrouded in total darkness. But still, especially with the help of countless explosions, there are a few things the viewer can still make out.

When western targets are hit in Hong Kong, Malaysia, and fortuitously, the Philippines, where movies are cheaper to film and to pass off as Vietnam, Ross is conscripted to get to the bottom of it. As luck would have it, he's already traipsing around 'Nam looking for the son he fathered with a local village woman, since killed, so we don't need to trouble ourselves with a messy international custody dispute (and putting aside for a moment whether a child would like to be taken from his village, his family, his country, and his culture to be whisked away by a strange foreigner in combat fatigues he's never met who communicates mostly in grunts).

Double Target shoots off so many rounds of action/Vetsploitation clichés, an abandoned warehouse full of bandoliers in tactical ammo cans is required:

- We get a sweaty, asthmatic Donald Pleasence mopping his brow as Senator Blaster, who fills in our hero by reading from an IMPORTANT DOSSIER outlining what is unquestionably a suicide mission, in this case, finding evidence that Russians/Vietnamese are up to no good and are behind the spate of bombings.
- The hero belligerently questioning the feasibility of the mission. Here, a reluctant Ross saying he'll "shove that briefcase up your ass and make you swallow that inhaler."
- A ridiculous and very arbitrary timeline to complete said mission as a device to help propel the plot.

- The hero inevitably saying "I've got some unfinished business to take care of" when he realizes there are still a few people among the hundreds of extras yet to be mowed down in a hail of jungle warfare M16 fire.
- A leap out the window of a tall building, aided by several well-placed multi-floor awnings to break the fall.
- The villain capturing the hero, then instead of executing him post-haste, keeps him around Bond-style, for "the real execution, which is tomorrow."
- The hero beating the holy tar out of a henchman after a stern warning, "The man in front of you is a martial arts expert!"
- The Rule of Choppers: When leaping into a helicopter, you never make it but are forced to hang precipitously off the landing skids until swinging your legs in once it's airborne.
- Vietnamese-speaking villains who occasionally lapse into English, even when talking to one another.
- The ability to fool native Russian speakers with a two-word vocabulary of "nyet" and "da."
- A buddy compatriot who gets injured and insists the hero continue on without him, so he can do something heroic himself before dying in some sadistic manner.
- And of course, countless thatch huts wiped out by flame throwers and expendable henchmen sent flying through the air accompanied by Wilhelm screams.

FIVE

REVENGE IS A DISH BEST SERVED IN THIS CHAPTER

THE TIME IS OUT OF JOINT:

O CURSED SPITE

THAT EVER I WAS BORN TO SET IT RIGHT!

—HAMLET

Why have a separate chapter for this when EVERY SINGLE MARTIAL ARTS MOVIE EVER is about revenge in one form or another? Because it's our book, dammit, and we'll do what we want! If you take umbrage with that, come at us and we'll get involved in a protracted back-and-forth war that'll leave a huge trail of bodies in its wake. But don't; we're writers, not fighters.

If we can draw a scotch whisky analogy . . . much like all scotches are whiskys but not the reverse, all martial arts movies are revenge films, but not all revenge films are martial arts movies. So there.

Anyone who's ever been shoved into a locker in high school has thought about how nice it would be to slip laxatives into their antagonist's thermos. And there's science to back up why we have these feelings. It's in our blood.

According to a *Scientific American* article, "MRI scans have revealed that thinking about revenge activates the reward center—where the feel-good neurotransmitter dopamine is lodged."[23]

The piece goes on to point out that we don't wish revenge on just anybody. It's personal, usually involving someone we care about. In action movies, that's depicted by forlorn looks at a photo inside a wallet and bellicose proclamations to the heavens of the name of the person to whom characters wish to enact their furious vengeance upon.

Revenge as an impulse is so powerful, it can turn dull suburban dads into superhuman robot-killing machines. It can turn unassuming architects into a one-man army. They say that "He who seeks vengeance must dig two graves: one for his enemy and one for himself." We suggest that, rather than doing that, read this chapter twice instead.

There are conflicting interpretations of Jesus's Sermon on the Mount: forget turning the other cheek. Let's turn the tables and keep both cheeks face-forward. For in this chapter, we're comin' for you. REVENGE!

43

ROLLING VENGEANCE (1987)

According to a 2015 examination of US census data, the most prevalent occupation in North America is truck driver. While by no means glamorous, you can still smoke on the job and make your own hours, a claim few outside the prostitution trade can make. And every waking moment is like the non-arm-wrestling scenes from *Over the Top*.

However, the profession is dangerous, what with the tight delivery schedules, running cars off the road to meet those schedules, and still managing to get to the nearest truck stop in time for onion rings and a bathroom dalliance.

Logging hundreds of miles with nothing but conspiratorial talk radio or the odd maniac hitchhiker as company is a sure-fire recipe for self-destruction. Besides, the physical tolls are steep—sedentary lifestyles, poor diets, and a buffet of pharmaceuticals processed through kidneys and lobbed out the window in a plastic bottle.

Truckers' rigs in action cinema usually serve two purposes. The first is to provide an obstacle for the hero to nearly miss crashing into during chases. At other times, 18-wheelers will suddenly spin out, the trailer unit blocking the road at a perfect right angle. The hero's vehicle will then find a way to fly *over* the trailer while the evil pursuer's vehicle will fly *into* it. If truck drivers are lucky to have a speaking role, it usually consists of saying something lewd to a busty blonde in a convertible. Hence, *Rolling Vengeance* is a long time coming, giving truckers the spotlight they deserve.

In the film, an Ohio town is coping with a rowdy and disreputable local business, Tiny's, a hybrid used-car dealership, tavern, restaurant, and strip club.

It's the focus of an outreach campaign by the local chapter of Mothers Against Drunk Driving, whose efforts to corral some of the drunk and disorderly behavior associated with the place is met with rudeness by the bar's owner, tough guy Tiny Doyle. He's played by Ned Beatty of *Deliverance*, sporting a flat top hairdo and a too-tight leather jacket. He sends the ladies packing with the message that his patrons aren't drunk and dangerous but actually "intoxicated with joy" after last call, and graciously offers one of them a table dancing gig.

And the fermented apples don't fall far from this degenerate's un-forking family tree as Tiny's five sons are all drunk layabouts. And their idea of fun is squealing like pigs while lobbing beer bottles at townsfolk from the back of a pickup.

Far better father/son role models are Big Joe and strapping Joey Rosso, who share a family run big rig and are part of a wholesome, tightly knit household that includes Joey's two younger sisters. (Well, not too wholesome. We're still in exploitation country after all, and in a curious scene, the 10-year-old asks the befuddled dad if she'll develop "boobs like Dolly Parton's.")

One day, the five Doyle family ruffians are tailing Big Joe's wife and two daughters in their family sedan. The tanked-up hicks hurl bottles at them, and when the missus takes evasive action, a tractor trailer plows into her, killing all the vehicle's occupants.

Back in town, justice is willfully blind. The judge, while conceding Tiny's sons were all drunk as lords, can't see fit to dole out more than a measly $300 fine as the fivesome escape manslaughter charges and one is hit with a meagre court-ordered rehab stint. The scofflaws even mock the grieving Rosso family outside the courtroom.

But this is a revenge chapter and this is a revenge flick, so we can't possibly expect Judge Judy jurisprudence with a quick lock-up-and-throw-away-the-key.

Dejected Joey and his pa head over to Tiny's and try to punch it out like men. They're saved from a certain beating by the same trucker whose actions unintentionally led to the demise of three-fifths of the Rossos.

The Doyle family, as might be expected, isn't exactly overcome with remorse and contrition. They're whooping it up instead! And they're soon back to their old tricks; making life miserable for drivers with Ohio plates.

They haul a bunch of concrete cinder blocks up to a highway overpass and drop them, ambushing poor Joe, and when father takes evasive action, his brand-new rig hurtles into the ditch and he's hospitalized, setting the stage for son to exact revenge. This is another classic example of completely ineffectual community policing so prevalent in action films.

"Rolling vengeance" takes the form of a monster truck, a pugnaciously pimped out ride that Joey constructs via a very macho welding montage. The beast shoots fire out its top and huffs like it's gonna gore a matador. It even has a giant drill bit attached to its undercarriage.

Joey drives it over to Tiny's and flattens every used car in the lot, as well as a couple of Tiny's boys for good measure, tracking one of them with a monster truck POV through a cornfield as the hapless fellow flees for his life. It's soon lights out for the rest of the Doyle family, as in the very best vigilante movies, law enforcement decides to take a very hands-off approach to investigating the case when they realize the whole town benefits. Without spoiling it, the drill bit in a drain pipe scene is not to be missed.

DEATH WISH 3 (1985)

Nobody slugs anyone with a roll of quarters anymore, and that's a shame—an art lost for the ages. In the first *Death Wish*, the Grand Poohbah of gritty revenge films, one of the victims of vigilante Charles Bronson does get a sock wallop of coins for his troubles, getting off pretty easy all things considered.

When we first meet Bronson as family man and real estate developer Paul Kersey, he's a guy whose "heart beats for the underprivileged," recalling the Irving Kristol zinger, "a conservative is just a liberal who has been mugged."

That heart hardens though when his wife and daughter are brutally victimized in his New York City apartment, and the trauma of an indifferent to his plight NYPD, up to its eyeballs in crime and with no leads, causes Kersey to immerse himself in work as a coping mechanism.

On a business trip to frontier-town Tucson, straight-shooting business partner Ames gives Paul a reintroduction to his Second Amendment rights and opines, "Hell, a gun's just a tool like a hammer or an axe," even if you can't imagine for a second middle-aged Kersey wreaking havoc on the mean streets of NYC with a hammer.

As a going away present, Ames gives Paul a revolver and soon, back in New York, he's Bernie Goetz reincarnate, getting rid of the city's scumbags and becoming something of a folk hero whom the cops are reluctant to investigate.

Death Wish is an undeniable classic, though derided in some circles as "fascistic," as if wanting to avenge the murder of your wife is some impulse that exists purely in the realm of speculation. *Death Wish 3,* however, further erodes the legacy of the first film which *Death Wish 2* had already kick-started.

Paul Kersey is back in The Big Apple and apparently down on his luck too. After all, what man of his means would take a lowly bus into New York's Port Authority?

He goes to visit his heretofore unmentioned "best friend" Charlie (a conceit few folks other than the Cannon boys could dream up), only to find he's been beaten and left for dead. Charlie, we hardly knew ya!

Suspected vigilante Kersey is immediately hauled in for questioning, despite lacking any kind of motive. With the lousy homicide clearance rate of police in the *Death Wish* movies, perhaps their new strategy is to just bring anyone into custody who is even remotely related to a crime scene, hoping that some sort of charge will stick?

Kersey is offered a deal by a police big-shot: either work for law enforcement as a hitman-for-hire or face jail time as "the vigilante." This is an unbelievably slipshod, silly premise that actually does fit the "fascistic" epithet critics had lobbed at the first film, as Kersey's given carte-blanche to waste anybody even tangentially related to the drug trade. Unlike the reticence to take matters into his own hands in the darkly ambiguous first *Death Wish*, here Kersey relishes in his street justice. It's actually a bit creepy how he fetishizes the firepower of each weapon he'll use to blow away the usual assortment of *Warriors*-styled tough guys.

Death Wish 3 though, isn't just sullied by dismal politics. It's also got the stamp of Cannon all over it.

There's a tacked-on love interest with a blonde public defender who takes an interest in Kersey despite the duo appearing to be three presidential administrations apart in age. The sparks fly between them, though, and Kersey accepts her offer of a home cooked meal, offering sizzling banter like "Chicken's good. I like chicken."

There's a hopelessly ridiculous scene with elderly Russians allowing their place to be booby trapped with a nail board. And a World War II vet offers Kersey use of his massive Browning machine gun to blow away Brooklyn's criminal element, maybe apropos as *Death Wish 3* has a higher body count than *Saving Private Ryan*. The gangsters look like Ash Wednesday penitents with bizarre forehead paint. They're lead by Fraker, the world's scariest Caucasian, who's got a stripe shaved into his skull like a Bizarro World mohawk.

It's Fraker's demise that's one of the most outstanding in the action film canon. With Kersey cornered in the living room of a second story walk-up, Fraker announces via chest thump, that's he's "bullet proof, asshole," on account of the Kevlar vest.

Unfortunately, this protection is no match for Kersey firepower. And Fraker gets blown through the tenement window by Kersey, who happens to have a bazooka where the reading lamp should be.

Zeppelin guitarist Jimmy Page once again supplies the keyboard-heavy soundtrack awfulness, and this one really goes down like a lead balloon.

MASSACRE MAFIA STYLE, A.K.A. THE EXECUTIONER (1978)

"You see these hands? You know what they smell of? Oregano, pasinigol, beautiful herbs! These hands gave you mostaccioli, lasagna, pizza—some of the most appreciated foods in the world! But what did we give her, Chucky, eh? We gave her violence! We gave her death! We gave her dishonor!"

From the mouth of would-be mafia kingpin Mimi Miceli in 1978's *Massacre Mafia Style* (also known as *The Executioner*)—a film that suggests what *Goodfellas* would have been like had it been crafted by the misguided meat hooks of *The Room*'s Tommy Wiseau.

The Executioner practically defines the term "Grindhouse." It's super sleazy, ultra-violent, amateurish, and bursting with casual racism. It also lacks anything remotely close to unity or coherency. But like outsider art, *The Executioner* rises above those debits (or are they credits?), and the final product is a sort of incomprehensible genius.

A labor of love for popular LA nightclub performer (and amazingly, Fred's singing voice in *The Flintstones*) Duke Mitchell—billed here as Dominico Miceli—this film was intended to educate the world on what the mafia was *really* like, since that hack job *The Godfather* steered us all so wrong. Like all auteurs, Mitchell wrote the screenplay and directed, produced, and starred in the film. (He had hoped his good friend Frank Sinatra would costar, but upon seeing the script, Ol' Blue Eyes remarked "Duke, I love you, but I get paid real money to do real movies.")

Mitchell plays Mimi Miceli, the son of Don Mimi, a mafia head sent packing back to the old country while Mimi was just a little linguini. As Mimi Jr. matures, he yearns to return to the States, both to avenge the wrongs committed against Papa and also to grab a slice of the Mafia pie for himself. Back on US soil, he immediately reunites with his childhood friend Jolly Rizzo, who bears an uncanny resemblance to Wolfman Jack.

With a motto of "Tonight we eat, tomorrow we shoot!" Mimi and Jolly cut a swath of terror and destruction through the criminal underworld of Los Angeles. Their rise is marked by a propensity to kill anything that moves in gruesomely creative ways such as impaling rivals on meat hooks and rolling a wheelchair-bound foe into a bathroom, shoving him into a urinal, tying an electrical cord to his leg brace, then demonstrating the conductive properties of metal when they plug the cord in.

When Mimi isn't killing indiscriminately, he's going off on lengthy spiels about the plight of Italian immigrants in America. (See the genius "You see these hands?" soliloquy above.)

But alas, like Icarus, Mimi and Jolly fly too close to the sun, and their rapid rise is followed by an equally precipitous (and rather convoluted) fall. Soon Mimi is hitting the mattresses, hiding out, and shooting pornographic movies! Jolly gets whacked. When Mimi discovers his friend's lifeless body, he picks up Jolly's own arm to make the sign of the cross.

Massacre Mafia Style is filled with terribly executed ethnic accents of all stripes as well as horrendously awful '70s haircuts and fashions. Mitchell stands roughly 5'2" tall and cuts quite the figure with his graying pompadour, gigantic medallions, highway-wide lapels, shirt unbuttoned past his sternum, and pants hiked up to his nipples. Nonsensical Italian-sounding words such as "Sazulla" and "Maro-Mamina" are bandied about faster than an antipasto tray at an Italian wedding.

To compound the lunacy, the scenes purportedly set in Sicily look as if they were shot in a Hoboken backyard. Still, you have to admire Mitchell's hubris. He sold a supper club that he owned to fund the film, and sent out real invitations to get extras to populate a wedding scene. Mitchell then sold the gifts the "guests" brought to fund the film further.

Massacre Mafia Style is crazed filmmaking at its finest. Come for the broadly drawn ethnic stereotypes and gratuitous violence, but stay for Mitchell-composed and -sung songs featuring titles such as "Tic-a-Te" and "Rigatone, Mostacoioli and Spaget."

DEATH FORCE, A.K.A. FIGHTING MAD (1978)

With a samurai sword protruding upright in the sand like a B-movie Iwo Jima, we find ourselves again deep in South Asia, tantalized by lush orchestration and a lovely beachside vista, in another Filipino lensed exploitation cheapie from the always entertaining Cirio Santiago (*TNT Jackson*) oeuvre.

That's Luzon Island, the Philippines, formerly Clark Air Force Base, where we've got three grateful G.I.s just back from 'Nam and ready to resume a peaceful suburban existence stateside. Or not. In a bar with "hot women and cold beer" they're already plotting a criminal caper. This involves transporting gold bars stashed in coffins for "The Chinaman," a fixture of the local underworld, played by the ubiquitous Thrilla from Manila, cherubic Filipino genre staple Vic Diaz.

But African American Russell is a reluctant participant, keen on seeing the missus and his young son back in California. The other two, McGee (*Penitentiary's* Leon Isaac Kennedy) and Morelli, prove that there is no honor among thieves in heist movies. Just once it'd be nice to see brigands separate the loot equally and be off on their merry way.

On a boat in the South China Sea, Morelli convinces the other African American McGee that racial solidarity is for suckers, and the only color that matters is the one on the bill. The duo double-cross Russell, stabbing him and dumping him overboard.

Little do they know, Russell is made from tough stuff. He washes up on a South Pacific island inhabited by two self-sufficient Japanese soldier castaways, neither of whom is aware their war is over.

The kindly duo nurse the man back to health, then press him for details about all the history they've missed, and are disappointed to note that decades have passed since either DiMaggio last suited up in the major leagues.

Death Force is a one-size-fits-all genre-bender: Blaxploitation, martial arts, mafia, Vetsploitation, heist movie, and revenge flick. It's the closest film we've come across which could conceivably fit into each and any of our chapters, save for Kick-Ass Women. There's even an inane nightclub crooner act in the form of Russell's long-suffering wife, as if producers felt they'd short-changed the audience by not making this a musical as well.

Back on the tropical island, Russell is the most exciting thing to happen to these Japanese in eons. They speak in stereotypically broken "Eng-Rish" and teach him the ways of the samurai sword by pitching coconuts at him baseball-style (years before *Fruit Ninja*).

While they're resigned to their fate, Russell is still convinced he'll get off the island, and sure enough a Filipino navy search party lands on their secluded oasis, perfectly timed so Russell wouldn't have to Robinson Crusoe it for any longer than necessary. He heads back to the States. On his person is the formidable samurai sword given to him by his oddball mentors, one of whom has committed Seppuku rather than fall into enemy hands. This is quite the overreaction given how swimmingly they got along with American Russell.

Back in LA, McGee and Morelli are gunning down every underworld flunky with a sex-offender mustache and a fedora, often in third-rate trattorias and complete with *Godfather* knock-off

music. The 'Nam vets have eaten into mafia territory by wasting an Ellis Island boatload of guinea stereotypes, but have no fear; this film is an equal opportunity offender: the Japanese guys are played by Filipinos in whiteface!

To add insult to injury—make that the attempted murder of Russell—McGee has been putting the moves on Russell's singing wife (Jayne Kennedy, the first African American actress to grace the cover of *Playboy* albeit fully clothed inside, top-billed here despite her scant screen time and unwillingness to doff her top).

When a steamed Russell (who, after what couldn't have been more than two weeks on the island, is now both fluent in the ways of the Bushido *and* the Japanese language) returns a "cold calculating killing machine" (at least according to the trailer, the bad man with a large sword) cuts and parries his way through corrupt cops and dull-witted Mafiosi, all in an attempt to track down the duo who wronged him. If you "wanted to hang on to your head" and were in a ten-mile radius of Russell, you were in a bad way.

Overlong, improbable, and with a downer of an ending that truly comes out of nowhere, *Death Force* is nonetheless prime genre fare served up well-done, Santiago style.

THE ONE ARMED EXECUTIONER (1981)

The title almost sounds like some Confucian parable: "He who shakes hands with a one-armed man . . . ," something, something. After all, in the land of the blind, the one-eyed man is king.

However, a film about a man who cannot symmetrically flag a cab leans heavily to the side of the goofy: the first scene features a midget shaken down inside a phone booth by a henchman, then dumped off the end of a pier.

When authorities fish the little man out of the bay, nobody can understand how the "small-time hustler" (pun not intended here) ended up dead or what his connections to the lucrative Philippines' drug trade was. And it's up to our hero, Ortega, to find out.

What *The One Armed Executioner* lacks in hyphens, it more than makes up for in MacGuffins. And boy is this one a doozy. A dead drug dealer conveniently leaves behind a diary that somehow survives a fiery biplane crash. Didn't figure heroin dealers were the introspective type.

Interpol agent Ortega is able to use the pages as bread crumbs which lead to evil dealer Edwards, who is hell-bent on retrieving the incriminating tome. It's a work that rivals *Fire and Fury: Inside the Trump White House* in its popularity.

Like the best movies set in the Western Pacific, *The One Armed Executioner* has some Vanilla in Manila. And that's the usual assortment of evil white guys. One of them, a mobster in a bathrobe, has an inane right-hand man who feeds him synonyms: "I'm surrounded with idiots." "Idiots? Might I suggest numbskulls, sir?"

Much like in a thousand other cop movies, the drug dealers set their sights on someone close to Ortega: his bodacious blonde wife, who favors shower caps even during lovemaking scenes.

Thugs in ski masks storm his tastefully decorated home, by the garish standards of Filipino B-movies. They tie up his wife and see if they can get Ortega to blab.

But Ortega is a tough mutha. The gang whips out a samurai sword and bam, the movie's title. No arm, no dash. No wife. We're left with a hero who won't be able to do the "Y-M-C-A" anymore.

From the confines of his hospital bed, Ortega vows revenge. He then seeks comfort in a lonely honkytonk piano bar, a lugubrious exercise in self-pity and self-medicating, where it's gotta dawn on him that he can't double fist drinks anymore.

Luckily, this is a martial arts movie, so his despair won't last too long with the looming presence of. . . a DOJO!

He learns to "be a man," through extensive martial arts training. Ortega is forced to discover and confront "the world of darkness," admittedly not the most useful thing in the world as he's missing an arm, not blind. He's also urged to "listen to sound" (one of the better things to listen to) and finally, "to become one with all the elements of your soul!"

After an exhausting limb-asymmetrical martial arts montage, and the sensei declaring that he's ready, Ortega is prepared for action.

Luckily, there's a second MacGuffin in this film in addition to the memoir containing all the best-kept secrets of the heroin mob. And that's a gold ring worn by one of the perps, a woozy detail that gradually becomes clear to Ortega as the movie wears on (and clearer to the audience as well: the idiot camera zooms in on it ostentatiously so only the most ADHD-addled would miss it).

And before you think it's a tall enough order to take on a criminal enterprise, and using only one arm to do it, Ortega faces another obstacle: they're apparently Nazis! At roughly a bit past the hour mark, as Ortega is laying waste to one baddie after another, all failing to deduce that perhaps they should try attacking from the left side as he's using his right arm exclusively, one of them escapes in a boat marked with a Swastika. That there is no previous reference whatsoever to them being Nazis just adds to the charm.

Machine-gun-wielding guards in thatch huts prove no match for a one-armed man in a chopper + grenades. And like their brethren all over the globe, these henchmen die in slow motion while falling into bodies of water. One thug also dies trying to hide in a mud bath (the bubbles from his breathing tube give him away).

The One Armed Executioner is a Bobby A. Suarez production, a Filipino national responsible for a slew of terrible features like *They Call Him Chop Suey* and *Warriors of the Apocalypse*. Watch it as a double feature with *Crippled Avengers*.

STRIKE OF THE PANTHER, A.K.A. FISTS OF BLOOD (1988)

It's a martial art chestnut that the protégé always casts his mind back to the dojo for some somber life lesson bestowed by his sensei or a timely reminder from beyond the grave of some training system that's somehow quicker than any instinctive reaction. It's rare that the messages are delivered telepathically unless it's *Strike of the Panther*, an Ozploitation "mahh-shall ahhts" flick.

Strike's aged mentor, whose telepathy is pretty tele-pathetic as it only seems to kick in when he's about to kick it, utters this from his hospital bed: "REMEMBER THE TEACHING; REMEMBER THE TEACHING!" This as the hero is being ambush-garrotted by a goon lying in wait on the catwalk above. Sorry, what kind of training prepares you for THAT? And given that the mentor has been telling his pupil to "watch out" and "look behind you" as he fights his way out of (where else?) an abandoned factory, why get all lazy with the specifics now? If your charge's life is literally hanging in the balance from a catwalk, damn well pretend you're cornering an MMA fight and tell him how to get out of it, not some blarney about remembering the teaching!

Either way, by the looks of it, our hero, Jason Blade, seems like he started learning the deadly arts in the first trimester. He's a kind of Down Under David Duchovny-Italian in high-waisted pants, schooled at the Panther dojo, a secret Hong Kong kung fu school that graduated him and cattle-branded their insignia into his forearm. Perhaps to give him something to think about when the alumni association calls asking for their yearly contribution?

Blade is played by Eddie Staszak, who is now apparently a gigging accordionist in his native Perth, where *Strike of the Panther* was shot. Hopefully he hasn't become a statistic—another life claimed on the dissolute and unforgiving polka circuit.

The first twenty minutes of *Strike of the Panther* is dialogue-free, a voiceover spectacular that was shot and released consecutively with its predecessor *Day of the Panther,* so as not to confuse people who hadn't seen that one. Like us.

Blade shows us he's worth every word of those V/Os by getting a judge's heroin-addicted daughter out of a brothel. She kicks the habit like Bruce Lee roundhousing a nun, in about, oh, ten minutes.

He accomplishes the rescue by going undercover as a nattily attired John, flipping through the talent registry book, then finding the woman in question. He then proceeds to wipe the floor—if you'll forgive the expression; this is a house of ill repute—with its assorted bodyguards.

We've spent years wandering the action movie landscape with our pilgrim sticks, but we can safely say we've never seen an assailant break a hand on an opponent's abs. What makes the brothel throwdown particularly odd (besides the fact that, of all people, a cathouse Madame is testing our hero's abdominal strength), is that Blade is a real stickler when it comes to staying in character. When the Madame bursts into the room with fresh towels a mere two minutes into his paid session, Blade as the john is really into the role, carousing quasi-naked with the judge's daughter to keep up the ruse. That seems a bit unprofessional for someone you're supposed to rescue. At least he didn't bang her.

Eventually, of course, they must fight their way out of the building. They dodge wide-swinging suits in bad mustaches while the resourceful

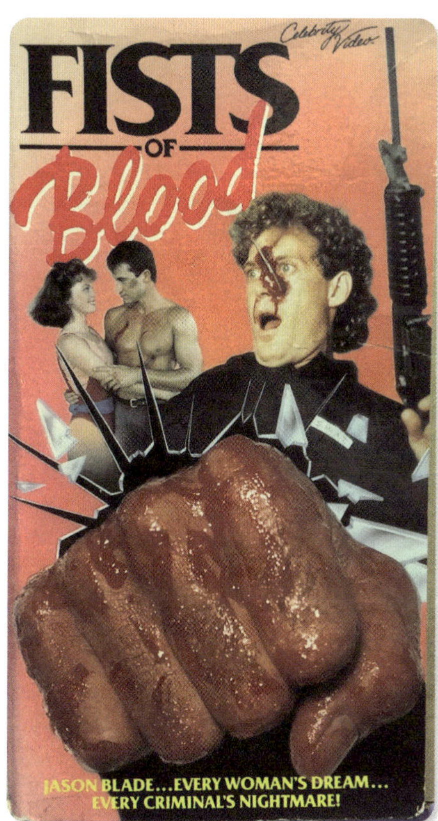

"rescuee" beats on her assailants with a riding crop, something some people would pay a lot of good money for. Blade also gamely uses a newel as a weapon. What's this? Well, we newel-Googled to find out. A newel is an upright post that supports the handrail of a stair banister.

And as they're about to exit, Blade opens a door to a john dressed in a full chicken outfit, to which our hero opines, "You're sick." Talk about judgmental. Couldn't he have quipped to the hooker, "Does he taste like chicken?" That, ladies and gentleman, is why we write books and not movie dialogue.

With the girl rescued and her evil "kidnapping specialist" Baxter sentenced to life in prison (which "everyone knows is a flexible term" according to the voiceover), Blade can get back to the business of training his task force, a bunch of out-of-shape nobodies who run around the desert in white karate *gis*, going through some rudimentary moves.

Baxter, who has since bolted the Big House using tied-together sheets like it's a *Bugs Bunny* cartoon, has "kept the casualty wards of Perth full of people." He's also taken Blade's girlfriend hostage and run over his mentor with a car door.

Don't let the name fool you. While he shares a name with Ron Burgundy's dog in *Anchorman*, Baxter is a mean bastard who's got an army of hockey-mask-wearing ninjas with baseball bats, and while they might be confused when it comes to North American sports, they're nonetheless ready to do Baxter's bidding and fight to the death. And he's ready to do battle with Blade, in the setting that's like water for fish in action movies, the abandoned factory.

Strike of the Panther provides whiz-bang action of the highest order. It's a one-stop shop for everything we've come to expect from an action film: heroin, hookers, the mob, an abandoned factory, ninjas, a love interest (one who even does a courtship dance in a gym), a mentor/guru, special forces, workout montages, and of course, a bare-chested stud-machine who's not to be trifled with. There's even a scene where Blade and a goon scale the balcony of a high-rise apartment, a stunt that looks especially dangerous, especially with a rickety corrugated rooftop.

Much like the Canadian tax-shelter era, which spurred so many great Canuxploitation horror films, so too did Aussie government tax breaks help launch the country's action and thriller scene in the '80s.

OF NOTE:

Strike of the Panther (a.k.a. *Fists of Blood*) was directed by our pal Brian Trenchard-Smith, and when *Kill Bill: Volume 1* premiered in Australia, mega-fan Quentin Tarantino dedicated the film to him.

BAM! A Ninja Star is Born

Baseball pitchers spend years honing their craft to be able to reliably place a ball in the area between a batter's shoulder and knee. Yet ninja stars (or *shuriken*), while much harder to throw, as a universal rule always land in drywall or—BAM—right between the target's eyes (and always horizontal too, never vertical.) You never see an errantly thrown ninja star lodge in someone's hamstring or ping off a brick wall. With that degree of accuracy, it's a wonder no ninja has ever been called up to the majors. Must be the concealed identity thing. Also, considering how sharp and pointy *shuriken* are, there's got to be some special way of carrying them, so the ninjas don't just cut themselves randomly as they're walking around. All in all, a pretty confusing mechanism.

POCKET NINJAS (1997)

Pocket Ninjas shoots out of the gate with clichés lifted right out of a Yogi's *Instagram* feed: silhouetted poses, setting suns, and serene beaches. But this isn't a film to slow your heart rate even if it does dull your other senses. No, this is another one of those up-with-people roundhouse karate kid movies where gutsy youngsters save the day. Of course, this was a decade removed from the era that saw dojos popping up on every corner like wack-a-moles and the "wax on" Miyagi stuff was nearly as long in the tooth as Ralph Macchio was when he played a "teenager" in the first *Karate Kid*.

And *Pocket Ninjas* gets its dojo mojo from the ridiculous figure of real-life London kickboxer Gary Daniels (*Skin Traffik* and the most expendable in the original *Expendables*) as a sensei-by-day/vigilante-by-night. In his day job, he sports a scrunchie and a ponytail like Tonya Harding, and is just as dangerous to opponents' kneecaps in his night job as the "White Dragon" vigilante.

Being a lone crimefighter is taxing. At least when Batman took a mental health day, he had the admittedly underwhelming Robin to carry the freight.

Similarly, White Dragon needs some help fighting the forces of evil. And not from prisons, boxing gyms, nor NFL training facilities does he look, but rather from the very dojo where he schools prepubescent babyfaces in the deadly arts, a place that doesn't look like it'd be the source of anything particularly lethal unless a staph infection broke out. Maybe we're being needlessly harsh. After all, in "the war to end all wars," many who served were under the official age of nineteen. Then again, it's no doubt they at least shaved. Nonetheless, White Dragon's succession plans include sourcing talent for the "next generation" of urban karate vigilantes—vigilantes who apparently shop in the children's department of their local Old Navy.

He picks three young charges from his dojo, Tanya, Steve, and Damien, each several inches shy of five feet. And White Dragon has nothing but fulsome praise for each as he presents every one of them with a mask. ("Your light is an inspiration to others!" and "You must conquer your inner demons that are keeping you from true happiness.") The sight of ripped competitive kickboxer Daniels bestowing solemn gifts to a bunch of back-lit, spindle-armed pimple-faces is something to behold.

Tanya, Steve, and Damien each get their own color-coded dragon façade, with hair sprouting out the sides like Riff Raff from *Rocky Horror*. Now masked, they proceed to go through their not-quite-synchronized paces putting light dents into heavy bags. With moves as pitiable as those, it's probably for the best that the trio is unidentifiable. Nonetheless, the same training montage is repeated throughout in order to max out the supermodel-lean eighty-minute run time.

Soon, the three ninja Dragons are taking to the mean streets and enforcing the law—on roller skates,[24] the single most impractical piece of crime-fighting clothing imaginable short of a terry cloth bathrobe and some Birkenstocks.

Not before long, they come upon some car-thief toughs and wipe the floor with them (not leaving a streak either, as that'd be slippery). The thugs, once they've comported themselves, tail between their legs, report to their boss that the Dragons were "huge" with "big muscles!"

You might've guessed that *Pocket Ninjas* is played for laughs . . . and the uber-boss isn't old enough to legally Uber-drive. He's just another kid whose name is Cubby Khan, and he promises to "wipe the Dragons off the map." Cubby trains his henchmen, all of whom look like gas station attendants, through a series of slapstick moves punctuated by screeching electric guitar.

One of the funnier parts of *Pocket Ninjas* is the crowbarred-in environmental messaging. From the confines of their treehouse fort, the Dragon kids banter awkward green-friendly exposition like "Have you noticed the dead fish by the beach? Toxic waste. That's why they had to close the beach up. That's why I became a vegetarian!" Turns out that pint-sized Cubby, much like the modern-day mafia, is involved in the illegal disposal of toxic materials. His team hustles barrels of the stuff out of warehouses and onto tanker trucks. (Despite the wanton environmental destruction on display, it's actually refreshing to see a warehouse used for warehousing for once, rather than sitting empty waiting for the next shootout like in just about every other action film.)

Cubby's chief henchman/enforcer is Cobra Khan,[25] played by a chest-beating and always-appreciated genre stalwart Robert Z'Dar. Here, he wears a cheapo chain around his neck but won't win a "Who wore it better?" against the likes of Rampage Jackson, Mr. T, or The Junkyard Dog.

The only one who can defeat him is White Dragon (and we only have White Dragon's word about this, no explanation). Cobra Khan's battles with White Dragon include a really oddball tilt at a carnival, or at least exterior shots of a carnival as the battle takes place inside the cozier confines of a very obvious soundstage. There, in a fight complete with balloon pop two-stepping and slide whistles, the broad-shouldered Z'Dar trades Three Stooges' rope-a-dope while bouncing on colored inflatables. After escaping, Z'Dar later does battle virtually, as *Pocket Ninjas* exploits the '90s VR fad that had firmly taken hold.

About halfway through, White Dragon says "This was all a big mistake. I have to ask the three of you to give up being the dragons . . . what if that lucky punch had been a knife or a bullet?" And at the end, we see outtakes of the goons whooping it up, presumably to show kids that it wasn't real—not that this was exactly needed after White Dragon and Z'Dar's sped-up slap-fight.

Despite the kid-friendly proceedings, one of the Dragons does get a black eye, but we know that everyone's in a safe space. There's even the time-honored cross-eyed KO when a baddie gets dropped.

50 CRIPPLED AVENGERS (1978)

The Tian Nan Tigers aren't some Asian corporate softball team. They're the cripplingly evil villains we're introduced to in *Crippled Avengers*.

You know the phrase "Women and children first"? It originated back in 1852 when the HMS Birkenhead sank off the coast of South Africa. What does this have to do with a Shaw Brothers Hong Kong action movie from the '70s? Well, the Tian Nan Tigers are nasty sorts who "don't fancy killing women and children," but do it anyway. Just for sport.

The Tigers break into the stately mansion of a nobleman and his family. We've seen his name variously rendered in different iterations of the film as Tian-du Dao, Du Tain Dao, and a half-dozen other variations. It doesn't matter. He's uberscrewed. We'll call him Pops.

The Tigers lop off his wife's legs at the knee (don't even get us started on her name). And the bastards leave her there to die, some three-quarters the woman she used to be. They then sever the young son's arms at the elbow. Pops arrives, albeit too late, and an awkward father/son pause ensues.

The young son (Tao Sheng) bravely whimpers: "So, they cut off my arms, still they couldn't make me beg."

Another awkward pause.

"Good. When your arms heal up I'll get a blacksmith to make you iron hands. And then you'll practice until you're invincible!" He's no Atticus Finch in the fatherhood department, that's for sure. Still, all the makings of your standard father/son revenge flick, perhaps? Not so fast. . .

Fast forward ten years and the now grown Tao Sheng has been set up with his promised prosthetic iron hands ("I tried seven pairs. But these are the best. They also shoot darts.") You know how those spring-loaded prosthetic death hands are . . . You can't just get 'em off the rack like a suit. Bespoke is all the rage.

Now that son Tao Sheng is all kitted out, Pops teaches him the tricks of the trade. He's a master of three Tiger Styles of kung fu: Forest, winged, and windmill. What these have to do with an orange predatory feline is unclear. No matter.

Then, in some of the wildest exposition you'll ever see, Pops explains that he "killed all the Tian Nan Tigers to avenge your mother" and captured the Tiger sons. The sons are to be granted their freedom if they can best ol' Iron Hands Tao Sheng in battle. They can't. That's some *Merchant of Venice* "Sins of the father are to be laid upon the children" shit right there. Seriously, what do the sons have to do with all this? They can't help it that the Tigers were murderous sadists. But it does give everyone a chance to see those kick-ass hands in action.

Soon, Pops and his wrought-iron hand-clad power-mad son rule like despots over the villagers and torture anyone who dare speak up against them.

Tao Sheng blinds a hawker with his custom gloves. "I have no hands, you have no eyes, we're even." (We don't mean to quibble, but what does that have to do with anything? He was just some random guy with a noodle shop who didn't care for how the village was being treated.)

Pops makes a mouthy local blacksmith mute by forcing some weird-ass potion down his throat. He then makes him deaf with a devastating double strike landing perpendicularly to his eardrums.

And henchmen lop off a village drifter's legs

just below the knee.

It just so happens a stranger is in the neighborhood for some blacksmith services. Wang,[26] referred to by everyone in the village as "stranger," as is the custom, intervenes on behalf of the crippled men. The white-clad stranger promises to avenge them, and to "get rid of this evil man."

All the makings of an avenging angel revenge flick? No!

Try as he might, he's no match for Pops, Tao "Iron Hands" Sheng, and a slew of henchmen.

While Pops and Tao Sheng enjoy their tea, their goons shackle the avenging angel/Good Samaritan. They then shove Wang's head into a vice and squeeze and squeeze and squeeze around the temples until he's rendered "slow-witted" and giggling like an idiot.

He does break free though, eventually reuniting with his crippled brethren as the guy with the "fourth disability," for those of you counting along at home.

NOW it's revenge time!

But how are a blind, deaf, amputee, moron foursome expected to enact their vengeance? Especially when one of their comrades is prone to making stupid pratfalls, which include dumping his comrades out of a wheelbarrow and clapping to himself like a fool?

The four crippled avengers need to learn the ways of the deadly martial arts, techniques that can be incorporated for the sensory deprivation/Paralympic set. They rifle through Wang's belongings for information. (Remember, he's an idiot now and can't respond to simple requests like "Where does your sensei live?") Success! They track down the sensei, otherwise known as a "sifu" in Cantonese. Basically a tutor (usually with a wispy grey beard) with impossibly lithe reflexes for someone pushing seventy.

He trains each one of them, developing a heightened sense of hearing for the blind, sight for the deaf . . . you know the drill. He also teaches his charges how to spike falling leaves with branches, punch through fire, roundhouse kick sticks lobbed in their direction, etc.

Suddenly, the crippled avengers can get to the business of avenging, destroying every useless henchman in their path as they make beelines for Pops and son. Why don't henchmen ever run when they know they're facing superior foes? Why don't henchmen work together and use their sheer numbers to overwhelm their opponents? Why don't henchmen ever use the element of surprise? Because they're useless, stupid, incompetent henchmen, that's why.

This is an absolute cracker of an action film. There's a spectacular fight featuring hula hoops that's one for the ages, a Bolshoi ballet of gorgeous sinuousness. And all the kung fu is off the charts. And that's no surprise. After all, it's directed by "The Godfather of Hong Kong cinema," Chang Cheh, who also gave us *The One Armed Swordsman* (we're sensing a theme).

Crippled Avengers, a.k.a. *Mortal Kombat* and *Return of the 5 Deadly Venoms*, has many limbs a-lopped and many eyes a-gouged, but it's strangely empowering. It's not to be confused with *The Crippled Masters*, which came out the following year. That one's about two men—one without arms and another with shrunken legs—who develop their kung fu abilities to seek revenge against their evil teacher who disabled them.

OUT FOR JUSTICE (1991)

Seagal has incredible range. As in human if not as a thespian. The man has literally logged thousands of miles shooting shitty movies in Romania and other assorted Eastern European locales because he can no longer get them financed here, but ask him to register a facial expression beyond "squinty constipated" and you might as well be asking Sisyphus to keep that boulder atop the mountain.

We kid, but you can't fault the Hoarse Whisperer for trying (or you can actually, if you're us). He's solemnly murmured his way through countless ex-CIA op/cop roles, variously portraying a Cajun mercenary, Alaskan oil rigger worker (who's possibly Native American insofar as he looked like he fished Dennis Hopper's fringed *Easy Rider* jacket out of the trash), and a Russian novelist. Incidentally, if you think Seagal is a good fit for, say, Tolstoy or Pushkin, we have a money-laundering production that's set to start filming in Omsk.

Luckily, before he was expatriated to Eastern Europe, Seagal made some unforgettably violent art on these shores. In *Out for Justice*, Seagal is (once again) back on familiar turf: playing yet another Italian-American cop who plays by his own rules.

The opener will have the Gods of Action smiling from high atop their perch on Mount Fire Escape. Some dissolute pimp starts talking smack in an alley. Seagal grabs the guy by the tie and hurls him over some oil drums. He then back body drops him right through the windshield face first. Cue dramatic music, the poor bastard's legs sticking out of the car like those stupid elf legs they sell every Christmas, and the words "STEVEN SEAGAL" in freeze-frame as horse face with a ponytail looks back into the vehicle to survey his handiwork.

Out for Justice is one of Seagal's canonical "four films, a cop, and three words," films, the others being, *Hard to Kill*, *Marked for Death*, and *Above the Law*. (Alternatively, add the phrase "Steven Seagal is . . ." before the title to figure out the best of the man's oeuvre.) In *Out for Justice*, Seagal plays "Gino Felino," a name which can't possibly be serious in the way any name that rhymes isn't serious—a Brooklyn NYPD with ties to the neighborhood. He's got a cute son to throw the ol' apple around with and that staple of cops-in-action cinema everywhere: the estranged wife.

Gino's childhood friend, mob boss Richie Madano (a rather corpulent William Forsythe), has murdered Gino's partner, Bobby Lupo, firing hot lead into him and sending Lupo careening into a fruit stand. Nice to switch things up and see a person, even a deceased one, destroy a fruit stand for a change rather than an out-of-control cab.

Seagal takes out a personal vendetta against Richie and his crew, fitting a bunch of pasta fazool bowling shirt shitstains for toe tags along the way.

Large swaths of the movie involve Gino yelling, "Where's Richie? Anybody seen Richie? I'm going to keep coming back until someone REMEMBERS seein' Richie," and "Anybody know why Richie did Bobby Lupo?"

The trail leads Gino into two great bastions of masculinity: a meat shop and a billiard hall. In the former, Seagal sticks a meat cleaver into one goon's back and whacks another over the head with a large wrapped salami! Gotta give credit where credit is due—using an oblong slab of cured pork as an instrument of blunt force

And Gino drops him below the cash register and between the eyes with a well-placed elbow, the kind of thing you'd see in the UFC. (Speaking of which, MMA fans delighted in making sport of Seagal's claims that he helped champion fighter Anderson Silva front kick KO an opponent in the cage, "perfecting a kick he learned 30 years ago in Japan." This failed to impress many YouTube wags, as a front kick is taught in every basic karate class, and it's certainly not something that would've been a novelty to Silva.)

trauma is pretty darn ingenious. As for the latter? If you thought *Above the Law* had a great bar fight (and it does), well hold our drinks for a moment. *Out for Justice* has the best bar fight in cinema history, save for perhaps the inspired punch-up at the Double Deuce in *Road House*.

Gino swaggers into some Brooklyn dive favored exclusively by bookmaking mamalukes, and they're none too impressed that he's dressed like a flamenco dancer from some horrible tapas restaurant. Undeterred, Gino, his oleaginous ponytail and NYPD badge slung between his pecs, begins talking smack to the *Jersey Boys* crotch-grabbers in a language they (but not us) can understand.

The proprietor welcomes him with an "Offisah Big Shat come to bust my boles," and Gino dispenses with some choice homophobic remarks before kicking the barstool out from under some greaser. They all protest that he's nothing without the badge and the gun. (This sentiment, or a variation thereof, occurs at least four times.) Gino proves this to be patently untrue, in a scene that'll go on the Mount Rushmore of ass-whoopins.

For some variety, Gino switches to Italian-language homophobia, shoves aside some biker from "Attica," and sets up shop behind the bar, admiring the boxing memorabilia lined up along the wall.

"Who's da boxa?" Gino asks.
"Me," replies the bartender.
"You a tough guy?" queries Gino.
"Yeah, tough enough."
"What could you do?"
"To you?" (Isn't that implied?)

Seagal then takes a bar towel, slings some billiard balls in there, wraps it around his forearm, and proceeds to whip the holy tar out of a half-dozen "fanooks" in the place.

Biker Attica comes back to bait him with a "You wanna get by me? There are only two things stopping you: fear and common sense," and for his troubles (or maybe for his lame and lousy taunt), gets a cue ball to the mug, knocking out his teeth, which he spits onto the billiard table.

The bar proprietor then summons "Sticks," the only Asian in the place, whose specialty is . . . swinging billiard cues like a stick-fighter. You know. Being Asian and all.

The assembled yell "poke his fuckin' eye out," but little do the assembled know, Seagal is a beast with the sticks. Heck, might as well call him Neil Peart. Or Burt Peart as would be more befitting the monikers handed out to characters in this film.

Director John Flynn wowed us with *Lock Up* and followed up that one with this heart check for Seagal, who proved he was, at one fleeting point in time, the man. In the end, Gino's family reunites, for as it is written, in action cinema, bad fathers and husbands become good again after whipping enough ass. He even adopts a puppy, Coraggio (Italian for "courage"). But given *Out for Justice*'s dialogue, not to mention Seagal's dopey beret, maybe Formaggio might've been more appropriate.

SIX

MY FIST, YOUR FACE

YOU PUNCH ME, I PUNCH YOU. I DO NOT BELIEVE IT'S GOOD FOR ANYONE'S SELF-RESPECT TO BE A PUNCHING BAG.

—ED KOCH, FORMER NEW YORK CITY MAYOR

Mike Tyson famously said, "Everyone has a plan till they get punched in the mouth," which is a pretty pithy declaration coming from a guy who's taken that many blows to the head. His fisticuffery belies his wordsmithery.

In the *Journal of Experimental Biology*, the authors of a study about metacarpal bones say that "the human hand presents a biomechanical paradox . . . The capacity for precise and delicate manipulation requires that the hand be relatively fragile . . . Yet, the hand is also our most important anatomical weapon, used as a club to threaten, beat, and sometimes kill other humans."[27]

We've seen that there's a certain set of expectations for martial arts movies. They've got a dojo and septuagenarian senseis with bad facial hair and incredible kung fu that is at odds with everything we know about gerontology and life expectancy. And these films generally involve someone skilled in one type of discipline. Think Seagal's aikido or Van Damme's kickboxing. But that's just one type of film where villains catch enough beatings to justify universal healthcare. What about the rest of those non-black belts, like bouncers and wrestlers? Can't they get in on the action, too?

My Fist, Your Face introduces us to quick-tempered sorts—brawlers who don't have the time to throw on a *gi* and sit on a beach cross-legged to balance their *qi*.

The force of a fist equals mass times acceleration, but timing is the most important part of a punch, and these folks here know all about that. To quote that famous action film, *The Breakfast Club*, this chapter is really about "Two hits: Me hitting you, you hitting the floor."

ROAD HOUSE (1989)

Will cooler heads prevail? No, you didn't ask, but we're gonna tell you that a "cooler" is a professional doorman whose job it is to manage other doormen. It's the top rung in the bouncer profession, which is a bit like being the savviest guy at the annual Flat Earth Society meeting, but still.

As guys who've been, ahem, given a personal escort out of the odd drinking establishment, we recognize the importance of a good bouncer. After all, without a lug in a three-sizes-too-small suit and a clipboard who can ring bar denizens' heads like bells should they get out of hand, evenings out would be a lot less safe. Simply put, they're key entertainment establishment figures, on par with porno set directors, the guys who blow up balloons at state fairs, and the entrepreneurial fellows who wheel their hot dog carts outside of nightclubs at last call.

Road House is the *Gone with the Wind* of bouncer movies, a genre narrow enough that Lara Flynn Boyle could fit through it sideways, and in it is our cooler character—the incomparably cool Dirty Dancer himself, Patrick Swayze.

He plays Dalton, a strong, silent type who lets his quick-draw extremities do the talkin' while he sends belligerent barflies a-walkin.'

In *Road House*, a Missouri bar owner who owns a bar so shit-kicking the resident house band has to play behind chicken wire lest they got cracked in the skull by an errantly hurled Michelob, goes on a talent search to New York City to find just the guy to clean up his violent saloon. Why this requires an international talent search you'd expect for a Google CFO is a question best left to idle speculation.

The cause of his bar's violence (The Double Deuce, which sounds like something one might suffer through after enjoying one too many roadside tacos) isn't half-off happy hour margaritas but sleazy businessmen and the world's tiniest crime boss, Wesley (indie icon Ben Gazzara), who naturally has a slew of goons at his disposal. Gazzara, the inestimable Cassavetes regular, has never looked more uncomfortable than he does here, wearing bolo ties and giving faint shit-eating grins like a failed congressional candidate giving a concession speech.

Hey, art films seldom pay the bills, and he's working for a lot more than tips in the relatively big budget offering here.

His character Wes, though small in stature, wields a big stick and an even bigger Napoleonic complex. He has a stranglehold on the entire town and wants to squeeze out all the existing establishments so he can bring in a mega-mall. And if this involves blowing up a slew of mom-and-pop operations and sending dozens of town denizens to the hospital or the morgue, so be it. Nobody said gentrification was easy.

Or maybe Wesley has his sights set on a ski resort, as despite this supposedly being set outside of A-cup Kansas City, there are towering D-cup mountain ranges visible in the background. The type that added, shall we say, a "unique" topography to the similarly horizontally challenged Haddonfield, "Illinois" in the horror film *Halloween*.

Unfortunately for Wes, the Double Deuce stands in the way of an urban sprawling strip mall empire. Naturally, he rains holy hell down on the bar as a means of intimidation rather than making the owner a reasonable offer and retrofitting the saloon into a Starbucks, something

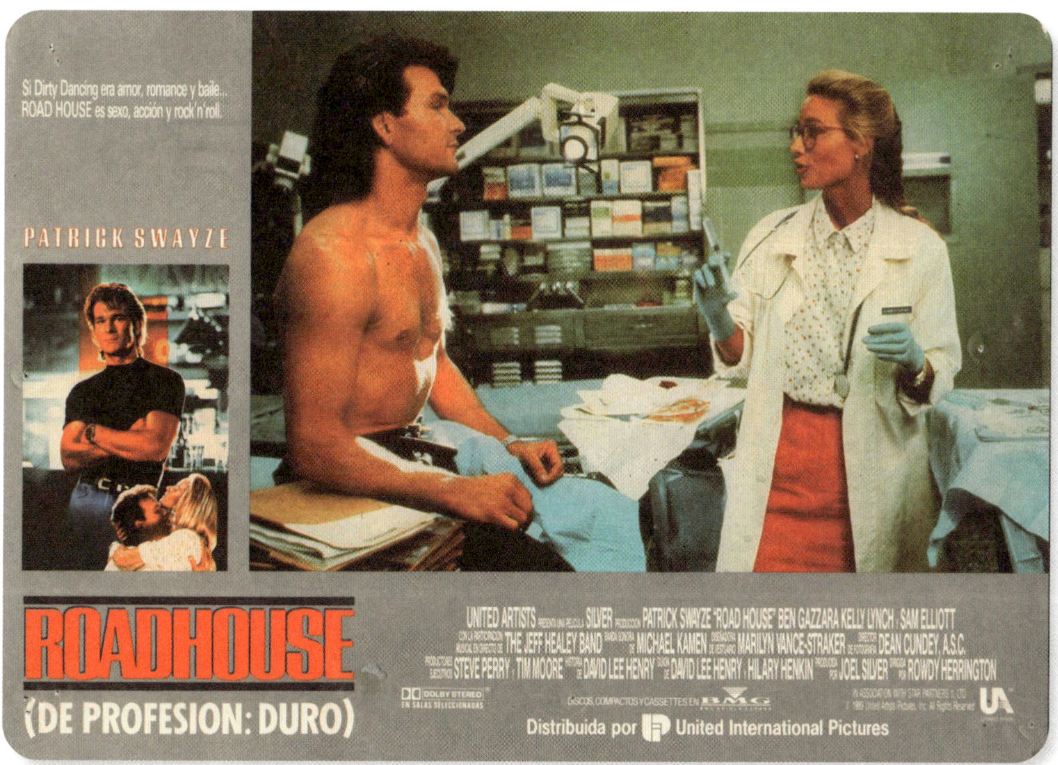

which would've reduced the film's runtime to, oh, about twenty-four minutes.

In *Road House*, only the towering force that is the modest 5'10" Dalton/Swayze (a man who carries his own medical records with him; records which inexplicably list his educational background along with his blood type) can stand in the way of this crooked entrepreneur. Suave as he is, Dalton still finds the time to settle down in a barn walk-up as well as bed the town's resident doc, Elizabeth Clay (played by Kelly Lynch, a role which weirdly was supposed to have gone to Annette Bening/Mrs. Warren Beatty, but who producers fired from the set).

Dalton's all set to go *mano a mano* with the gangster Wes, after setting up his own crack team of bouncers and taxing the small Missouri town's after-hours emergency dentistry services.

Goes without saying there are bar brouhahas galore in *Road House*. A whole wack of people are slugged in the face. And since this is an action movie, if two guys brawl, gosh darn it, half the place has to jump in to duke it out, cracking chairs, breaking beer bottles, and all-around boosting insurance premiums.

There's even a cameo by wrestling great Terrible Terry Funk, who busts a lippy guy in the liver and sends him ass over tea kettle into a bunch of innocent bystanders. The film also showcases a really greasy-looking Sam Elliott as a bouncer mentor. (Wait, those exist? Somebody, please schedule a TED Talk.)

Featuring some of the most quotable lines in action movie history ("Pain don't hurt," and "I want you to be nice until it's time to not be nice" being two of our favorites) and other philosophical musings by the tai-chi practicing yet bare-handed-throat-tearing-out Dalton, who has to make up for the ten-year education gap with his doc paramour somehow, *Road House* will kick your behind. The film will also cut you off and send you packing. Four upturned beer-stained tables out of five for sure.

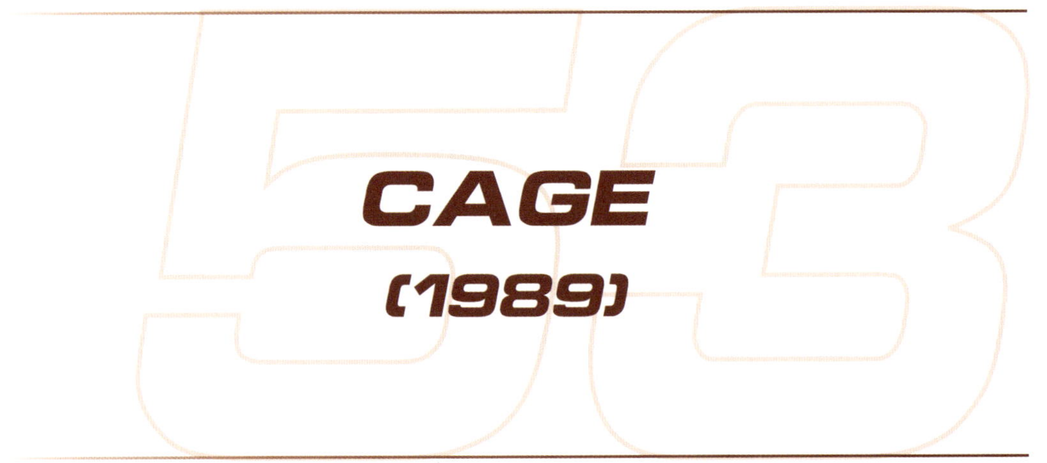

CAGE (1989)

In the deep dark tropical jungles of Vietnam . . . ah, who the heck are we kidding? In the Mexican desert just across the California border, so obvious a mariachi band might as well be tuning up in the bushes, Billy and his captain Scott are fighting the Viet Cong. The enemy is attacking all in a row in accordance with action movie style, which should indicate they're courting certain death. However, this is the film's opener, so we can't have our heroes winning right out of the gate. No sir, that wouldn't do. A formidable obstacle is required in action movie first acts, from which our heroes must heroically overcome in order to be, well, you know . . . heroic. Thus, despite the predictable attack gambit, which results in Marines mowing down a slew of Vietnamese like a hedge clipper to a bush, the baddies do eventually force the Americans to beat a hasty retreat.

With things faring poorly for the boys, a rescue chopper is summoned. Billy (Lou Ferrigno) avoids bullets whizzing by his ears to clamber aboard, but before the chopper is able to put distance between itself and the ground and return to the nearby Hollywood backlot, Billy shouts to the pilot, "What about the captain?"

O Captain! My Captain! is Scott, portrayed by perpetually jovial Reb Brown. He singlehandedly uses his machine gun to dispatch with a dozen or so Viet Cong advancing in poor formation before Billy extends a veiny, pulsating super-arm and drags him aboard the chopper. (Hey, you don't get called "Mr. America" nor get slathered in green grease paint to portray *The Incredible Hulk* for your ability to do long division.)

Suddenly, Billy's shot by the Viet Cong and his blood pours out of his left temple like the arc from a late-night pee. He lingers on in survival mode and is hastily deposited at the local veterans' hospital.

Have no fear, though; brass instruments are being tuned for a heavily sax-ified convalescence montage—a cacophony which would make Mr. Ferrigno glad he's partly deaf.

Back in the duo's hometown, two low-end goombah typecasts are up to their ears in mafia trouble. They're in hock to a Chinese gangster stereotype over mounting cage fight gambling losses. Unable to figure what to do about it, they decide to cool out at the local tavern, not coincidentally the one now owned by civilians Scott and Billy. Over "beers," that go-to beverage order before film product placement fully came into vogue, the underworld figures weigh their options in a jerry-rigged exposition-fest.

Now, who should arrive at the very same bar? Why it's a bunch of Latino stereotypes (notice a pattern?), who announce themselves by punching a few of the barflies into the next zip code and slapping their women. Urged to leave by a now fully recuperated Billy and business partner Scott, the greasers just can't help themselves and get into it physically with our guys.

The brawny barmen make short work of the Mexicanos, who are left licking their wounds and picking glass shards out of their mullets.

Naturally, this impresses the Olive Garden-variety Mafiosi, who figure they've witnessed the next Randy Couture in the making; burly men who they surmise will take the cage fighting world by storm and help them pay down their debts.

They press Scott to sign up as a cage fighter, but he demurs, both for himself and on behalf of brain-damaged Billy. You see, the injury Billy sustained on that ill-fated helicopter jungle ride has made him simple, childlike, and trusting (and fond of ice cream), in one of the more regressive treatments of people with disabilities you'll ever see or hear in a film.

With no other way out of their dilemma, the mobsters kidnap Billy, cajole him with sweet talk and an even sweeter submarine sandwich, and convince him that he'll make enough money to help Scott rebuild the bar, which has since been firebombed by the grudge-holding Latinos. Thus, before you can say "claptrap plot-device," Billy's forced into the brutal cage fighting circuit.

Naturally, it's caretaker Scott to the rescue. He's tasked with figuring out both where Billy's been taken and where the clandestine tournament is being held. Standing in his way: Rotund biker chicks, whatever assorted dirt bags still standing from their bar beat-down, and a bunch of toughs playing billiards. But luckily for Scott, it's an incontrovertible action film fact that holding a billiard cue means lights out, so those adversaries at least are soon left counting the cracks in the ceiling.

All roads don't lead to Rome but to a dilapidated octagon somewhere in a very rough and rundown part of Chinatown. Tough guy Billy has given a good accounting of himself in several matches, but the grind of the clandestine human cock-fighting circuit isn't easy on anyone, and Billy is ultimately injured and unable to continue. With no other recourse, Scott is compelled to fight in his stead, sporting ring regalia of blue-jeans; a fitting sartorial accompaniment to his danger-in-denim fighting prowess.

Eventually, when the dust settles, all that's left standing is the corny twosome while a bunch of ethnic typecasts waste each other in an epic shootout melee finale.

The *LA Times*, who it's hard to believe actually took the time to review this, called *Cage* "a sentimental macho fantasy about male bonding," and the film's women "peripheral." Hey, Reb Brown's character does KO a biker chick. That's got to count for something.

And while women don't exactly spearhead the plot, it's ethnic minorities that fare the worst in *Cage*, with its Chinese fortune cookie banter, frequent greaser "esé" droppings, and dumb, marinara-drenched guinea gabfests. But at the end of the day, it's the deaf subculture that gets the worst of it, as Ferrigno's unmistakable speech cadence is explained away as a brain lesion in this utterly braindead feature.

THE CONDEMNED (2007)

The Condemned is another fight-to-the-death tournament movie, featuring the combined star wattage of "Stone Cold" Steve Austin and Vinnie Jones, which is more of an asteroid in a far-flung galaxy where there's an entertainment value vacuum and oxygen to the brain is in short supply.

Since this is a WWE production, we get burly grappler Austin along with the man whose football hooligan visage is welded into a perma-sneer, Jones. With a duo like this, brace yourself for a lot of snarling. And throw on some shades 'cause there'll be even more squinting. Hey, would you expect the intricate wordplay of the musical *Hamilton* from this guttural twosome?

This movie was ahead of its time as far as knockoffs are concerned, as it ripped off *Battle Royale* well before *The Hunger Games* had a chance to do so.

Here we're condemned to watch convicts unwittingly starring in a bad reality TV show-cum bad movie. (To be fair, the phrase "bad reality TV show" is fairly redundant because other than the Gordon Ramsay hosted ones that these writers love, reality TV is something we'd like to see go the way of the Dodo, along with its movie corollary, found footage horror movies.)

Jack Conrad (Steve Austin) is wrongfully convicted and sitting in a Salvadoran prison. He's wrongfully convicted because producers don't believe an audience will be emotionally invested in say, an embezzler, pedo, or a mugger in a crappy prison genre movie such as this.

His freedom is bought by an unscrupulous reality TV producer (there are no other kinds) to fight in a very high stakes, *Survivor*-type game show set on an island. It's a fight to the death, and Jack's not alone. He has to battle a who's who of ethnically typecasted inmates, including an angry, blustering German, a hotheaded Italian, an Asian guy who dazzles with his martial arts prowess, and yes, the incomparably surly Englishman, played by Jones.

They're brought to the contest locale via helicopter and punted into the ocean; a move which ends one combatant's life (and contest) rather prematurely.

And just so you know, the guys can't loll about in the surf or attempt to build a raft and paddle away, as they're each affixed with an incendiary device attached to their ankles. If they have any designs on going AWOL from the course, ka-boom. There's a time limit too; the anklets are set to blow up, ideally to stir the viewer from their slumber.

This is *Battle Royale* with cheese.

The "winner" and lone fight-to-the-death survivor gets a big cash prize as well as their freedom. If you ever wondered under whose authority convicted killers can be released, you're not alone. Apparently, it falls under the auspices of a big-time TV producer. What kind of jurisprudence is this? Where's Simon Cowell to crap on the proceedings?

And of course we find out Conrad is a Special Forces op, the vocation-of-choice for Steven Seagal in seemingly every movie he's in—except this one, which he's not. Still, Stone Cold makes a pretty formidable Special Forces operative. This WWE production lets him cut loose with his patented wrestling moves even if we'd count this movie out.

BAM! Adjust your Aim

If you're a sniper henchman, your prey is escaping on fleet foot, and you find your machine gun fire hitting just inches away from their feet as the distance between your perch and you widens, just shoot a little higher. You won't get him in the foot, but you'll maybe get to hit something even more incapacitating. Just don't keep doing what you're doing as all you'll do is memorialize his getaway with bullet debris.

PARROLE VIOLATORS (1994)

Looking for an action movie where the hero/protagonist performs all his own death-defying stunts but don't want to be distracted by the grace, fluidity, wit, and charm of Jackie Chan? Then say hello to Sean P. Donahue and his film *Parole Violators.*

Donahue is credited as the stunt performer/coordinator on more than forty films, including Troma's *They Call Me Macho Woman!* and *Class of Nuke 'Em High Part II: Subhumanoid Meltdown.* His father, Patrick G. Donahue, directed the incredibly inane *Kill Squad* and the aforementioned *Macho Woman.* In 1994, they combined their formidable might and made the astounding *Parole Violators,* a film that replicates what it would be like to watch Homer Simpson leap the Springfield Gorge for a full ninety minutes.

Meet Miles Long, former cop, current host of the television show "Parole Violators." The show features clips of a balaclava-wearing vigilante who wields a video camera and goes out hunting scofflaws, hoping they'll reoffend. The vigilante, dubbed "Videocop" by the police, then kicks the recidivists' asses with sloppy karate and ties them to a tree for the cops to collect them. Videocop is actually Miles under the mask, although no one on the force can seem to figure that out (nor bother to question their ex-colleague about it either).

A Latino gangster/pedophile, Chino, who Long put away back when he was a cop, is receiving early parole and is greeted outside the prison by his second, the hulking, tattooed Toos. Although maintaining that he's a changed man, Chino also informs Toos that he wants "Girls, little girls, you know, little, little girls." (Yep, it's a pretty icky plot detail.) He also wants beer, a beverage which seems to carry quite the importance for this particular scumbag, as the phrase "Let's get a beer, man!" is repeated numerous times throughout the film. "We just kidnapped a girl from a playground and we're being chased by an ex-cop vigilante . . . Let's get a beer, man!"

There's a female officer on the force named Tracy who appears to be Miles' friend with benefits. She's in a police auto shop when Miles barges in to berate her for Chino getting out (not that she had anything at all to do with it). They have a long back and forth which concludes with an overture made by Tracy to come by Miles' for pasta and a little something extra for dessert. Trouble is, the mechanics are still working, and the two actors have to shout their lines at each other in order to be heard over the various sounds of car repair, something that elevates their stilted dialogue and flat delivery to the precipice of abject hilarity.

The crux of *Parole Violators* is Chino kidnapping Tracy's young daughter, Susan, then Miles and Tracy teaming up to rescue her, then taking down Chino and the two-dozen neo-Nazi skinheads he's enlisted for backup.

But it's not the destination that's important but the journey, and that expedition is chock-a-block of full-contact martial arts, unintentional laughs, risible dialogue, and ham-handed stunt work.

Some of the highlights of *Parole Violators* include:

- Miles rescuing Susan from "drowning" in a filthy leaf-covered backyard pool which could not have been more than three feet deep. At no point, does the water ever go above anyone's waistband, and that includes young Susan. Yet it's enough of an ordeal for Susan to fall into a coma.

- Miles getting hit by a car. This happens a lot. Twice even before the opening credits. (And by the same car!) And then again and again and again. In another scene, Miles leaps onto the roof of a car belonging to a parole violator who's attempting to flee. The driver abruptly and repeatedly puts the car into reverse and then drive. Each time the vehicle brakes, Donahue clumsily rolls himself over the roof, from the trunk to the hood and back again, with all the grace of an elephant on roller skates.
- There's a fight in the back of a moving van. With each kick and punch accompanied by a squib burst of blood, Miles kicks one of his assailants in the groin which hurtles him upwards, bruised and bloodied, right through the van's sunroof.
- Miles chases Chino and Toos on a motorcycle. Their lowrider hits Miles, and he bounces off the hood of the car (naturally). Toos then gets out, kicks Miles in the head hard enough for his helmet to fall off, then picks him up, throws him through the window, and bounces him off the car hood like a basketball. Next, Toos kicks our hero until he's hanging precariously at the edge of a cliff. But not for long, as Miles slides down the cliff side, only to come to a quick, safe stop. Donahue then clearly propels himself further so he can slide down the rest of the way.
- In the most *Simpsons*-esque stunt of them all, Miles is punched off another cliff. He slides partway down, then in the next scene is shown leaping from the cliff, accompanied by a Wilhelm scream. He falls through one canopy of leaves, then another, before landing with a sickening thud on a large tree branch. He then continues his descent, sliding down a completely different rock cliff and landing in a rocky riverbed. Watching somebody effectively kill himself for our amusement has never been so ridiculously entertaining.
- In the climactic shootout, Miles is atop a roof when Toos shoots him in the chest and knee. Miles drops his weapon and goes sliding down the roof, but is able to retrieve his sidearm, replace the ammunition clip, and shoot Toos twice in the chest. All this as he flies off the roof in a parabolic arc that defies all rules of Newtonian mechanics. He's then shown incongruously leaping off another completely different, much higher roof before landing on top of Chino's car.

And yet all those ridiculous moments still cannot prepare the viewer for the scene where Tracy, in the back of a pickup, tries to seduce her captors by thrusting and rubbing her very evident cameltoe. Unfortunately, her lubberly attempt at seduction breaks down when she compares a goon actually named Goon to a bird.

Parole Violators is a hoot. In addition to the graceless stunts, there's also hilarious malapropisms like "You son of a bastard!" To enhance your viewing enjoyment, allow us to propose a *Parole Violators* drinking game: take a shoot whenever Tracy utters "My baby!" in relation to her kidnapped daughter, and two shots whenever someone is thrown, kicked. or simply falls through a window. However, if choosing to participate in the game, make sure to have emergency numbers at the ready as alcohol poisoning is all but guaranteed.

56

FIRESTORM (1998)

The elevator pitch is basically *Backdraft* meets *The Right Stuff*, but in the event of a fire, elevators wouldn't work anyway. But you, the viewer, get the shaft in this one.

"Smokejumpers" are an elite team of firefighter paratroopers co-led by 6'5", 280-pound NFL Football Hall-of-Famer Howie Long (Jesse), who's basically an Easter Island statue with a crewcut.

In the film's opener his hulking form descends from the sky to battle a raging wildfire and rescue a cute little girl trapped in accommodations that can only be described as Unabomber chic.

The wildfire is so strong, it picks up a motor home and sends it flying onto Wynt (Scott Glenn), who emerges mostly unscathed, save for a slightly buggered up lower leg and perhaps a bit of lingering resentment for costarring in this. Not bad though, considering this is an RV that would've crushed both witches and most of the cast of the *Wizard of Oz*.

Because this is a terrible action film, and screenwriters frequently feel compelled to have one of the characters utter the movie's title, we get: "You don't wanna get caught in a firestorm!" This gambit would not work in *The Hudsucker Proxy*. And also because this is a terrible action film, Jesse has to swoop in and not only save the little girl, but risk life and limb and third-degree burns to his cinder block head to extricate her cute little puppy from the shack.

With Wynt now on the mend, it's Jesse's responsibility to train recruits, one of whom nearly drops an axe on his head from a high training pole, that madcap. But elite smokejumpers and trainees aren't the only ones battling fires in *Firestorm*.

There are also "volunteer" firefighters of sorts, volun-told Wyoming penal system baddies who risk life and limb battling raging infernos when they could easily be hammering out license plates or selling timeshares.

Cons in this pilot program are given axes and a trip out into the wilderness, what the cynical among us might call "a head start." When locals question the safety of such a program, bureaucrats counter with "The people aren't stupid; they're aware of the risk!" Perhaps not aware enough.

Sure enough, the cons use it as their get-out-of-jail-free card. Shaye (William Forsythe of *The Devil's Rejects*), too much of a loon to be considered for forest fire detail, sneaks his way into the program by shanking a guy who'd signed up and assuming his identity. He does this, in true bad movie fashion, by donning glasses and chopping off his hair. Why there was no lockdown post-shank is a question left to the guys who thought giving hatchets to inmates in the woods was sound thinking.

Shaye promises four con co-conspirators he'll give them a cut of millions of mystery dollars if they aid his getaway, and they quickly overpower the guards. Because there is no honor among whoever is serving federal time, Shaye leaves the remaining firefighting cons to burn in the prison bus.

The escapees, now dressed as firefighters, hack their way through the forest, hoping to find freedom, while Shaye surreptitiously offs a few of them for a larger share of the loot.

Along the way they encounter a female birder caught in the blaze, and another kind of flying species—bulky defensive lineman Jesse descending from the skies to battle the flames and rescue her.

When Jesse meets the undercover cons, he is immediately suspicious about how close to the blaze they've been wandering. Sensing this, crafty Shaye adopts a thoroughly unimpressive Canadian accent as cover. Jesse buys it and probably chalks up the cons' utter lack of firefighting know-how to the fact they're Canadian, eh?

As they all march through the forest to seek help at the trading post, Shaye figures he can't continue the firefighter ruse much longer and whispers for his second-in-command, a Russian galoot, to kill Jesse when they arrive.

But our hero is ready for it, and ready to showcase his NFL defensive skills, in a prolonged brawl, one of the silliest and most drawn out fight scenes in recent memory, where support beams are knocked over, shoulder tackles are thrown, and the Russian tries to set Jesse and the log cabin on fire. Savvy Jesse escapes via a motorcycle out the window. How utterly expedient that a trading post in the middle of the woods would have a fully operational, fully gassed up motorcycle for sale on its premises.

Speaking of convenience, we learn that the birder mentioned earlier is not just an admirer of rare spotted owls but that she is . . . A COMBAT MEDIC WITH SOME MARINE TRAINING! That's a shoehorn large enough to help Paul Bunyan don his boots.

We also discover that Jesse is afraid of water (charming and ironic, right?) as he and the birder escape the twin dangers of angry cons who don't want the authorities tipped off about their whereabouts as well as a scary conflagration.

We also learn that when another new recruit nearly drops an axe on his head toward the film's end, Jesse is bemused rather than irate. That's the kind of temperament you'd want in a firefighter instructor (or a kindergarten teacher).

57

LOW BLOW (1986)

Delving into the world of second-, third-, and thirtieth-tier action films quickly reveals that the contemporary perception of the '80s action hero—the towering figure with muscles upon muscles, each bulbous massed assemblage of soft tissue threatening to rip through the thin epidermis saran-wrapped over their bulging veins and ripped striations—is but a myth. Sure, the top action marquee actors were larger than life and jacked to the gills, but in the wilder and woollier world of straight-to-video, where product was being churned out at an astonishing rate, action heroes came in all shapes, sizes, and types. Hence, when fifty-eight-year-old Leo Fong caused a tiny ripple in video stores in 1986 with *Low Blow*, the sight of an aged protagonist with a wardrobe more befitting a retiree kicking back and feeding pigeons on an autumnal Sunday than an ass-kicking action hero fazed no one.

Written by Fong and directed by Frank Harris (*Killpoint*), *Low Blow* opens with a going-out-of-business scene right out of *Dirty Harry* sequel *Sudden Impact*. Fong, playing ex-cop, current PI Joe Wong (a character he would reprise four years later in *Blood Street*), overhears an armed robbery occurring in a sandwich shop a block away from his garishly decorated second-floor office. He tells his secretary he's stepping out, then saunters over to the besieged boîte, a sharp-dressed man in his de facto uniform of tight denim, white button-down, and gray, zipped-up Member's Only jacket (a look in keeping with his vintage to be sure). Wong enters the shop, orders a ham sandwich, then casually takes a seat before blowing the criminals away with a revolver so tiny it makes Harry Callahan's .44 Magnum look like a damn bazooka.

And is that Cameron Mitchell sitting over there? Of course it is, since there was that provision indicating that no straight-to-video genre cheapie of the '80s or '90s could have been made without him. He's like the staff of life for these films; they'd wither and die without him. Here, he plays Yarakunda, the blind and lame head of the "Universal Enlightenment" cult. With the Star of David tattooed on his cheek, the Hindu bhindi painted on his forehead, the cross around his neck, and his rambling but beatific sermons which mix bits of Taoism with verses from the Bible, Yarakunda is looking for unspecified redemption wherever he can find it. Either he's really confused, or as is more likely when considering Mr. Mitchell's personal life at the time, extremely drunk. And with his second, the beautiful Karma by his side, they make their disciples hoe arid soil while Karma incessantly and psychotically bellows "Yarakunda" into a megaphone.

One of their newest initiates is Karen, the daughter of wealthy industrialist John Templeton (B-movie stalwart Troy Donahue), who is shocked when informed that his daughter hasn't attended her college classes in over two weeks, but not as shocked as his wife, who registers an expression so exaggerated you'd think her daughter was turning tricks on the Sunset Strip rather then just having missed a few advanced trig classes. Nonetheless, Templeton decides to seek the services of a private investigator to determine her whereabouts.

Now, Templeton is this supposed captain of industry with unlimited means at his disposal, so he could have hired the best of the best[28]—not to mention go to the relevant authorities, which, as is par for the course in these films, he does not—but he hires this *schmoe* Wong simply because he witnesses him using his inelegant, drunken-uncle style martial arts to dispatch with a couple of purse snatchers—a minor act of heroism which nonetheless convinces Templeton that Wong is the right man for the job. And talk about a list of qualifications! Wong's office door has this useful inscription: "Mr. Joe Wong, Inc." (there's no way this dingy two-person operation is listed on the NYSE, especially as it's evident that Wong is living out of his office); "Private Investigation" (fair); "Bounty Hunting" (we'll give him that one); "Knife Fighting Lessons" (weirdly illegal thing to advertise); and the absolute kicker, "World Headquarters Wei Kuen Do Association" (a martial arts style developed by Fong himself). But who are we to judge? In an unpredictable market, it's always good to be diversified, and Wong is nothing if not diverse.

Sneaking onto the cult's compound will not be easy, especially with the dozen or so armed guards patrolling the perimeter, one of whom is played by future action superstar turned Tae Bo magnate Billy Blanks, here making his film debut. Wong attempts to infiltrate the compound/farmhouse, posing as a journalist, but is greeted with a welcome less than hospitable. He does manage to escape with a teenage runaway in tow, but then lets the kid go without doing any actual investigating. At the very least, he could have asked him if there had been any new initiates who joined, say, two weeks ago. We think that info might have proved useful since locating the Templeton girl is what he's actually getting paid to do, not rescuing strung out teens bound for the casting couch.

In a haphazardly edited segue, we next see Wong sitting at the breakfast table at his secretary's farmhouse. (Why does everyone live on a farm in this film?) She's cooking him breakfast, which can only lead the audience to infer that it's the morning after a night of sweet, sweet love, so Wong it's right (and for that awful joke, your humble authors plead for your forgiveness). It is confusing though, as nothing prior indicated that their relationship was anything other than professional and platonic. Karma's men descend with machine guns (How did they know he'd be there?) but prove little match for Joe. So forceful is Wong's attack that the assailants hop back into their Caddy to retreat but are stymied when Wong pulls some sort of plug out from underneath their hood, rendering their vehicle immobile. He then gleefully grabs a bandsaw and channels his inner Leatherface by sawing off the car's roof, only to let the baddies run away. A hilarious scene to be sure, but pointless all the same.

The climax does little to establish any more of a serious tone. Wong decides to hold a "Toughman Contest," with the promise of $25,000 to the winner. But it's all one big ruse, with Wong withholding the prize money unless the winner helps him reinvade the compound. Further proof that anyone wanting to enter a no-holds-barred underground fighting competition really needs to read the fine print. Nonetheless, the only one who seems to object is one African American boxer who Wong uncomfortably calls "boy," then puts him in his place by standing his entire 5'8" frame up to the boxer's 6'3".

At last though, the final invasion and the battle we've all been waiting for: the enigmatic Leo Fong vs. the formidable Billy Blanks! Trouble is, their fight lasts all of thirty seconds and is lit so poorly, you can't make anything out anyhow. After vanquishing Blanks' "Guard" character with ease, Wong then puts the cherry on top of the whole ridiculous sundae by ostensibly crushing another guard's cranium with a single punishing blow, turning the "head" from an actual watermelon to an actual pile of mashed potatoes.

As a matter of interest, the poster for *Low Blow* has to be one of the most disingenuous in the history of VHS box marketing—an industry not known for its veracity. It features a muscle-bound Caucasian standing shirtless and ready to strike in front of a city silhouette. The illustration does not resemble any character in the entire film, and certainly not Leo Fong. Evidently, *Low Blow*'s distributors had little faith in Fong's façade to shift units and decided to dupe the audience instead, which really is a shame, as Fong's head on top of that same jacked-up body would have been an image so epic it surely would have adorned thousands of '80s' college dorms right alongside cheesecake swimsuit shots of Christie Brinkley.

The Deadliest Weapon is Still Your Fist!
LOW BLOW
ACTION COMMUNICATIONS INC. presents a FRANK HARRIS Film
"LOW BLOW"
Starring LEO FONG • CAMERON MITCHELL • TROY DONAHUE • DIANE STEVENETT • STACK PIERCE
and AKOSUA BUSIA as Karma Produced by LEO FONG Story and Screenplay by LEO FONG
Associate Producer HOPE HOLIDAY Directed by FRANK HARRIS
A CROWN INTERNATIONAL PICTURES RELEASE
R
VESTRON VIDEO
AVAILABLE DECEMBER 10

NO HOLDS BARRED (1989)

When it comes crashing down
and it hurts inside . . .

And so begins "Real American," Hulk Hogan's theme song during his glory years atop the WWF roost. And also a perfect encapsulation of how many hearts felt after first viewing the Hogan/WWF vehicle *No Holds Barred*. The year was 1989, and young, full-fledged "Hulkamaniacs" were beyond hyped to see the larger-than-life hero up on the big screen. But alas, for every child, there comes a time when rose-colored sanguinity vanishes. . .

Vince McMahon Jr., Grand Poobah of all things squared circle, had wanted to make his golden boy (literally . . . the man uses more tanning bronzer than all of Venice Beach combined), Hulk Hogan, a crossover movie star for years. Made sense. The former session bass player[29] did first enter the public consciousness playing wrestler Thunderlips opposite Sylvester Stallone in *Rocky III*. And the mainstream knew who Hulk Hogan was. He had hosted *Saturday Night Live* alongside Mr. T, and his trademark thinning yellow mane and handlebar mustache had adorned everything from action figures to trading cards to T-shirts to the cover of *Sports Illustrated*. Imminent movie stardom seemed assured.

That is, of course, until the public actually *saw* the movie. Hulk and Vince, who both co-executive produced, reportedly hated the original draft of the script so much that they checked into a hotel and stayed up seventy hours straight rewriting the thing. That is accepted fact. What is apocryphal, though, is that they also consumed enough cocaine during that stretch of unbridled creativity to bring down a herd of mastodons. And while that may be apocryphal, it's also very believable, since the influence of Bolivian marching powder can be seen all over *No Holds Barred*.

The film begins with what can only be described as a Bizarro version of a WWF show. The arena looks familiar, "Mean" Gene Okerlund and Jesse "The Body" Ventura are at ringside calling the action, and the announcer is WWF stalwart Howard Finkel. And the champ is the Hulkster. But he's not Hulk. He's Rip. Just Rip. Seventy-two hours locked in a hotel room and that's seriously the best name they could have come up with? They could have at least called him Rip Roar or some such for a little more pizzazz and some alliteration. But he's Rip, just Rip, and he's the WWF champ.

Rip looks like Hulk Hogan, acts like Hulk Hogan, has a move set as limited as Hulk Hogan, but he's not Hulk Hogan. He's Rip; key distinction. Thus, instead of Hogan's trademark red and yellow, Rip's colors are white and blue. He still delivers the big boot (dubbed the "big foot" here) but rather than follow it up with his trademark leg drop finisher, he instead knocks his opponents silly with the "double axe hammer." Furthermore, he's accompanied to the ring by his trainer, Charlie, and his whiny twerp of a brother Randy. His catchphrase is "Rip 'Em," and he throws an inane hand gesture, which is a slight derivation of the Hawaiian *Shaka* sign, or "hang loose" gesture.

As Geno and The Body call the action, Rip rips into his opponent—number one contender Jake Bullet, played by Bill Eadie (known better to wrestling fans as Demolition Ax). Bullet has an unfortunate hairstyle and even more unfortunately applied eye makeup. Watching the match along with his boardroom cronies is maniacal television executive Brell, played with manic, bug-eyed intensity by Kurt Fuller.[30] Brell is the head of the World Television Network and is livid over getting trounced in the ratings. Or as he puts it, "Every time this jock ass decides to strip down to his sweet nothings and wallow around like some sweat hog, we eat it!" As Brell stalks his boardroom, brandishing a large crystal sculpture, his ferocity is such that you expect him to go all Dick Jones on someone.

Although his "word is his bond," Rip does take a meeting with Brell, who offers the "jockstrap" a blank check if he signs with the network. Rip sticks to his (24-inch) guns, and Brell makes the mistake of pushing him not once but twice. Big mistake! Rip takes the check and stuffs it into Brell's mouth, quipping "I won't be around when this check clears!" and throwing the "Rip 'Em" gesture as he exits.

Rip then gets into the Brell-provided limo, but notices much to his consternation and repeated reminders, that the driver is going the wrong way. It's a trap! If Brell can't get Rip to sign, he's gonna resort to vehicular kidnapping and a little assault and battery. Rip's taken to an empty warehouse where a number of weapon-wielding toughs await. Defying all rules of physics, Rip bursts out of the car's roof and destroys the henchmen. Then, after dispensing with the assailants, Rip makes his way to the driver's side, laughing and snorting maniacally all the way. He tears the car door off its hinges and grabs the driver by the scruff of his collar. The camera then pans down to show that the driver has clearly soiled himself. "What's that smell?" inquires Rip. "Dookie" is the driver's pitiful response, to which Rip then looks at him with that rabid glint in his eye that only Hulk Hogan can muster and growls back "Doooo-kiiiieee." Shit jokes in a Hogan movie? That shit ain't right.

And that's not all about *No Hold Barred* that ain't right. The sexual innuendo between Rip and Samantha (Joan Severance), an account executive assigned to enhance Rip's brand, is particularly discomfiting. Leering looks at Hogan's barely clad buttocks; Samantha waking up to sounds clearly meant to imply that Rip is pleasuring himself when he is merely doing push-ups clad in a skimpy pink Speedo. Wrong, wrong, wrong!

Yet this is all undercard, for the main event is the climatic no-holds-barred (but of course!) battle between Rip and his nemesis, Brell's new "champion" Zeus. Portrayed by Tommy "Tiny" Lister, a prolific actor turned born-again minister (perhaps best known for playing Deebo in the *Friday* series), Zeus is a cross-eyed, unibrowed behemoth, bald save for the letter "Z" shaved on the side of his head. He calls Rip out at a charity event and challenges him to a match. Instead of saying "You name the time and the place, Brother!" like any sort of champ should, Rip cowardly backs down like a little chump. It takes Zeus beating the stuffing out of and sending brother Randy to the hospital for Rip to finally step up and accept the challenge. But not before a brief montage showing Zeus punching cinderblocks into dust while Rip tends to feeble Randy, nursing him back to health by assisting with his physical rehab and hydrotherapy. Not exactly running up mountains in Siberia, are you Rip?

And what madness is this? The final fight, the one the entire film has been leading up to, is contested not in a stadium holding 93,173 screaming fans[31] but rather in a rinky-dink studio surrounded by silver Christmas tinsel. One would think a Machiavellian businessman such as Brell would have gone for a larger gate, but apparently even he didn't have much faith in the drawing power of Zeus vs. Rip. As such, even with the hundred or so attendees dressed in formal wear to give the event a little élan, the climax can't help but feel somewhat anticlimactic. Wheelchair-bound Randy is at ringside, but even with that added encouragement, Zeus is dominant for the majority of the fight. Without spoiling the winner (though it can't be too difficult to surmise), the climax of *No Holds Barred* also features the infirm Randy knocked out of his wheelchair and kicked a few more times by Zeus for good measure and Brell going to the great network in the sky after fatally electrocuting himself.

No Holds Barred is a bizarre beast. It's wrongheaded from start to finish, and its tone is dichotomous to its intended audience (ostensibly Hulkamaniacs aged 6–16). While not an out-and-out flop, *No Holds Barred* fell way short of expectations and effectively ended any conception of Hulk Hogan as a viable box office draw. It should have also meant the end of "Tiny" Lister's ridiculous Zeus character, but Vince wasn't about to let that creation go without a (no pun intended) fight. Hence, Zeus was soon seen stepping off the screen and into the squared circle, challenging Hogan in a number of pay-per-view main events. No four-star mat classics those, but that's another story for another day.

SUPERFIGHTS (1995)

"Styles make fights" is a maxim as old as boxing itself. In the early '90s, UFC decided to put this to the test, pitting fat wrestlers in unitards against little guys in karate *gis* to see which style prevailed. Fighting style that is, not fashion. And it's no accident the WWE's "Attitude Era" sprung forth soon after, featuring more adult themes, gestures, and moves in an effort to make fake fighting look more in line with the real thing.

Superfights is a marriage of pro wrestling and martial arts movies that probably should've been annulled. It's a fighting federation of baby-face stars "No Mercy" Budokai and Dark Cloud, and lots of backstage camaraderie.

And like other cage combat-type movies of this ilk, we're meant to believe that blood sports are incredibly popular with the vox pop, even if the producers couldn't fill an arena with enough extras so what we're left with looks like a barely filled to capacity high school gym.

Superfights' superfighting is overseen by Svengali sleazeball Robert Sawyer, a Vince McMahon surrogate right down to the bad haircut and the, ahem, "vitamin" pushing.

And who's that looking to join the ranks of the federation? Why, it's young marquee-friendly, all-American-face, he'll-get-bums-in-the-seats Jack Cody, a man who just so happens to have the great grace of working in a warehouse large enough for him to train after the working day is done. He does this by jerry-rigging a back room with punch dummies that he can manipulate with rope and pulley like a jacked Jim Henson, swinging them to and fro so he can time his uppercuts and roundhouses.

But it's Cody's exploits defending a pretty young woman from an ATM mugging and subsequent appearance on the 6 o'clock news that makes him a hero in Harrisburg, Pennsylvania. And soon we find out that, as luck would certainly have to dictate, the victim's grandfather is a (choose one):

a) Town comptroller
b) High school principal
c) Respected haberdasher
d) Retired martial arts instructor.

If you answered d) you'd be correct, as every martial arts flick worth its smelling salts needs a sensei/mentor (although a haberdasher wouldn't be missed should one appear in one).

The eighty-plus granddaddy beats up the young upstart in the family's living room, with age- and gravity-defying flip kicks, and essentially does what every other sensei has done since the beginning of time: beats humility into his student while teaching him all about *qi*, that ever-important inner force that can be summoned in flashback form when danger is around the corner.

News of Cody's heroics spreads through town like a brushfire, with school kids shouting out to him from bus windows, and soon fight promoter Sawyer is sniffing around. "Do you have an agent?" to which Cody replies, "Should I?" and Sawyer answers, channeling his inner Don King if not his *qi*, "Not necessarily."

And hence the new Superfighter signs on the dotted line.

Cody is put through his paces by Angel, the pumped-up female champ whose training facilities are equipped with the latest in young-upstart training technology, including a column of blue light which, when breached, calculates punching and kicking force and spits out the results on a computer screen. Memo to self: develop an app that does just that. Cody is revealed as a promising fighter with panther reflexes that belie his geek physique.

But signing a Superfights contract might not be the panacea it seems, something viewers might have clued into earlier with the musical foreshadowing of the theme lyrics, "*You've entered a world of drugs and corruption, murder, extortion, lies and seduction. SUPER FIGHTER!*"

After a particularly grueling workout, Angel rubs her leotard-clad rack into Cody's back and checks her "favorite vital sign" by grabbing his crotch, surprising given that youth-friendly karate fare usually ducks adult sexuality. And we find out most of the Superfights roster is on the take, pops pills, and that its leadership is mobbed up.

And it's up to Cody (a one-and-done performance by Brandon Gaines) and his jingoistic Stars & Stripes harlequin ring attire to fight and then expose them.

But as is often the case, it's the heels that make this movie so scrumptious. The cast includes The Enforcer, played by "The Giant Killer" Keith Hackney, a stocky two-hundred-pounder and footnote in mixed martial arts history, who TKO'd a 616-pound sumo wrestler in UFC 3. Then there's Cody's childhood hero and focus of a feature article in *Martial Arts* magazine "Where's Rocco? Superfighter disapears (sic)." He's since become a crooked Sawyer enforcer and is played by All Japan Pro Wrestler Jungle Jim Steele. And finally, squared circle fans will also get a kick out of a brief appearance by Rob Van Dam, ex-WWE/ECW man known for his innovative aerial moves, slight resemblance to the more-famous Van Damme, and infamous affinity for THC.

Superfights, the brainchild of director Siu-Hung Leung (*The Legend of Drunken Master*) features that classic '80s retort, "You and what army?" and has every bit of '80s fromagerie despite being lensed in the '90s. *Rocky* fans will take umbrage with a training montage up the steps of another Pennsylvania mainstay, the State Capitol building, where Cody jumps in the air for a pause mid-jump, like a bad *Instagram* vacation photo.

OF NOTE:

Pioneering Hong Kong director Patrick Lung-Kong is fun in the grandfather role. Lung-Kong was a highly respected director and veteran of Cantonese-language action films who wanted to elevate the genre above its "wonton noodle" roots—when directors took an indifferent approach to their craft, purportedly going out to grab a noodle bowl while the camera ran.

BAM! Flipping Out

There are few moves in martial arts movies as ubiquitous as the kip-up. What's that, you ask? Well, it's an acrobatic flip done with a person lying flat on the ground, so they can launch themselves quickly up to their feet. It's a staple of breakdancing, wrestling, and action fighting sequences, and it also looks hella-cool. There's a bunch of videos and a *wikiHow* tutorial. Proceed with caution and please don't even attempt a kip-up less than thirty minutes after eating.

PENITENTIARY 2 (1982)

Jamaa Fanaka's *Penitentiary*, released in 1979, was a low-budget yet surprisingly well-executed hybrid lock-up/boxing flick. Starring the undeniably charismatic Leon Isaac Kennedy (*Death Force*), *Penitentiary* told the tale of Martel "Too Sweet" Gordone, a man sent up river for a murder he didn't commit. There he dons the gloves and joins the prison boxing league in hopes of earning early parole. The Blaxploitation hit crossed over and grossed more than $13 million, paving the way for a follow-up. And while *Penitentiary* did have its share of goofy moments, it looks like a Bolshoi ballet compared to its successor. *Penitentiary 2*, released three years later, takes the grittiness, social commentary, and credibility of the first one and KOs them decisively; pretty much in the opening round.

Penitentiary 2 picks up almost immediately where the first film left off, and capitalizing on Blaxploitation's undeniable science fiction roots, begins with a *Star Wars*-esque vertical crawl (set to a peppy pseudo John Williams score to boot), lest the viewer feel lost. Too Sweet has been living with his sister's family and working as a roller-skate messenger, violating the conditions of his parole which state explicitly that he must work for boxing promoter Cunningham. But Too Sweet hates boxing. (Funny that, as there was no indication whatsoever of his distaste for the sweet science when he was gleefully knocking chumps to the canvas in the first film.) To add to our hero's woes, "Half Dead, a vicious killer who had become an obsessed enemy of Too Sweet's after Too Sweet fought off his nocturnal amorous advances in a prison cell [has] escaped . . . [and] vows to kill Too Sweet."

Gordone (We'd call him "Too Sweet" here, but since his nickname was used so much in the opening crawl, let's take a small break and refer to the protagonist by his surname—in this paragraph at least) needs to report to Cunningham forthwith, or he'll be sent back to prison. And so Gordone rolls his way into Cunningham's gym. There, sparring in the ring, is former bouncer turned bodyguard to the likes of Diana Ross and Muhammad Ali, Mr. T. And he's playing . . . Mr. T! (We pity the fool who takes no creative chances in their first major feature film role.) T takes a break from punishing his sparring partner, who later pulls a straight-edge razor on the soon-to-be Clubber Lang before T kicks the living shit out of him, to inquire non-sequiturly, "Hey Sweetie, where's my pizza?" Since Gordone refuses to box, Cunningham puts him to work mopping floors.

After a hard day's night making those floors shine, Too Sweet is chilling on his sister's futon, waiting for his girl, Clarisse, to exit the bathroom. Half Dead comes out of the shower, now played by Ernie Hudson, replacing Badja Djola (*The Serpent and the Rainbow*) who played Half Dead with frenzied intensity in the first film. Half Dead has his way with Clarisse and ultimately kills her. Too Sweet does bust in, but Too Late for poor Clarisse. He grabs Half Dead and the two recreate/pay homage to the nearly nude brawl between the two in *Penitentiary* (upping the ante a bit, this one features a near drowning in a toilet bowl). Before a decisive victor can be declared, the bare ass brouhaha is broken up by the police.

A broken and despondent Too Sweet wants to avenge Clarisse, but rather than going after her assailant directly, surmises instead that he needs to learn to box. (Something he was able to do quite handily in the first *Penitentiary*. They say prison changes a man, but c'mon.) Sobbing, he tells his sister "I'm gonna be somebody . . . I'm gonna get respect . . . I'm gonna talk to kids about the insanity of this world . . . I'm gonna make a difference . . . for Clarisse!" There's faulty logic in an ex-con boxer becoming a role model, seeing as how nobody looks up to Mike Tyson as any sort of aspirational figure.

Mr. T is assigned to train him, and another character from the prior film returns: Two Sweet's former trainer and cellmate, Floyd "Seldom Seen" Jackson. Despite maintaining he was "institutionalized" in the first film, thus refusing release, Seldom Seen is now out and tearing up the streets. Also recast, Seldom Seen has morphed from a wise, erudite elder-statesman into a loud lecher who's at least twenty years younger and sixty pounds heavier. (Again, prison does change people.)

Gordone's first bout as a professional is fought in the same penitentiary where he once was incarcerated. Seems the prison bouts are still going on, yet what was once a *Fight Club*-like, clandestine bit of brutality has now gone global. The prison fights are now inexplicably televised, complete with ringside commentators. (One doing his utmost to impersonate the cadence of the late, great Howard Cosell.) It's Too Sweet vs. Jesse "The Bull" Amos, but it's truly hard to pay attention to the fight due to a number of preposterous distractions. First, there's Mr. T at ringside, dressed in a purple genie outfit and brandishing an Aladdin's Lamp which emits purple haze when rubbed. Second, there's the inmate in the audience playing his saxophone throughout the duration of the fight. Finally, there's the little person inmate who interrupts his game of dice to shimmy under the ring and across the arena to proposition a prostitute. Too Sweet gets his ass handed to him, yet like a certain Southpaw from Philly, has "captured the hearts of America" due to his tenacity in defeat.

The rest of the film is a bountiful bag of insanity, so let's unpack, shall we?

There's the police officer guarding Half Dead in the hospital who "doo-doo[s] in his bowels" when Dead's lackeys bust him out. There's Mr. T, this time in a gold genie outfit, leading a conga line in a park while chanting "Let's go!" There's the rapidest rise to number one contender status of any fighter in cinematic history (the story of which told by that hoariest of cinematic clichés: the spinning newspapers.) And there's T again, now in his third genie outfit (a black one), knocking the stuffing out of a rainbow-colored-afro-wig-wearing Half Dead. (And to think, Hudson would be busting ghosts alongside Dan Aykroyd and Bill Murray just a scant two years later.) There's a cameo by Dolemite himself, Rudy Ray Moore. And of course, there's the obligatory rematch, which is second verse, same as the first: Same venue, same sax player, same little person shimmying under the ring to get some "poontang."

Penitentiary 2 is a clear, albeit entertaining, step down from its predecessor. Jamaa Fanaka had to be in on the joke, or else he had lost the plot entirely (1987's *Penitentiary III* lends credence to the latter.)

The film ends with a dedication from Fanaka: "This film is for my parents, Bea and Bob." One wonders just what they did to their son to piss him off so.

DOLEMITE (1975)

"Dolemite is my name and fuckin' up other mutha fuckers is my game!" Who could not love a rhyming couplet like that?

Doing serious pen time for trafficking in illegal furs (really) as well as half a mil in blow, Dolemite (Rudy Ray Moore) is thrown a bone and offered a way out by the warden: in exchange for his release, he has to take out drug kingpin Willie Green along with the corrupt white mayor, both responsible for bringing the "4th Ward" of whatever fictional city this is to its knees. Last count, there were eight such 4th Wards in the United States alone. The only people in on this plan: the warden, whorehouse Madame Queen B, and an unnamed FBI agent.

Once the deal is done, and following unnecessary flashbacks and some shaky exposition, Dolemite doffs his peels for a dapper jumpsuit. Not even waiting to get home to change, he strips down to his tighty whities right outside the prison gates, brought to him by limo by his bitches. (This, as the less-than- impressed cornball Caucasian guards call out, "You'll be back, Dolemite!"

Meanwhile, the newly freed warrior is harassed by two cops on the take while he goes about his business.

He gets the lay of the land from Creeper, a.k.a., The Hamburger Pimp, a shuffling base head who's promptly assassinated. We learn that Willie Green has taken over Dolemite's Dolemite-themed nightclub, and big D has to get rid of WG, an original OG. Just what kind of audience a Dolemite-themed nightclub would attract other than the admittedly hefty orbit of his entourage is anyone's guess.

Along with this colorful cast of characters—a reverend who runs guns, a karate-kicking all-female militia force, dancer Chi (short for Chicago)—the omnipresent boom mic is a character unto itself, visible at the top and the bottom of many a frame.

At the center of the mess is Dolemite, a man who carries BB King's girth and drops Grandmaster Flash's rhymes; an urban poet who delights assembled street toughs and captive audiences alike with parables about monkeys and lions as well as what might've gone down on the Titanic had the racial politics been different.

But there's business to attend to, including avenging his nephew Lil' Jimmy's murder. He lays waste to much of the 4th Ward's criminal element with half-baked karate chops and elephantine spinning back kicks.

The semi-comatose Dolemite, who looks like he's perpetually recovering from invasive surgery, is still good for the odd line like "You no good rat soup eatin' honkey mutha fucka!"

Where can you dine on this specialty? Nobody knows for sure, but Rudy Ray Moore has a gift of gab and a grab bag of put downs that could skewer a dozen Yo Mama wannabes. See, we have skills too.

As an introduction to Blaxploitation, Rudy Ray Moore is no Ron O'Neal, can't hold a lighter to Fred Williamson, and sure as hell ain't Richard Roundtree (though he's plenty round).

As inept as it is hilarious and beguiling, Dolemite is kind of must-see material—basically an excuse for Moore to showcase his less-than-stellar stand-up, his band, and of course, the Dolemite Dancers.

Rudy Ray Moore
is
DOLEMITE
Bone-crushing
Skull-splitting
Brain-blasting
ACTION!
FEATURING
• SHINE AND THE GREAT TITANIC
• THE SIGNIFYING MONKEY
STARRING RUDY RAY MOORE AS "DOLEMITE" CO STARRING D'URVILLE MARTIN WITH JERRY JONES
INTRODUCING LADY REED AS "THE QUEEN BEE" PRODUCED BY RUDY RAY MOORE & T. TONEY DIRECTED BY D'URVILLE MARTIN
WRITTEN BY JERRY JONES MARTIAL ARTS CHAMPION HOWARD JACKSON
R RESTRICTED
UNDER 17 REQUIRES ACCOMPANYING PARENT OR ADULT GUARDIAN
A DIMENSION PICTURES RELEASE
A XENON ENTERTAINMENT HOME VIDEO RELEASE.
XENON
HOME VIDEO
VHSCOLLECTOR.COM

THE DEVIL'S SWORD (1984)

Being a villager is tough. If you're Chinese, some Manchu thug is going to trash your noodle shop and burn down your temple. But if you're Indonesian, you must contend with something even scarier. Crocodiles. And unlike Qing enforcers, crocs can't be bought off by protection money. And if that ain't enough to contend with, the villagers in *The Devil's Sword* also have to deal with a Crocodile Queen, a ruthless monarch in a baby blue bikini whose handmaidens rock reptile tiaras.

The she-demon's bed is inside a crocodile skull, and her boudoir is decorated with what look like used condoms. And they might as well be. You see, this South Asian Cleopatra takes men hostage to use as her sex slaves, depopulating local villages of menfolk and "weakening them," according to the grousing elders (who may just be grousing because they're not the ones being selected).

In her aquatic lair, she enjoys orgies on effigies (say that three times fast) and gets her crocs off reclining on a translucent reptile sculpture while half a dozen gents pleasure her in awkward fashion—welcome comic relief when the plenitude of chopsocky mayhem, smoke bombs, and purple verbiage threatens to get stale.

To ensure the supply of villagers equals her demand, the queen's got a right-hand man, evil warrior Banyujaga, who sweeps down from the heavens astride a papier-mâché boulder and proceeds to slice the domes off villagers who refuse to yield to her demands (this includes browbeating a young prince whose betrothed is standing awkwardly by while the "you've gotta *shtup* the Queen, or else" message is relayed).

The queen clearly gets what she wants but is unable to get what she needs, and the monarch is desperately seeking the Devil's Sword, if only to justify the film's title. The titular weapon is a magical (but not satanical) piece of steel forged out of a meteorite, then melded into a rock-solid plot device by an old wizard.

The queen wants village pimp Banyujaga to source the sword before heroic warrior Mandala does, the virtuous combatant who we first meet when he's rushing to the aid of the villagers whose ranks are about to be turned into unwilling gigolos. And who'da thunk it, the two warriors were once students of the very same sensei.

Dojos are dangerous places—remember that. Now granted, they can set wayward youth on the straight and narrow by providing guidance, life direction, and the ability to knock an opponent silly with a well-placed crane kick, and they're also the places you come to find your "inner *qi*," that magical force which, like your cell phone, is always in the last place you look. But someone really needs to investigate those damn dojos. Why? Because as we see in *The Devil's Sword* and a whole host of other martial arts movies, a sensei will invariably teach the deadly arts to one morally upstanding student (which is good) and one evil student who'll break ranks to wreak havoc (which is bad). There's always got to be one obligatory Goofus and one requisite Gallant, right? If action films have taught us anything (and boy have they taught us everything), it's clear that more dojo due diligence needs to be done. And here we have good disciple Mandala against evil one Banyujaga. They're the odds-on Vegas bookmaker favorites to claim the sword.

Banyujaga, certainly no slouch in the martial arts department, can also conjure up warrior "crocodile men" as backup, a nude-from-the-

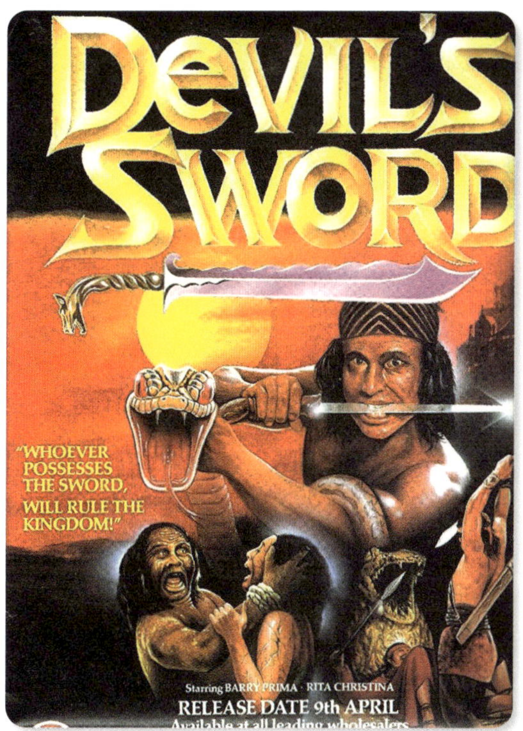

waist-up fighting force who wear latex croc masks and swing flopping rubber chainsaw blades. While these silly guys popping out of nowhere certainly surprised us, hero Mandala seems less than impressed. (Maybe it's because actor Barry Prima's face, much like Dorothy Parker's famous remark about Katharine Hepburn, "runs the gamut of emotions from A to B"). He looks at them, mutters "hmmm . . . Crocodile men" like Homer Simpson ogling the Gummi de Milo, then off goes their heads as the arterial sanguinity sprays. Like a hero from Greek antiquity, Mandala must also face a formidable cave-dwelling stone pig cyclops whose maw resembles Gypsy's from *Mystery Science Theater 3000*.

But lest you think this is a contest of only two, there are some longshots vying for the coveted weaponry, including female warriors who fly around with parasols, *Mary Poppins* style. (Incidentally, Julie Andrews once told Stephen Colbert that she could feel the harness wires nearly giving way when filming that iconic scene, and she fell to the stage floor, narrowly escaping serious injury.) There's also a graying warrior lady who "smells like death," and her strongman ally who slings a conical hat like a *Master of the Flying Guillotine* villain (and whose shoulders Old Warrior Lady hops on midfight to gain a competitive height advantage against swordsman Banyujaga).

The warrior battles yield much bloodshed and some spectacular dialogue right out of old wrestling promos. You could easily substitute "world championship belt" for the title weapon here and utter in your best Randy Savage growl: "Old woman, there is room for only one tiger in this jungle. There is only one sword, and I must be the one to possess it!"

The Devil's Sword is one profoundly messed up movie, a woozy pastiche of sword and sandal adventure, martial arts mayhem, and Harryhausen-esque stop motion effects. But when it comes to the devil sword itself, a piece of magical steel which can "change the world as we know it," it's pretty underwhelming. From what we can gather, its most practical use is as a big shiny scalpel to slowly saw off the sensei's legs at the knee to prevent "poison of the snake" from spreading to the rest of his wracked body.

The '80s were a fruitful, and yes, truly magical period for Indonesian film. Rapi Films was a kind of Cannon of South Asia, a ballsy can-do crew who financed movies like *The Devil's Sword* which fused black magic and butt-kicking. And their leading man Barry Prima[32] put the production house on the map with 1981's *The Warrior*, subsequently becoming Indonesia's biggest action star of the '80s. And as an exemplar of Indonesian action-fantasy at its finest, the hallucinatory *The Devil's Sword* is pretty hard to beat.

LOCK UP (1989)

A guarantee of three warm meals and a bed, or "three hots and a cot" comes to us from the military, then moved its way over to prison. We say "us" but neither the military nor prison are especially accommodating to late risers.

The worst part of prison, apparently, is not the raping, the lousy food, the beatdowns, or the lack of sunlight, but the boredom. OK, it's the raping, but if you can avoid that, it's the boredom. But for whatever reason, Sylvester Stallone is a prison movie recidivist, appearing in a whopping ten movies that prominently feature the Big House. The man's been incarcerated in roughly twenty percent of his major roles, including *Tango & Cash*, *Demolition Man*, *Judge Dredd*, *Victory*, *First Blood*, *Rambo: First Blood Part II*, *Rambo III*, *Over the Top*, and *Escape Plan*. Ironically, he wasn't imprisoned in *The Prisoner of Second Avenue*. Still, his Oscar lifetime achievement award should be presented on a metal tray.

If you're as short as Stallone that you need an apple box or "man-maker," as those in the film business call it, to give you height, then you better damn-well be built like Stallone if going to a real prison. But luckily for all involved, *Lock Up* is fiction—martial law when it comes to taking liberties with realism.

Every prison movie needs a hero, and it's always someone undercover or in the joint on trumped up charges. Why? 'Cause while antiheros are praised for being morally ambiguous, no audience will stand up and cheer for someone who embezzled an old lady out of her life savings or stuck a knife in a bodega owner. Hence, in *Lock Up*, Stallone as hero Frank Leone is in for vigilantism—pounding the snot out of street toughs rather than lurking around an elementary school in a trench coat.

Lock Up's primary antagonist, despite everything popular culture tells us, isn't Bubba, the 6'8" light sleeper in the bunk above. It's the warden. A lot of prison movies have sadistic wardens, but in *Lock Up* the evil warden is Donald Sutherland, of all people, in a performance that would justify the electric chair. He plays Drumgoole, a warden who saves his vindictiveness for escapee Frank, and one would hope, more serious transgressors like guys who've shanked guards.

Through some plot device, Drumgoole, even though he's not a federal judge, makes sure Leone is sent to Gateway Prison, a maximum-security facility.

Drumgoole enlists the help of scary lifer Chink, a name which has not become less racist in the interceding decades since filming, to make Leone's life a living hell. And speaking of race, apparently Gateway is one of the most tolerant prisons ever. Stallone is able to heal age-old racial grievances, getting along so well with everyone you'd think a United Colors of Benetton photoshoot was in the offing.

There are a few other key things we learn in *Lock Up*:

- The warden takes such an unnecessary and ridiculous personal interest in Leone's stay, as does everyone at Gateway (when Leone is finally released, hundreds gather at the gates to see him off like he's heading to Western Europe to fight the Germans).
- When Leone and Drumgoole have a heated physical altercation, Leone points and asks, "do you recognize that [electric] chair?" Stands to reason he does, after

all, he's the goddamn warden. And strapping him into it isn't gonna jog his memory.
- It's apparently really easy to operate an electric chair with no training. It's even better for sight gags!
- Gateway has the worst prison-to-guard ratio ever. It's more like the odd security guard you might find wandering around the concession stands at an NFL game. And those few guards all know Leone's name and face like he's O. J. or the Son of Sam.

- Prison movies need to have at least one of the following: a lifer who feeds birds; a guy who can source any kind of contraband imaginable, liquid or solid, large or small; and of course, some young inmate weeks from release who gets the short end of the pointed toothbrush.
- Prison ID numbers are a mere three digits long. In one scene, where guards put Leone "in the hole" (solitary) for some minor transgression, they torture him with light every hour and force him to recite his three-digit prison ID. Sorry, but there are not enough number permutations for a prison this large. That is unless Stallone is so notorious he gets a special three-digit number. For those of you looking for a pen pal, federal US inmate IDs have a five-number-dash-three (12345-678) number format, which, let's be honest, sounds far cooler to recite. Imagine how lame it'd be being 123?
- Gateway has a full-scale auto repair garage that's lightly policed. This has to be just so we can have that action movie staple, the "macho fixing stuff" montage. (Typically welding as it's the manliest of all repairs, what with all the sparks flying around and such, but can include carpentry in a pinch.)
- When you're doing maintenance work under the hood, it's important to have the soundtrack play that hoary chestnut "Vehicle" by The Ides of March to avoid confusion and ambiguity. It's the same rule that dictates the obligatory playing of Thorogood's "Bad to the Bone" to demarcate anyone who's bad . . . to the bone!
- You so long for a taste of freedom that you drive through the garage door just so you can do doughnuts in the prison yard.
- Everyone can have free weights in the yard (stranger danger!), and gym time is available to everyone at once. This is not good. See point number one.

So, will Leone prevail? We he be able to reunite with his girl on the outside, instead of flexing his acting rage by looking forlornly at her photo from his bunk?

For *Lock Up*, Stallone was unfairly Razzie-nominated against Patrick Swayze in *Road House*, another legit actor in a Graphene-strong classic. In true action movie form, that lousy Razzie bunch clearly has a vendetta against Sly, nominating him a record nine times in a row, when there are way less capable one-note thespians around. (Here's lookin' at you, Chuck Norris, Mr. Botox No-Expression). As an every-mensch fighting against injustice, Stallone has the face and the acting chops to generate sympathy in any role, even if he looks like Pope Gregory IX, the Inquisition pontiff. (Thanks, Internet.)

OF NOTE:

As guys raised on TV, we were delighted to see the dad from *Good Times*, ex-NFLer and Golden Gloves boxing champ John Amos as a guard. And much like *The Longest Yard*, *Lock Up* has a sizeable portion of its running time devoted to football (you won't be surprised to learn Leone is a star of the yard flag football gridiron).

FURIOUS (1984)

Salvador Dalí once said of his art, "It is not necessary for the public to know whether I am joking or whether I am serious, just as it is not necessary for me to know it myself." The same sentiment could be applied to filmmakers Tim Everitt and Tom Sartori and their 1984 opus *Furious*, which depending on your perspective, is either the most brilliantly surreal or patently ridiculous martial arts film ever made. If Alejandro Jodorowsky or Luis Buñuel made a chopsocky, it would be *Furious*: a film replete with hypnagogic imagery, incongruous sound elements, and a non-Euclidian narrative that exists in a time, space, and logic all its own.

The film begins conventionally enough with a *gi*-clad woman being pursued through a forest by a horde of what, judging from their attire, look to be Mongolian nomads. She runs while one pursuer periodically stops to warble the "coo-loo-coo-coo-coo-coo" theme that Bob and Doug McKenzie used to begin the "Great White North." OK, that's sort of strange. They're also predominantly white, but that could be forgiven since Mongolian extras might have been hard to find in Southern California (where the film was shot "entirely on location" as touted by the exclamation-point-heavy VHS box). She has a tusk that they want, and though she fights them off admirably, she's eventually overcome and her tusk taken.

Without any form of natural segue to orient or clarify, we move to the treehouse abode, overlooking a sort of martial arts gulag where out-of-shape children practice the deadly arts 24/7, of her grieving and contemporarily garbed brother Simon (Simon Rhee). Wait, so this ISN'T a period piece? Um, now our head's starting to hurt a little. As he's skulking around the compound, the same white "Mongol" warrior who killed his sister pops in liberally and summons Simon to meet Master Chan.

Chan, played by Simon Rhee's brother Phillip,[33] runs a dojo incongruously housed in a high-tech office building complete with automated guards at the door and a steady stream of people in white hazmat suits smuggling live chickens in and out at all hours of the day. (Chickens are a recurring theme in *Furious*. In addition to the poultry smuggling, random clucking sounds are heard intermittently on the soundtrack, perhaps foreshadowing the fowl play to come.) He takes a break from his usual pastime of floating a few feet off the ground to convey sagacious gobbledygook to Simon such as "You're now between an anvil and a hammer" and "The dove is a gentle creature." He gives a pendant to Simon emblazoned with Asian characters, then sends him on a journey to find others who have the same symbol.

Upon leaving, Simon runs into his posse, which includes a woman giving him serious stink eye and two mustachioed string beans, both wearing Hawaiian shirts. Hawaiian shirt #1 recognizes the lettering as belonging to a Chinese restaurant and the group march over to see what's what. They're attacked by a bunch of goons (who were delivering—you guessed it—chicken) to the closed eatery, and what starts as a standard kick-and-punch encounter turns deadly when the chef runs out of the kitchen replete with apron, chef's hat, and a kitchen knife, which he throws into one of the Hawaiian shirt guy's backs. Simon wrests the knife away and slits the chef's throat. Suddenly, assailants are everywhere, throwing

empty cardboard boxes off rooftops, shooting guns, and leaving Simon as the sole survivor.

He retreats through a forest where the wind stops crying Mary to whisper "Simon, beware!" (It's later revealed to be a small Buddha statue delivering the communiqués, a revelation that does very little to mitigate the weirdness.) Then the Mongol guy returns and the two have a stick fight in a meadow. Simon notices that his opponent has the same necklace as him. This leads him back to the Chinese restaurant which, unlike last time, is open for business, but where every diner seems to be foregoing eating to watch a buff white guy doing a sword swinging/nunchuk demonstration. Everybody, that is, except the one old lady who the camera keeps coming back to as she's eating . . . fried chicken! Before he's even had a chance to peruse the appetizers, a waiter in a kabuki mask brings Simon a cloche. A lift of the lid reveals a dish unworthy of *Master Chef*: the severed heads of two of his friends. Simon's screams clear out the restaurant and it's clobberin' time! And it's a great melee too, especially when front-of-the-house reinforcements enter to chuck rice bowls at him.

As the film continues, the weirdness remains in top gear. There's more forest whispering, threats of opening an astral plane to other dimensions, and Master Chan (who's revealed to be the evil mastermind behind the whole *meshugas*) flying through the air like Superman. There's even a few glorious seconds of Simon beating on a giant papier-mâché fire breather. (Talk about Enter the Dragon! This fake lizard's appearance is so out-of-left-field that if you haven't checked your sanity by this point, you certainly will now.) But everything really is just dress rehearsal for the glorious lunacy to come—Simon's battle with Mika the Sorcerer.

Mika is a cackling villain with a Fu Manchu mustache. He and Simon circle each other as Mika makes contorted hand gestures and shoots fireballs from his fingertips—fireballs which turn into . . . wait for it . . . chickens! As far as combat weapons go, poultry has got to be the least effective. These chickens simply scurry away, barely so much as grazing Simon. But don't close the barn door just yet, for Mika has yet to unveil his finishing move—the one where he turns into a pig! Simon gives the porcine pugilist a quick kick to the snout, effectively turning the poor beast into bacon. But before Mika shuffles off this mortal coil, he's got a few words for his combatant. Yep, this pig can talk! (Would you expect anything less from this film?) And talk he does, babbling on about nonsense such as how "fast food franchises" have turned Master Chan evil and how only Simon can stop him from taking over the world. (Come to think of it, swine Mika is squealing both literally and figuratively!)

The methodology of *Furious* is so out there that trying to piece it all together in any coherent way would make your brains ooze out of your ears like a milkshake left out in the sun. It just cannot be done. Instead, the best way to experience *Furious* is to turn off the rational mind and forget that Newtonian physics and any other established law, natural or otherwise, even exists. For the world of *Furious* is one where anything truly goes: a world where pigs talk, sorcerers summon chickens, and frantic new wave bands in white Devo-like outfits pop in at random intervals.

BLOODSPORT (1988)

The word "arena" is derived from the Latin for sand, for it was that granular material that sopped up blood, urine, and water atop an elevated platform that held combatants in the Colosseum. Roman fighters even wore *caesti*, ancient leather analogues to modern MMA/boxing gloves that were wrapped mid forearm. The key difference? Sometimes they were fitted with lead balls or spikes. Ancient Rome was also known for their baths, and if we were called to the arena, we'd be throwing in the towel pretty quick. Please, not the face.

Frank Dux (as in, "put up your_______," not "get your _____ in a row") is off to fight in an underground no-holds-barred fighting tournament in Hong Kong, much to the consternation of his US Army plot device superiors. It's a testament to how much fat needs to be trimmed at the US Defense Department that his two bosses fly all the way to South Asia to intervene on behalf of Uncle Sam and ensure Dux isn't hurt. Yes, one single solitary US Army Captain is just that valuable. Of course, it's Jean-Claude Van Damme, so maybe he's a long-term investment. He's the Muscles from Brussels whose great line from the film, "Use any technique that works, never limit yourself to one style," is wonderfully applicable to the modern-day blood sport that is the UFC (and to a certain extent, the boudoir).

Bloodsport is a pit fighting film, but at its heart it's a kung fu film. And what good is such a film if there aren't elaborate training montages a hero can flash back to? *Bloodsport* has backstory aplenty. It'd have to, just to explain how someone barely intelligible in the English language could move so high up the ranks of the Army Corps.

Young Dux and some pals are caught breaking into a home. But it's not just any home; it's that of a Japanese-American family whose father/son must've been a lark at school picnics, breaking wooden boards and such.

The son plants a front kick into Dux's ribcage, crumpling him into a quaking mass. But instead of beating him like a rented mule, the fam takes him in. Dad Tanaka teaches Dux everything he knows, much to the chagrin of son Shingo, whose words of encouragement include, "Why don't you quit, round eye?"(This is just part of the, shall we say, "interesting" ethnic portrayals in the film, the others being an African fighter who scurries monkey-style along the ground, and two generic Arab combatants in keffiyehs, garments which are designed to cool hot heads but here lack the desired effect.)

And at this point in *Bloodsport* we get one of the great joys of action films, the transcendent sensei[34] training sequence, taking the hero from bootlicking humiliation to eventual approval. Little by little, Dux gets stronger and better and can withstand various indignities—in this case, being beaten with bamboo sticks and drawn and quartered, but minus the horses. Seeing Dux roped up spread-eagle like da Vinci's Vitruvian Man is pure awesome. However, Tanaka also makes him fight blindfolded, that time-honored "develop the senses" cliché. But Dux must also deliver tea to the family dinner table blindly, which seems like the harder, not to mention more dangerous, of the two, especially if the scalding stuff ends up in someone's lap.

None of the other canonical Big Four Martial Artists (Seagal, Norris, Lee) could've pulled off Van Damme's humility and good-naturedness here. The childlike optimism as well as the wishbone groin pulls are what put JCVD in a league of his own.

When Tanaka's son Shingo dies, Dux is fighting for his adopted family's honor in a Hong Kong kumite tournament, where he meets some of his fellow combatants, á la *Enter the Dragon*, the similarities to which could fill a small volume.

On the kumite circuit, Tanaka's name apparently carries a lot of weight, and cage fighters are wondering, "Who's this gringo, fighting for Shingo?" (We're paraphrasing.) To prove he's connected to the Tanaka camp, Dux must demonstrate "the death touch" and crush a brick with his bare hands, which he does. Why would a fighter risk almost near-certain injury in a stupid stunt like that just before entering a major tournament? Cannon Films,[35] that's why! *Bloodsport*'s got the Cannon stinky-fun imprimatur all over it.

Dux's buddy Jackson is an Ugly American brute who swills lager and struts around in sweatpants. He duplicates the brick stunt but uses his head. To give you a sense of just how tough the kumite combatants are, this brick-crushing display doesn't send a single one scurrying for the exits: "Very good. But brick not hit back!"

Jackson is played by Donald Gibb, the lout who memorably menaced geeks in *Revenge of the Nerds* and tried to belch his way to a trophy in that film. He riotously refers to Dux as "kid" despite the actors' only six-year age difference. Chalk it up to the beard and the gut. And as the best friend, you know it's Jackson's role to eat leather and nearly die to dial up the revenge arc.

But in many ways, *Bloodsport* is all about Bolo Yeung, who plays Chong Li. It's "Two tickets to the Yeung show," a one-man pec-ing crew. We could go on. The bodybuilding behemoth, Shaw Brothers regular, and *Enter the Dragon* costar provides one of the most memorable villains in action history here. With single-nostril blowing aplomb, the wanton rhino snaps the neck of his first opponent but not before waving to the adoring throngs. He's the man to beat in the kumite, and the man who does the beating.

When they inevitably go head to head, Jackson seems to get the better of Chong Li, but forgets the old boxing maxim, "Protect yourself at all times," as Chong dusts himself off the canvas, gets up, and stomps Jackson's face like a cockroach.

Before the ultimate showdown between Dux and Chong Li, a fight fought to avenge some beer-guzzling oaf he met in a hotel lobby and barely befriended, JCVD gets in two more splits, one between two wicker chairs in a hotel room, the other atop concrete blocks overlooking beautiful Victoria Harbour.

This is all set to Stan Bush's awful karate chop to the cochlea, "Fight to Survive" and its chorus chant, KU-MI-TE, KU-MI-TE, KU-MI-TE.

SEVEN

THE LONG ARM OF THE LAW

I'M NOT AGAINST THE POLICE; I'M JUST AFRAID OF THEM.

—ALFRED HITCHCOCK

We cannot overestimate how important law enforcement is to an action film. Their response time inadequacy is absolutely vital, especially when restaurant patrons are being thrown through latticework or elaborate shootouts are happening in abandoned urban warehouses. Also, their inability to properly detain action heroes, not to mention even coming close to catching them in a high-speed pursuit, is paramount when it comes to advancing a plot.

The Thin Blue Line may not always represent a sizeable obstacle to action movie heroism, but every now and then, they're the heroic figures themselves. Steven Seagal, for example, burst out of the gate playing a cop in his first four movies. Now, he's bursting out of his suits as an enemy to any and all buffets.

Seagal has portrayed the LAPD three times, and Chicago PD twice. He's been a Detroit cop, Memphis PD, and probably many more. (The rest of the time, he's ex-CIA or DEA. The man's the king of acronyms, but when it comes to his background and mythology, he's mostly just full of BS.)

As we saw with enlisted men, cops are also frequently at odds with their superiors, who want them to "do it by the book," like a randy librarian. It's the tension between the savvy officer (who isn't savvy enough to know that shooting your mouth off won't get you promoted) and the chief that drives a lot of what happens in cop action movies.

Luckily, the officer usually wins out and is free to club whimpering criminals into submission, blow them off fire escapes, and roundhouse kick them into garbage bags piled up in an alley. (It's a mystery of mysteries how it is that heaps of garbage bags are always there to break someone's fall when they're beaten up.) These cops are usually judge, jury, and executioner all in one. Forget jurisprudence. Have you ever seen a super-cop in an action film single-mindedly pursue his perp for ninety minutes only to read him his Miranda rights? Pshaw! The only rights these cops give to crims is the right to bleed out all over the pavement. The average lawman will only fire his weapon once in the line of duty over an entire career. These cops fire their piece five times before breakfast.

Stay on the right side of the law, folks, and enjoy our badge-of-honor chapter.

HARD TO KILL (1990)

"Gonna take you to the bank . . . the BLOOD bank" sounds like it's straight from the marble mouth of *The Simpsons'* Rainier Wolfcastle, but it can only be one man—Steven Seagal. He's *Hard to Kill.* And hard to miss as well. He's the real "Il Divin Codino," or "divine ponytail," the nickname once bestowed upon Italian soccer hero of lore, Roberto Baggio. His magic mane contains all his sure-shot/martial arts/Lothario powers.

Here, everyone's favorite ethnically ambiguous aikido low-talker is kicking ass and taking names (and also fact-checking those names against a database, and kicking those people's asses again just to be certain).

And if you're gonna kick ass and take names, what better name to have than MASON STORM???

Hard to Kill is the apotheosis of moron '90s ass-kicking action films; here, the svelte and shockingly lithe Steven, who's since eaten his way up several weight classes, is a hard-bitten LAPD detective.

Much like Chuck Norris's *The Hitman*, Seagal's Mason Storm is attacked and left for dead. And he makes a near-miraculous recovery, but

not before morphing into Rasputin the Mad Monk while lying in a hospital bed. (What? They don't cut patients' hair who've been in a coma? What kind of long-term care facility is this?)

Luckily, nursing him back to health is none other than hot Kelly LeBrock, Seagal's then wife.

When he comes to, not realizing what presidential administration is in power, he does what many an action hero is compelled to do when recovering: go through an elaborate training montage set to piercing vibrato guitar.

Back in fighting form, he tracks down the mob bagmen and corrupt cops who tried to do him in (and there's a subplot with his son, but who gives a crap about that?) And naturally, he gets help from a partner cop everyone in the viewing audience knows is doomed to eat lead.

This is where we get Seagal in limb akimbo aikido mode. Every third-rate henchman better watch out for some leg sweeps as Storm is kicking up . . . a storm.

It's sad what Seagal's become these days: barrel-shaped and sounding like he's born in the Bayou instead of the south—of Michigan. We've subjected ourselves to *Submerged* and *Half-Past Dead*, two films that accurately describe his later career choices, and regretted both. Here though, it's full bore Seagal assault mode. And *Hard to Kill* has the greatest acupuncture scene in cinema history, not to mention that inimitable line from whence this book's very title came. Seagal, after beating up a bunch of generic stooges in a liquor store and taking one of their shotguns, is left with one holdup man still standing, full of piss and vinegar and brandishing a very silly little knife. Seagal gives him a withering stare and says, "Oh, I know what you're thinking. Mine's bigger than yours, right? It's not fair." Ever the sportsman, Seagal sets his gun on the floor, then snaps the guy's ankle bare-handed like it's a Christmas wishbone.

Since every bad action movie worth its salt mentions its own title in the dialogue, we thought we'd do the same for our book as a tribute.

BAM! Pictures of You

Action heroes usually have one facial expression per movie, so it's important to show dramatic range. What better way to do this then by opening a wallet with a picture of your wife (usually an ex, taken during better days) you can stare pensively at? Should a picture of a wife not be available, a photo of a now-estranged daughter makes for a fine substitution.

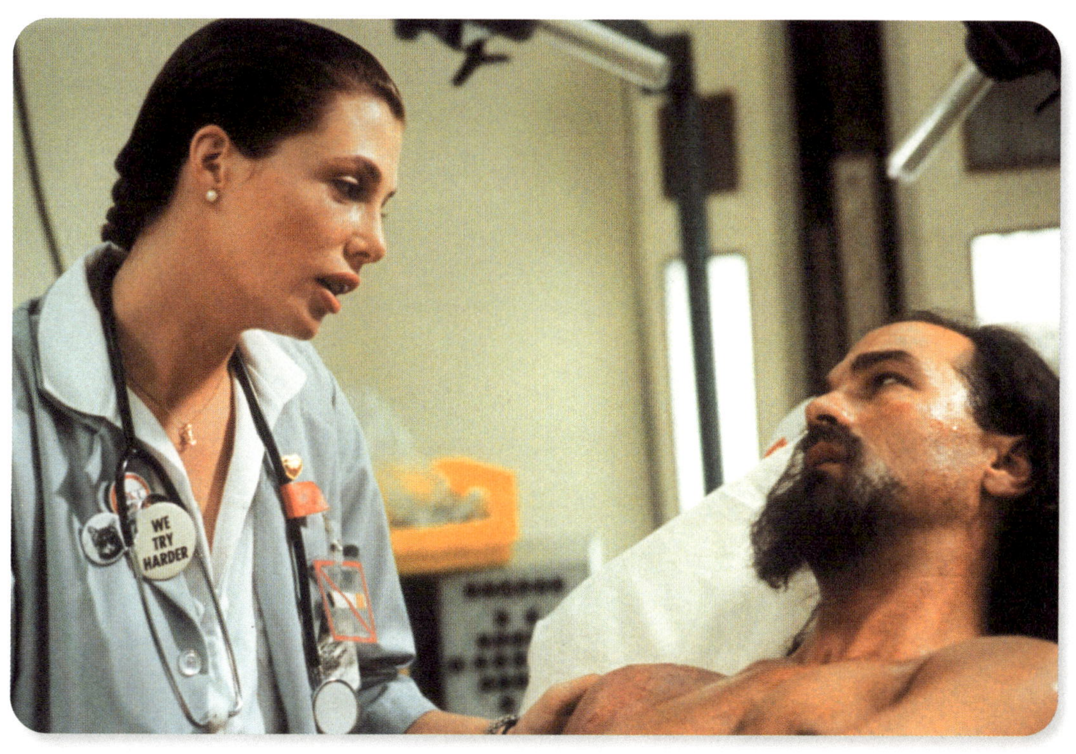

DANGEROUS MEN (2005)

If your movie makes less in its release than the cost of an average pair of shoes—seventy bucks to be exact—well, these things happen. Not every film can land with a cannonball splash.

However, if the project were two and a half decades in the making, time enough for wars to be fought, constitutions amended, and diseases to be cured, you'd at least expect a pristine finished product. *Boyhood* this ain't, and boy is this end result anything but a finished product. You can see why it caused merely a revenue ripple. The brainchild of John S. Rad, the auteur who did everything associated with this other than appear on screen—although we can't definitively rule this out without another viewing—*Dangerous Men* could've actually used *another* decade of tinkering, at least so the average viewer could understand what in God's name is going on. To the best of our abilities, here's our take.

We're introduced to two young lovebirds, Daniel and Mina, having a romantic rooftop green screen retreat with hissing ADR that's almost a character unto itself booing the proceedings. They're merely two of the film's nearly half-dozen protagonists. In an eighty-minute runtime, three separate story arcs are shoved into *Dangerous Men* like Tokyo subway commuters.

The male half of the amorous duo is then asking the father's permission for his daughter's hand in marriage, yet the patriarch looks like a near-contemporary of the suitor, which is to say about mid-thirties.

Mina and her fiancé then take to the ocean, strolling along the beach, their banter frequently drowned out by the surf. When they're attacked by two leather-clad bikers, Daniel gets the better of one, but is promptly gutted like a suckling pig by the other. Mina is carried off like in *The Creature from the Black Lagoon*.

Mina shockingly 1) thanks the surviving assailant for getting her out of her pending nuptials, 2) invites him down to a sleazy Sunset Strip hotel, 3) requests that he lick her knees as foreplay (!), then 4) shanks him with a steak knife she's smuggled from their romantic dinner and has hidden between her buttocks!

With a taste for vengeance, Mina then hires a prostitute to learn some of the finer points of navigating the world's oldest profession, then turns herself out to take revenge on johns, all set to lure them to their demise like sirens from *The Odyssey* except with fishnets.

Soon, the deceased Daniel's brother, a cop (let's call him Protagonist #2 and this, Story Arc #2), is seeking redress for his brother's murder.

This conventional narrative *seems* like a table setting for your straight-ahead revenge flick/police procedural, except that the reservations are cancelled and there's not even a restaurant to speak of.

Like a dine and dash, the "dangerous men and the woman doing away with them" premise is totally abandoned. It's as if director John S. Rad developed a post-production grudge against the Mina character.

Protagonist #3 (in Arc #3) is a police chief, heretofore unnamed and unmentioned, with no viewer investment whatsoever. He takes over from the avenging brother, who has now disappeared into the cinema ether. The chief immediately oversees the investigation, and the beach murder is pinned on an until-now-unmentioned biker gang leader "who's killed more men than 'Nam!" (We have to take this at face value as none of it is seen.)

The gangster turns out to be a belly-dance enthusiast, which is clearly a nod to director Rad's Persian heritage, as the director fled his home country during Iran's Islamic Revolution. And despite going by the moniker "Black Pepper," the Caucasian sensation kingpin is a few shades north of the banjo picker in *Deliverance*. He also happens to be the brother of the steak knife-murdered baldy, just so we're clear, even if his connection to the beach-massacre is tenuous if not wholly nonexistent. It's not like he ordered a hit or anything.

Temporal, ahem, "considerations" are frequently cast aside in *Dangerous Men*. Given that this film was almost thirty years in the making, it was difficult to cast the same people in all of the roles, making for a perplexing viewing experience to say the least. There are oil change windshield stickers from 1985 and police calendars from 1995 separating the viewer from recognizable reality like milk solids from butterfat.

Ages, styles of clothing, and automobiles morph over time, and in one meandering scene which occupies at least one eighth of this film's runtime, a hitchhiking Mina turns the tables on a lecherous *Monty Python*-esque Good Samaritan, marooning him nude in the foothills of Los Angeles. This extraneous throw-away character's journey back to town occupies at least a dozen minutes, ironic given he's the sole character in *Dangerous Men* who could've been done away with entirely.

TENEMENT, A.K.A. SLAUGHTER IN THE SOUTH BRONX (1985)

This is pretty low rent stuff. Or is that *Rent*? The gang here look like they could belt out a showstopper from the bohemian East Village AIDS musical. But we're going uptown for this one. WAY uptown. Up to the Bronx. And don't let their sexually ambiguous attire fool you, this junkie gang means business.

Residents of a standalone tenement in the New York borough are up to their eyeballs in gang activity. As if they didn't have enough to worry about, the place is beset by rodents, awash in graffiti, frequented by johns, is a flophouse for addicts, and the greasy, bigoted superintendent, Rojas, is perpetually drunk. Also, the view sucks.

In a futile attempt to set things straight, Rojas tips off the NYPD about the goings-on in his building. The cops sweep in and do a massive bust, but the dastardly crew isn't exactly sent down to Rikers.

Not familiar with 1980s jurisprudence, Rojas remarks "Now you're gone for good," and the residents gather in one unit to uncork the bubbly and breathe a collective sigh of relief. However, this is to be as short-lived as *Tenement's* grindhouse run. The gang, including its taciturn bulbous-headed leader Chaco, sporting a weightlifting belt girdle and a singlet underneath his leather vest, is released from the justice system before you can mutter "hug-a-thug." And he's hell-bent on taking over the building for himself and his gang. This is a group that doesn't have very high aspirations other than getting high. The building is so full of rats and roaches and almost certainly fast-tracked for demolition, so controlling it in full doesn't seem like a golden ticket up the crime ladder.

The gang returns, pummels gloating Rojas in the face with a piece of debris, and sets up shop again as squatters in the building's basement. The tenants again mobilize, this time for an emergency meeting, and one of them proposes witheringly, "The only way we're going to be safe over here is to move."

What we're left with is civilian ingenuity versus angry gangsters. The former holed up in the upper reaches of the complex, with the toughest among them, African American Washington, fending off the delinquents with a switchblade as if he's Duane Jones from *Night of the*

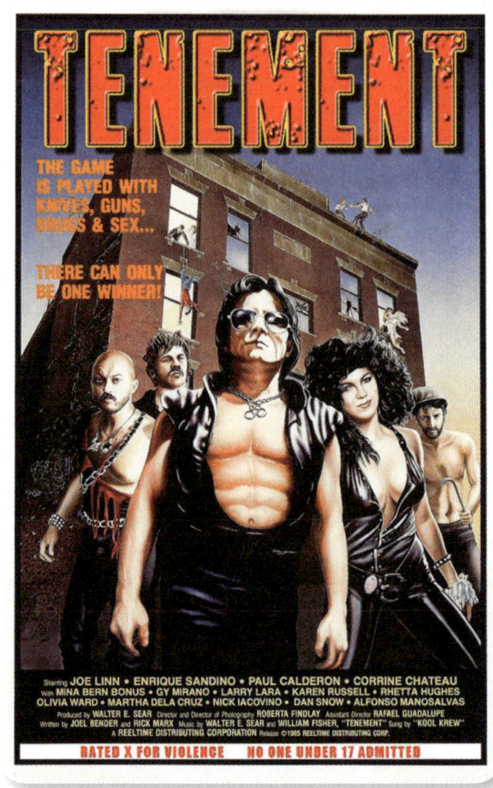

Living Dead. His compatriots eventually goad the goons up the stairwell. If gang leader Chaco were *Henry V*, he would've urged his henchmen on with "Once more unto the breach, dear friends, once more; or close the wall up with our Mexican-stereotype dead." Unfortunately for them, the residents have booby-trapped the stairwell. They've set up a refrigerator and a hutch to topple over and rigged a lamp and water as an electrical conductor to zap the baddies. The building's youngsters also get in on the action, using the element in its boiled form and pouring it over the siege men!

Tenement pulls no punches to say the least. There's an up-skirt shot of a pregnant lady. An old guy gets it. A turncoat gangster's balls get it. A blind guy's *dog* gets it. An old lady trying to rappel down to street level has her descent expedited by rope-cut.

Upon release, *Tenement* got an X-rating, not surprising as it was directed by the female half of the '70s husband-and-wife sexploitation duo, Michael and Roberta Findlay. They were known for adult fare like *The Clamdigger's Daughter* (Poster art: modify the Botticelli Venus and slap on a sexually suggestive tagline "All the fishermen want her") and *Mystique*, starring *Adult Video News* hall-of-famer Samantha Fox.

The softcore aesthetic of *Tenement* is visible here in all its skanky glory, with a building so squalid it makes Travis Bickle's flophouse accommodation in *Taxi Driver* look like casa Von Trapp.

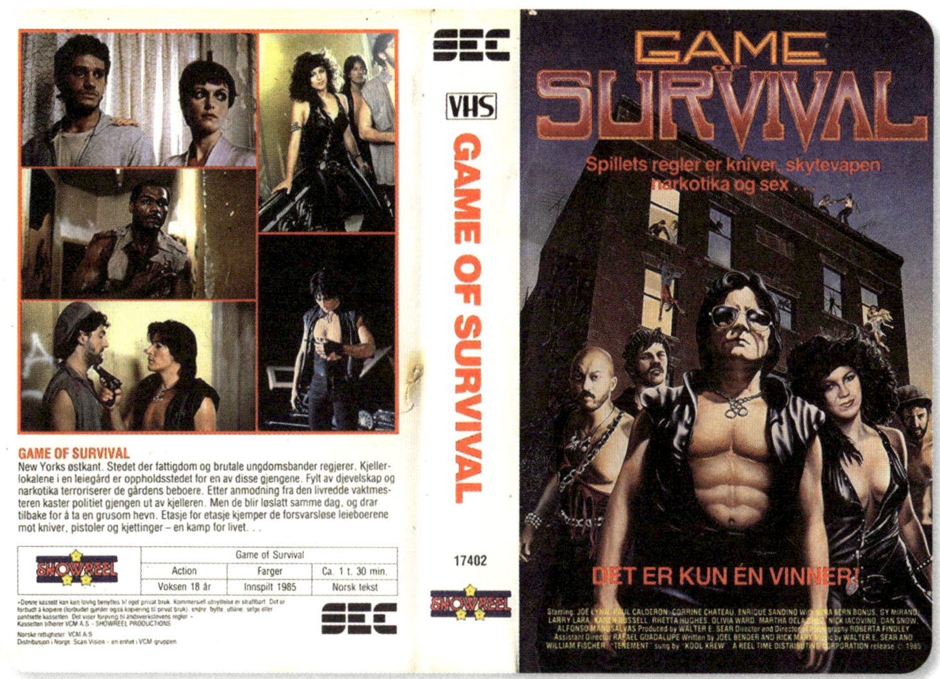

GETEVEN, A.K.A. ROAD TO REVENGE (1993)

The search engine confounding *GetEven* [*sic*] goes by "Get Even" if you sound it out and not "Good Evening" nor "Get Evan." Its tagline, "Will courage overcome corruption," could either be a question (but there's no question mark) or a statement if you put a comma after "will" and turned it into a possessive proper noun instead of a future tense. Will it make sense then? Will watching it twice help? Who knows? But where there's a will there's a way, especially if you want to make a full-length action feature but your day job is a California trial attorney and you have zero directorial or acting experience whatsoever.

Geteven is the brainchild of real-life barrister John De Hart, who looks like a grinder from the Broad Street Bullies goon era of the Philadelphia Flyers. He even sounds Canadian, mumbling in a humble hockey player bur when mouthing action hero shtick like "Here's a quarter, go buy yourself a personality."

And speaking of loose change, De Hart is responsible for producing this on the cheap, with day-for-night continuity errors and cameras woozily aimed out of moving vehicles doubling as dollies.

The film is such a vanity piece, its opening credits should pour out of a washbasin. De Hart also starred, co-directed, and because he had full creative control, inserted himself into love scenes he had no business being in. He even warbled the tunes in the hallucinatory anti-malarial drug nightmare that is *Geteven*.

He plays ex-LAPD SWAT team cop Rick Bode, and we're introduced to him after the movie's title appears on screen in quotation marks—certainly a cinema first—taking out a backwoods meth lab. He then appears at home, sizable gun protruding from his black *gi*, feeding a white poodle, which is spinning on its hind legs.

Bode, a self-styled martial artist given more workout montages than men half his age—that is, men who'd realistically hook up with the blonde costar Bode beds or be cast in this movie—becomes embroiled in a cult ring. And this ring is a sinister, Satan-worshipping, infant-murdering coven, the details of which are casually revealed to him by his girlfriend while lounging on a backyard swing:

"We sacrificed a human baby, so I had to leave LA."

So, tell me about your day?

This unexpectedly insane exposition makes *The Room's* breast cancer revelation seem matter-of-fact. And *GetEven* could even one-up the Wiseau masterpiece for hubristic silliness because Tommy had the good sense to delegate soundtrack responsibilities to someone else as opposed to Mr. De Hart, who has the temerity to warble over his own love scenes.

There's also a set-up job by the leader of the evil cult, a corrupt police officer ex-colleague of Bode's who instantly becomes a judge for some reason, bypassing years of experience as a trial lawyer, who's trying to take down Bode and his partner before they blow his cover.

Bode's sidekick is none other than the great Wings Hauser of *Deadly Force* and *Vice Squad* fame. He plays a wastrel ex-cop constantly at war with his ex-wife and his sanity. Appearing coked out of his gourd, he gives a monologue waist-deep, fully clothed, and in a backyard pool ("Huck's Haven.") It's one for the ages really, featuring stream-of-consciousness blather about "leading the Israeli-a-lites (*sic*) wherever they

came from, into the promised land. . ."

Huck Finney espouses "noble noises of Huckism," a personal philosophy based on, you guessed it, *The Adventures of Huckleberry Finn* by Mark Twain, one of two giants of the western canon of literature, along with Shakespeare, celebrated in this film with a syntax and grammar-defying title and tagline.

And speaking of The Bard . . . With Huck and Bode hanging out at a nearby saloon, which you'd be hard pressed to differentiate from the rec room basement of a youth drop-in center, Huck demands, yes, demands that Bode recite "that thing Hamlet wrote" to "class up" the joint. Bode corrects him, then graces the captive audience barflies with the famous soliloquy.

The honky-tonk, with dart holes in the wall where Huck missed the board, also doubles as a strip joint and has discerning female patrons who grumble "I did not come here to be grossed out."

The house band is fronted by none other than Bode, who's practically begged to get up on stage by a coterie of what look like porn star extras. The result: the glorious "Shimmy Slide," something Johnny Cash would have crooned after downing a bottle of Nyquil. (It has an accompanying line dance routine, both nude and otherwise, that mere words can't do justice. It *begs* to be seen.)

Suffice it to say, *Geteven* is a phantasmagoric experience. Wings Hauser is like a bad movie paratrooper dropped behind enemy lines, seemingly acting in another film altogether, louder and more vociferous than his costars, whom he occasionally acknowledges by looking them in the eyes. As a counter, John De Hart seems barely alert and risks even being woken up at any point.

With one surreal set piece after another, there are gems galore, such as a romantic Mexican restaurant scene nearly drowned out by a water fountain, taco mastication, and the plucking of a mariachi guitar. It's also where Bode regales the maître d' with two pointless, unfunny dirty jokes featuring a horny doctor and a duck.

Then there's the dialogue chopped off mid-sentence, and nuptials where Bode foregoes a tux in favor of white track pants and a rugby shirt. (He also visits the grave of a loved one in a stars and stripes denim shirt.) Huck also receives bedside counsel in hospital from a Mother Superior and says "You're very pretty for a nun."

The cult high priest hilariously goes by "Normad" and Bode's girlfriend says, "I thought that name sounded familiar!" Probably because it sounds like a typo, just like the film's title.

HUNTER (2015)

Good god, where to begin? Ron Becks is Hunter, serene Zen overseer of the LAPD's International Sex Crimes Unit. He wears a Gold's Gym weightlifting belt, yet judging by his physique, he's more likely to do curls with cheeseburgers.

He has a "sacred spot" in the foothills where he plays a trumpet, which upends viewer expectations by actually being an overdubbed saxophone. Hunter has a "front door" to his home that in fact opens into a hallway. How any of these blunders made it past the rough cut is a question best asked of the line producer. (Assuming there even *was* a line producer. In the infamous flop *The Room* costar Greg Sistero was tasked for the role, almost after the fact, and by then it was too late).

Hunter is one hilarious set piece after another that'll make you lose your equilibrium and maybe your lunch—a cheap stinker of galactic proportions.

We meet the title character, who looks like a Thin Blue Line fat Bo Diddley, at a crime scene that's ripped right from the headlines—a girl's body found in the water tank of the Cecil Hotel (based on the tragic real-life death of a University of British Columbia student there). We then meet his captain, Goodwill, who brings a bit of Martha Stewart's hair-helmet to her role as a do-gooder cop helping out runaways, with sagely advice like "If you are being attacked, you yell 'I have a disease!'"

We're not law enforcement officials, but we can presume this works in exactly zero percent of all dangerous situations.

Goodwill provides counsel to Kelly, a street kid who hails from the TENNESSEE BACKWOODS (that's the actual caption), and when the camera shows her homestead, it's basically somewhere in LA, pretty much around the corner from where they were shooting the rest of *Hunter*. The captain's lectures to Kelly also include this howler: "I wouldn't expect a high school hillbilly dropout with a crime record to understand matriarchal culture!"

Soon, the captain cajoles Hunter into looking after the young stray and taking her in for a few days, interrupting the lieutenant's drug dealer robbing, Makers Mark shot-gunning ways.

While this drama is playing out, cops con-

nected to Hunter are being found dead. Who is to blame?

And speaking of pointing fingers, who is responsible for this??? *Hunter* is absolutely mesmerizing, a few Sherpas short of scaling the summit of good-bad moviedom.

Hunter babbles self-help speak as a kind of Robin Hood who robs hoods and goads criminals with "How are you gonna make your point if you're dead?"

And then there's his sidekick, Sergeant Baran, shown chatting on his phone in what might be Farsi or Pashto, for an extended discussion sans subtitles, which is frustrating for anyone who doesn't speak those, not to mention the Persian music soundtrack frequently drowning out the dialogue (in and of itself, not necessarily a bad thing, all things considered, especially when saxes sub for trumpets). For good measure, there's also a fraternal duo of nunchuck-wielding meth-heads.

The cop killer's MO is to shave down lollipop sticks and jab them into victims' jugulars, and there are green screens aplenty, used to represent both the beach (weird, as this was filmed in Los Angeles), Tennessee, and many other scenes. The CG blood is among the worst you'll ever see.

Oh, and George Lazenby is in this! He, of course, was James Bond in 1969's *On Her Majesty's Secret Service*, and he'd probably want to keep his work here on the down low.

None of the promotional materials indicate whether this film about a "mystical cop, deadly force, and champion of people" is intended as a comedy. We can't really tell.

HARD TICKET TO HAWAII (1987)

How is "A bird in the hand is worth two in the bush" part of the popular lexicon and not "If brains were bird shit, you'd have a clean cage?" That's just some of the excellent patter in Andy Sidaris's *Hard Ticket to Hawaii*, a study in big boobs, big guns, even bigger plot holes, and yes, inane dialogue like that.

Hard Ticket to Hawaii wastes no time in establishing that we're in . . . well, Hawaii. But instead of leis and luaus, you get DEA agents cavorting with D-cups in a hot tub.

The film begins with two beat cops, a veteran and a rookie, taking a leisurely stroll through a Hawaiian jungle towards a local marijuana grow-up. The elderly cop is explaining the particulars of the weed trade to his young successor, when it probably should be the other way around. With only a month to go before retirement, we, as viewers well-versed in police procedural banalities, know that the elder cop will soon be shot to shit and indeed, he and his young charge do not make it off the island fully intact. Expecting to find a small, family run operation, they instead stumble across a huge drug cartel with underpaid brutes brandishing machine guns. The two get caught in a booby trap and are blown to bits.

Over in Molokai, two buxom bottle blondes, Donna and Taryn, are posing as cargo pilots but are actually undercover agents for the DEA. Their sassy shorts and teased hair make them look like they just stepped off the Sunset Strip. And why do cargo pilots need to carry nunchucks? Never mind. They're conscripted to fly two honeymooners for a private excursion to an island before delivering some crates, one of which contains an enormous, virally contaminated snake! And

why shouldn't the island be the very same one where the cartel holds its operations?

After dropping off the lovebirds, the girls discover a remote-controlled helicopter housing two boxes. They grab one box, but the other gets lost in a melee when two overweight henchmen attack them. The girls mange to flee, then convene at their apartment to assess the events. Naturally, their post-mortem is conducted in a Jacuzzi because, as Donna says, she does her best thinking there. Makes sense; we all know nothing facilitates restful contemplation like soaking topless in a hot tub. They open the box and discover several diamonds.

Crime kingpin Seth Romero is the man to whom the diamonds belong to—a man whose French accent is so thick, he'd lose a rap freestyle to JCVD. Naturally, he wants his diamonds back, so he sends a henchman and a henchwoman (or is it henchperson now?) to attack the two in their home. The blondes turn the tables, and Donna gets off a shot which grazes Romero in the face. The girls need backup STAT, so they enlist the help of himbo pal Rowdy and his ponytailed partner Jade to take down the evil drug lord.

Hard Ticket to Hawaii is the very definition of the word gratuitous. Besides the copious boobs, butts, and sex, the film also features:

- Gratuitous bazooka blasting when simple machine gun fire would do.
- Gratuitous sumo wrestling. [Editors' note: you can NEVER have enough sumo wrestling.]
- Gratuitous unbuttoned pastel dress shirts for men.
- Gratuitous oiled-up bodybuilder henchwoman dancing and flexing with nunchucks. (Again with the nunchucks. Was there a half-off sale at the army surplus?)
- Gratuitous leisure: A guard who takes time out to play Frisbee.
- Gratuitous razor-bladed Frisbee which kills aforementioned guard by throat incision. (Talk about your truly Ultimate Frisbee.)
- Gratuitous exploding toilet with contaminated cobra emerging.
- Gratuitously large explosions, so immense they'd likely level a medium sized suburb.

But it's precisely all that gratuitousness which makes *Hard Ticket to Hawaii* so endearing. (And really, when it comes to action films, there's no such maxim as "too gratuitous." This is action cinema, folks, not the Vienna Boys Choir.) And how can you not love a flick which contains chatter like "She's so dumb, she went home early to study for her pap test"? Simply put, *Hard Ticket to Hawaii* doesn't take itself seriously for a second. It's loud, dumb, ridiculous, and full of fun.

72

ACTION USA
(1989)

If heat were crap, *Action USA* would be a kiln. But still, you can't fault this *Lethal Weapon* cousin (complete with world-weary black guy and hot-headed ladies' man cops) for trying. It's rip-roaring fun even if its gene pool has been drained.

What's so great about the action genre is that even in a movie with a list of clichés so numerous an office temp could be hired to document them, *Action USA* provides the hilarity, the energy, and the chutzpah of a movie ten times its budget (although when you do the math, ten times nothing is still nothing).

The proof? You mean apart from a movie that has the gall to call itself *Action USA* despite having nothing whatsoever to do with Chuck Norris? In minute two, a shady diamond thief who's two-timed some baddies yells to his unwitting accomplice girlfriend, "Hang on baby, we're going airborne!" sending his roadster heavenward with impossibly great hang time. It's one of several gap-jumping heroics that would make the General Lee look stuck in the muck.

Then, with goons still in hot pursuit, the girlfriend leans her torso sideways out the car door like she's catching a wind gust in a sailboat race. The thief is subsequently captured, dangled, then dropped very convincingly from a helicopter before being filled full of lead. There's a lot of G-forces at work in the stunning opener.

The diamond thief's demise sets in motion the *Lethal Weapon* duo's participation. The deceased's hot "I can take care of myself!" girlfriend joins them, forming an unlikely triumvirate, and they're left trying to find out both what's up with the diamonds and which "ten-cent hoods" want them back. Seriously, this is the '80s and that kind of tough talk would've been edited out of an Elmore Leonard book.

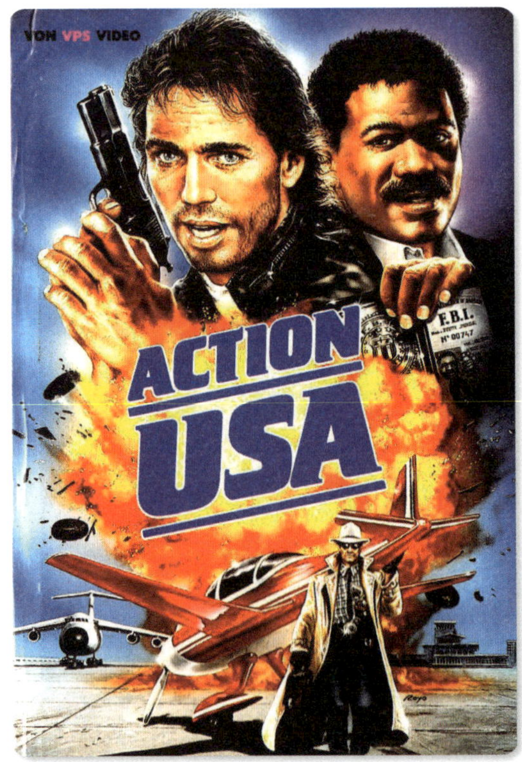

While the plot may be *nori*-thin, there's still much in the way of nutritional sustenance for action hounds.

Action USA's chase effects are dynamite and look suspiciously unsafe. But it was all overseen by director John Stewart, a long-time stuntman who credits a background in basic math(!) and gymnastics for his lengthy career in the stunting arts.

But the film's more than double-crossing and death-defying pursuits in and above Waco, Texas. There are exactly four scenes which vault this unconventional buddy pic into B-movie nirvana: 1) a honky-tonk band breezing through their chorus, *"Love is like a cruise missile headin' straight to my heart*; 2) a bar fight where an unlucky victim is body slammed onto a pinball machine; 3) the Danny Glover-type cop is thrown through a restaurant's decorative lattice work twice in quick succession, with just enough time to brush himself off and make an unfunny quip; and the coup de grace, 4) a john plowing a prostitute in the bathroom stall and warning another bar patron to "Wait your turn, asshole!"

Curiously, *Action USA* also features a car crash immolation where one of the perps stumbles out of the burning vehicle, pulls out his pistol, and starts blasting random rounds while he's charring to a Cajun crisp. It's idle speculation when it comes to how we'd act if we were barbecued alive, but we'd like to think we'd have the wherewithal to turn the gun on ourselves. It's ironic, given the pin-point accuracy that's always a mainstay of action shoot 'em ups, that this guy wouldn't even be able to shoot himself when it mattered most.

OF NOTE:

Of interest to genre fans is that everyone's favorite drunken uncle wanders his way into this one, the indefatigable kingpin of bad moviedom, Cameron Mitchell (*Night Train to Terror*, *Terror in Beverly* Hills, *Rage to Kill,* and at least a half-dozen films that appear in this book.).

OF SPECIAL NOTE:

The black cop is named "Panama" and there's absolutely no explanation as to why this is so. A fondness for canals, perhaps? Or maybe the hats of the same name?

OF EXTRA SPECIAL NOTE:

One member of the evil criminal syndicate is the towering goon Drago, who wears a ten-gallon hat and a full-length duster coat straight out of the Old West. And this is his getup of choice for piloting an incredibly effete little glider plane.

SAMURAI COP (1991)

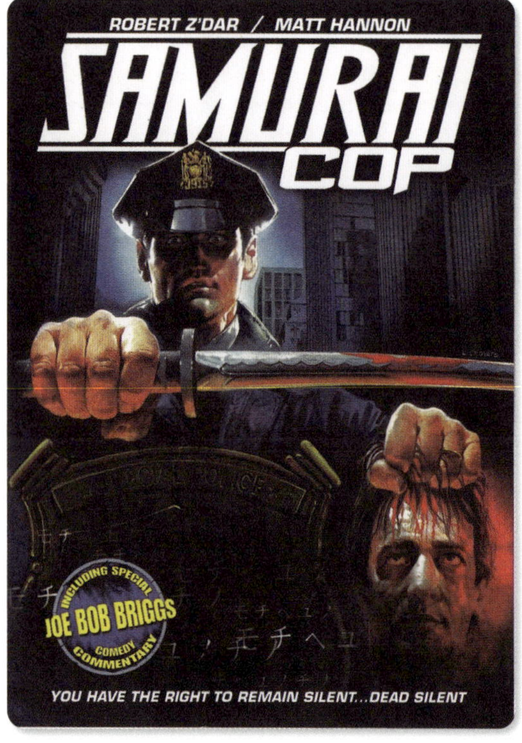

Watching *Samurai Cop* is a fundamentally disorienting experience, not unlike being severely jetlagged. With more pickup shots and reshoots than a basketball game at the Y, it's a perplexing experience to say the least. An almost hallucinatory smorgasbord of chopping board editing, jaundiced film overexposure, curious sexual innuendos, and every conceptual misfire imaginable. There's also way too judicious use of the "noddy," that lazy cutaway shot favored by cheesy journalists who want to seem deeply interested in their interviewee by, well, nodding.

Cop buddies Joe and Frank (Matt Hannon and Mark Frazer respectively) are hot on the tail of Japanese coke dealers in LA, one of whom, their leader and corrupt lawyer Fujiyama, has a mullet that's the map of Florida in profile.

And an interior vehicle shot of shaggy Joe behind the wheel is used five times over the course of the first fifteen minutes. Whether he's en route to the wharf, on the freeway, by the marina, or bearing down on a suspicious van in the mountains, the background never ever changes. Makes location scouting easier.

And the van might as well have been (and very probably was) in a different season. Maybe even a different time zone.

And it's not even clear Joe's cop buddy Frank is even in the same car with him as he's exhorting Joe to shoot the bad guys. Then there's the baddies opening the van's rear door to attempt to machine blast the two cops. It's the same exact shot duplicated twice within minutes, but all things considered, a pretty minor oversight given the cascade of continuity errors to come.

These gangsters mean business, and the LAPD needs help. That's where Joe comes in. Brought in from the Ancient Walled City of San Diego, California, Joe is a meathead cop who, according to the chief, is supposedly fluent in the culture, customs, and language of the Japanese. A suspect claim at best since he never utters a solitary word of the language save for pointing out that "katana" means "Japanese sword." He also stumbles over the tongue twister "Fujiyama" and utters the vaguely ethnic slur "Omaha, Yamaha." (Also suspect is why the LAPD would need to bring in an outside Japanese-expert cop for assistance. There are more than 35,000

Japanese-Americans living in the City of Angels, and not one is on the local police force? And is the Japanese culture really that obscure and exotic that they had to outsource? And this is the best they could get? As the film grinds on, it becomes tragically apparent that the sum total of Joe's Japanese experience is maybe tasting a California Roll once.)

Joe's elegant mane is a combination of actor Matt Hannon's lovely locks and a less elegant impromptu and very obvious wig fashioned for reshoots when the actor had already cut it. Frank is the black cop partner with whom it must have been hard to establish a buddy cop rapport when they were seldom in the same room together. He is resigned to inhaled pickup cutaway "oohs" and shameless mugging when Joe blathers on about his sexual conquests. This includes whether Joe's manhood is the "size of a jumbo jet," whether it's circumcised, and other bits of ostensible jocularity that should've been cut short as well.

Samurai Cop is a mess, a miasma of ineptitude on the grandest scale. Indie guerrilla filmmaking at its finest with cameras shakenly pointed out of moving vehicles and voiceovers duct taping it all together to make it a (barely) cohesive whole. And we're all the better for Iranian expat writer/director/producer Amir Shervan's creation.

Now a common trope of cop buddy films is the key witness or perp who's in grave condition and may not pull through. In this case, it's a henchman badly burned after an altercation with the two lawmen. He is recuperating in what is clearly a dentist's office. That's some medical malpractice continuity right there. And the poor guy is lying there in this makeshift hospital room wrapped up like *The Invisible Man* and bleeding profusely through facial bandages, even as minutes earlier, you can clearly see Joe and Frank stamping out the fire and covering him with a blanket, his face free of blemishes.

Regardless of the state of his injuries, it's still possible he may squeal. Ergo, Fujiyama figures he'll take him out and "put his head on this piano" in one of the film's many celebrated lines. Tasked to finish the job is Fujiyama's second-in-command, Yamashita, the very un-Japanese Robert Z'Dar, the hulking genre legend who's built to dance the Beer Barrel Polka and whose head looks like an Inuit sculpture.

Yamashita adopts one of the more interesting gambits we've ever seen: hiding his massive frame in a wheeled garbage container while undercover as a doctor. Wouldn't it be easier to just walk into the intensive care unit *dressed* as a doctor? But then again, something clever had to be done to conceal the samurai sword murder weapon he's carrying to lop off the poor chap's head and stuff it in a bag. Who are we to quibble with the methods of a guy that imposingly large? Plus, the sight of Yamashita emerging from the container in a lab coat brandishing his katana is worth the price of admission in itself.

But the centerpiece of *Samurai Cop* is a ridiculous encounter between our police heroes/zeros and the Kitana bigwigs, their girlfriends, and their lawyer in a Japanese restaurant. Joe, in a speech where he looks like he's ready to undergo concussion protocol, blankly stares at nobody in particular (this was done in post) and utters these immortal lines: "I'm telling these son-of-a-bitches that we respect the Japanese in this country who are honest businessmen. And yeah, this is the land of opportunity for legitimate business, not for death merchants who distribute drugs to our children in the schools and on the streets." Pausing midstream for a line-reading check, he then continues with a bunch of jibber-jabber about Swiss bank accounts and body bags and is obviously differently lit and made-up during the same monologue.

Samurai Cop has too many *mise en scène* miscarriages to count: a shot zooming up through a glass coffee table at Robert Z'Dar's formidable chin, a martial arts showdown on a California hillside clearly occurring at various points in the afternoon (according to changing daylight), and squibs that could pass for heirloom tomatoes (if they are even squibs at all as some bullet wounds are clearly the actor being shot at with a red paintball gun).

OF NOTE:

"Gaffers" are electricians whose job it is to light sets. This could not have been a complicated job on *Samurai Cop*, which was shot entirely during daylight hours to save costs. Still, there are gaffer gaffes. During a love scene between Joe and LAPD chopper pilot Peggy, grey gaffer tape is clearly visible blocking the blinds and it's also visible inside Joe's car, holding the interior above the passenger seat together.

HOLLYWOOD COP (1987)

Four years before Iranian director Amir Shervan pinched out the delightful turd *Samurai Cop*, he was already beginning to circle the drain with *Hollywood Cop*.

It begins at the home of crime boss Feliciano, who unfortunately never once breaks into a rendition of "Feliz Navidad." Feliciano is played by James Mitchum, son of Hollywood legend Robert, and it's immediately apparent that the apple fell as far away from the tree as Pluto is to the Sun. Whereas Mitchum *pater* appeared in dozens of great films, including stone-cold classics *Cape Fear* and *Night of the Hunter*, Mitchum *filius* shows acting ability only a fraction above a fast-food restaurant in-house training video.

A cluster of goons, with names such as Russian, Animal, and Spaghetti (and no definite articles either), are partying with some bikini-clad babes around Feliciano's pool before the boss swoops in and orders everyone to get serious. Someone in the organization has stolen $6 million and gone AWOL. He orders his underlings to descend upon the scofflaw's ex-wife Rebecca's home and kidnap their son for ransom in order to get the money back. (Seems kind of convoluted: Couldn't they just go straight to the source and find the thief, thus cutting out a number of needless steps?) Cut to a farm just outside of Hollywood (!) where a kid dressed as a live-action version of *Dennis the Menace* is playing with a goat. The thugs descend on the farm, sock the mother in the jaw, take the kid, and leave the goat.

Mom is understandably distraught and heads to Hollywood looking for help getting her kid back. She's sobbing at a hot dog stand when a strapping drink of water sporting an awe-inspiring, permed-blonde mullet (and poured into a pair of Levi's wrapped tighter than plastic cling) comes sauntering by to get his daily sustenance. Unfortunately, before he can enjoy his repast, he's alerted to a kidnapping in progress at a hotel directly across the street. This leads to this inspired exchange between Mom and Hot Dog Lady:

Mom: Who's that?
Hot Dog Lady: Turk? He's a cop!
Rebecca: He is?
Hot Dog Lady: He is! A good cop, really!
Rebecca: I wonder if he'll be able to help me.
Hot Dog Lady: I'm sure he can!

And that's when we checked *IMDb* to see if Robert Towne ghostwrote this sucker.

The rescue turns ugly, and the next scene is the requisite Turk and his partner getting read the riot act by their cantankerous chief on the verge of a coronary. Chief is played by Cameron Mitchell (again!) who bellows "You're a fucking maniac, Turkey!" After the umpteenth admonition of "Turkey," it becomes evident that our hero's actual name is Turkey. And his black partner's name is Jaguar. (Obviously named for his speed in solving cases and nothing else.)

And parked outside the station is the very same hot dog stand from earlier. Either Hot Dog Lady is stalking Turkey throughout Hollywood or he likes her wares so much he pays her to follow him around. Whichever it is, it's still rather discomfiting. They find Rebecca sobbing by the cart (evidently she really enjoys this lady's wares too) and ask her what's wrong. Rebecca recounts the kidnapping, and Turkey and Jaguar agree to help her out. Turkey even offers to let her crash at his place. (And we all know how that will end. Turkey, you dog!)

The rest of the film deals with the trio trying to track Rebecca's ex to get the money to pay off Feliciano and rescue the kid. Things naturally don't go quite so linearly, and we're treated to a riotous scene of the kid channelling the spirit of Dr. Doolittle and convincing a rabid Doberman to help him unlock a latch so he could escape. We also learn that the ex stole the money and ran off because he's dying from "blood cancer." Then there's Turkey losing his badge, being called no "Clint Westwood" by the chief, Jaguar mud-wrestling two babes in a night club and tearing off their tops, and more insanity than you'd find at your average Wal-Mart on Black Friday.

Hollywood Cop is the kind of low-budget lunacy we love. In many ways, it feels like a warm-up for Shervan's still-too-come magnum opus, but Shervan is not the first filmmaker to start with a test run. After all, before there was *Goodfellas* there was *Mean Streets*. Likewise, before Joe and Frank, there was Turkey and Jaguar (not suggesting that Amir Shervan is anywhere in the same universe as Marty Scorsese, but Hollywood Cop *is* leagues more entertaining than the stillborn *The Aviator*).

MR. NO LEGS (1979)

The dictionary definition of the word "exploit" is "[to] make full use of and derive benefit from. . ." While the connotation of the word may be positive, the denotation is inarguably negative. No one who feels exploited by their employee thinks "I'm so glad I'm being made full use of." In cinema, "exploitation" films have come to define a certain subset of movies that "often cheaply produced, are designed to create a fast profit by referring to, or exploiting, contemporary cultural anxieties . . . Ostensibly, exploitation films claim to warn viewers about the consequences of these problems, but in most cases their style, narrative, and inferences celebrate (or 'exploit') the problem as much as critiquing it."

In the broadest sense of the term, all action films can be read as exploitation, but for a brief time in the '70s, a very unique subset of films found some popularity/notoriety: Freaksploitation. These films highlighted the non-normative physiology of one of the protagonists to both market the film and arouse the viewer. The films of Weng Weng definitely fall into this category, as does 1979's astonishing *Mr. No Legs*, a film whose title refers to a character played by Karate Grand Master and double amputee Ted Vollrath.

Also known by the more hyperbolic *The Amazing Mr. No Legs*, the film isn't really about Vollrath's character, mob enforcer Lou, much at all. It's probable that first-time-last-time feature director Ricou Browning (the man in the rubber suit for the swimming sequences in *The Creature from the Black Lagoon* films) intended to call his film something else entirely, but producers, upon seeing the amazing henchman character contained therein and with dreams of lucre in their eyes, decided to exploit the incredible Mr. Vollrath to the hilt.

The uber-cheapie begins with a character played by Rance Howard (Ron and Clint's father) entering a private area demarcated by those flimsy orange-font-on-black "private" and "keep out" signs you can grab at any dollar store. There, a Geppetto-looking guy and a couple others are rolling drugs into cigars. The phone rings and a trade is arranged. However, once the transaction is complete, Mr. No Legs rolls out in his wheelchair, and using the two double-barrel shotguns hidden in the arms of his chair, blows the contraband buyers to kingdom come.

This is all on behalf of drug kingpin Mr. D'Angelo, who employs, among others, Lou and a college student named Ken. Ken returns home to find his girlfriend in the process of leaving him after discovering how her boyfriend pays for his tuition. The two tussle and she falls backwards, fatally hitting her head on a TV set. Lou and some other cronies are called for cleanup, and they figure it's best to shoot her up with enough heroin to make it look like an overdose. Lou also puts a bullet in Ken's chest.

Trouble is, Ken's now-deceased girlfriend's brother is a doughy undercover cop named Andy. Where supposed tough guys in action films often resemble WWF jobbers, in Andy's case it's actually true as he's played by Ron Slinker, a journeyman wrestler who competed for the National Wrestling Alliance throughout the '70s and whose biggest claim to fame is telling a young Rob Szatkowski to change his name to Rob Van Dam.

After tearfully identifying his sister's body, Andy heads to grieve at a garish watering hole

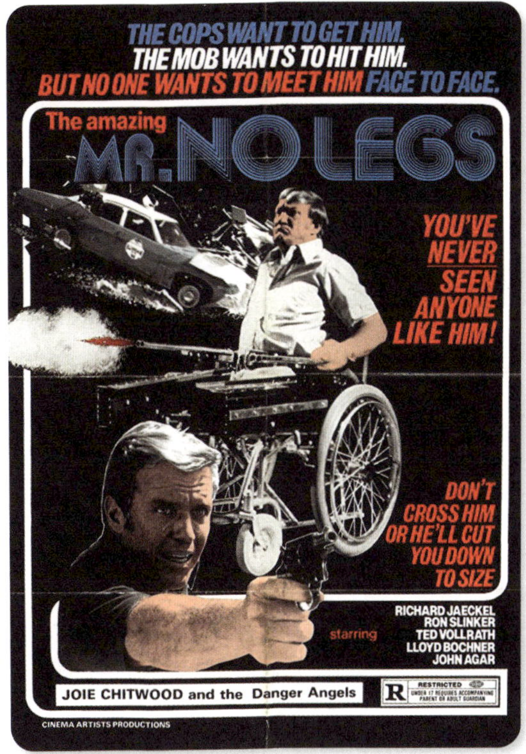

that wouldn't look out of place in *A Clockwork Orange*. He's there both to get right shit-faced and to watch "that million selling record group, Mercy" (consisting of a chubby guy dressed in a tux singing really poorly alongside a female duet partner) sing their "hit," a saccharine ballad entitled "I Still Remember Love." He then goes home with the bar hostess—a woman with an accent of indeterminate origin that turns phrases such as "cloak and dagger" into "clock and dagger"—and they make love on her wall-to-wall shag carpeting.

To find Andy's sister's killers, police captain Hathaway partners him with Chuck (Richard Jaeckel, *The Dirty Dozen*). Meanwhile, D'Angelo is getting tired of Lou's hotheadedness and orders him to fix things up. He tells Lou to meet with a woman named Bessie at a bar and admonishes his enforcer to "get this right this time or you're gonna find yourself on a street corner with a tin cup and a handful of lead pencils." Mr. No Legs, pissed, wheels off in a huff. Not the smartest move on D'Angelo's part; the man may have no legs, but he's built like a brick shithouse and keeps himself in tip-top shape by doing push-ups off his wheelchair!

Lou tells Bessie to get herself a drink. Unfortunately, she instigates a racially tinged catfight with "white-ass stoolie" Sereta, a woman missing one of her bottom teeth who's also an informant for Andy. Lou's midget companion hops on the bar for a better view of the melee as Lou sits silently and observes. The fight escalates, and Sereta sticks Bessie in the abdomen with a broken beer bottle. Lou pulls out a knife, stabs Sereta, then rolls away just as Andy enters the bar. This leaves poor Andy to use his dork-fu to take on the unruly patrons in a bench-clearing bar brawl which features chairs cracked against backs, beer bottles broken against skulls, and cardboard walls coming down like London Bridge. (One combatant who's thrown into a door by Andy creates a perfectly shaped square hole which was obviously pre-cut for him to go through.)

By this point, D'Angelo has had it with Lou and orders his no-legged enforcer to be taken out. As D'Angelo's thugs descend, Mr. No Legs springs into action. He removes the *shurikens* attached to his wheels and hurls them into an assailant, then hops off his chair, and with a mighty "hiyah," delivers a judo chop into the gut of another. He then hops back on, and using the chair arms for leverage, "kicks" the aggressor both forward and backward! Finally, he hops off again and chops the guy down like a tree before giving him a right pummeling in a must-see scene of slo-mo spectacularity.

Unfortunately, the law takes out Lou before the final act. A pretty spectacular car chase concludes the film, but it just isn't the same without our gruff, tenacious, bipedally challenged antagonist and his fabulous tricked-out wheelchair.

Mr. No Legs is an exploitation film, of that there is no doubt. But the question still remains: Does *Mr. No Legs* exploit Ted Vollrath's handicap? The answer is yes and no. Taking a side character that is non-normative and marketing an entire film around him when he registers, at the utmost, fifteen minutes of screen time is certainly exploitative. On the other hand, Lou is a compelling character and Vollrath is never presented as anything less than a complete badass. He's rough, tough, capable of kicking ass with the best of them, and is depicted doing things that we normally don't see the handicapped do. And in its own wacky way, that's something pretty special.

SHOTGUN (1989)

"She was just another hooker."
"She was your sister!"
"OK, she was a hooker. But she was once also a human being! You should know that better than anyone."

Once a human being?

Step aside, Aaron Sorkin. Put away that laptop, David Mamet. Here comes *Shotgun*, a genre-bending blast set on the mean streets of LA about a "basher," a guy who treats hookers rough. And he's mean to the eardrums too. His arrival in leather chaps and gimp mask is always marked by cochlea-piercing electric guitar that'll have viewers scrambling for the remote.

Luckily, two of LA's finest are on the case: Jones, a towering chisel-face whose hair is styled by the Geico caveman and whose sister is the working girl mentioned in the crackling dialogue above, and the other, milquetoast Max (or, er, chocolate milquetoast), a brother who openly admits his wife fantasizes about his partner to keep their marriage "fresh." *Lethal Weapon*-style, it's the white hot-head partnered with the black family man. With this buddy team on the case, the people of Los Angeles are in good hands.

But the movie isn't just about healing racial divides, casual wife-swapping, or the leather fetish scene. The Basher, it turns out, is an evil lawyer named Rivington. He, along with evil henchman Rocker (the names are to die for), are tied up with a Mexican drug cartel. But that's just a tacked-on subplot, included as an excuse to blow away a bunch of goons in a cantina and a gratuitous chopper chase.

To get to the bottom of the missing and/or whip-lacerated hooker case, our two cops, Jones and Max, strongarm the owner of a no-tell motel as well as a video store owner who sells kiddie porn on the side.

Eventually ladies of the evening start filing in to the station to report the incidents. In one particularly inspired bit of hilarity, three witnesses are allowed to look at a police lineup together and compare notes! With such a cavalier approach to evidence gathering and jurisprudence, it's clear these *Shotgun* cops are better suited to wasting bad guys without getting the pesky courts involved.

The investigation, however, is proving to be a bit of a challenge.

The Basher has been thwarting police by hiring a john to lure hookers to his room. And we're uncertain as to whether this is genius or stupidity, but the john bears a strong resemblance to the perp. If you were leading cops astray, wouldn't it be better to have someone visibly dissimilar to you? And that seems like a crappy gig anyway. Hopefully the guy was well-paid for being a potential murder suspect patsy.

Another challenge: Jones is kicked off the LAPD. The *Serpico*-style rogue cop who plays by his own rules is one thing, but to get an idea of just how lax standards are for frontline officers at the LAPD, Jones is only *suspended* for viciously beating an Internal Affairs colleague with a nightstick and putting him in hospital for a week.

Luckily, there's an avenue for psychotic officers in the US to make a bit of money when they're suspended without pay: bounty hunting. It's here Jones can operate outside the bounds of proprietary, if there even is such a thing for the LAPD, and to dispatch as many baddies as he'd like with a shotgun (he's called "Shotgun

Jones" on the street). It's also a milieu where he can call in favors and get access to an empty garage for a time-honored welding montage, that essential bit of action cinema where a hero jerry-rigs simple weaponry on a vehicle, transforming them into mass killing apparatuses.

In *Shotgun* we learn that Jones isn't the sharpest scalpel in the ER. He's informed of his sister's demise like so: "They did everything they could, buddy. But between the drugs and the beating, there was just too much internal damage. I'm sorry."

"WHAT DOES THAT MEAN?"

For a guy whose job it is to tell family members about a loved one's demise, Jones is pretty obtuse when it comes to English idioms.

But it's hard to fault him. With his Icelandic sweaters, propensity to shoot perps in the ass, and his hair-trigger temper, he cuts a memorable (and very quotable) figure: "We were in a situation that would've given you the Hershey squirts!"; "Open your mouth. Let me shut it for good and save the taxpayers some money!"; and "Anybody ever tell you you make too much noise? Only faggots, pimps, and bad-tempered desert hermits!"

On *The 80's Picture House Podcast*, Stuart Chapin, the actor who played Jones, reported that as the lead, he made $100 a day on this $100,000 budget, ten-day PM Entertainment production. Chapin acknowledged that *Shotgun* was "The nadir of '80s entertainment" and that "there were no second takes . . . except on special occasions." The ethos on set was "good for picture, good for sound, moving on." Suck it, Stanley Kubrick. Also, in what too was par for the course for this type of film, the poster art featured a woman who walked in and wanted to be in the movie but wasn't.

BAM! Workin' Hard

Never underestimate the power of a welding montage! As we know, action heroes get little in the way of perks. Besides the notoriously unsteady labor market for a guy or gal who can suture their own wounds and mow down entire advancing armies with one round of ammunition, they unfortunately have to cope with hazardous working conditions, lack of health insurance, and no pension plan to speak of. At least they have the construction trades to fall back on. At least 98.3% of action heroes are experienced welders, capable of jerry-rigging and mounting M60s on tanks, mountain bikes, helicopters, city buses, and all sorts of other conveyances. All it takes is a mask, a torch, an empty garage, and a sleeveless getup to show off their sinewy, sweaty muscles.

DEATH WARRIOR (1984)

Wordsworth said in the preface to his *Lyrical Ballads*, "the human mind is capable of being excited without the application of gross and violent stimulants." Good thing we're not him, and not just 'cause he's long dead. But we're gonna wax poetic about *Death Warrior* in his honor. The thing is, with such a non-stop, nonsensical exercise in mayhem, you gotta stretch first or you might pull a muscle.

Europe is under assault. But unlike the Siege of Vienna, it's the Ottomans as the saviors rather than the invaders. And their present-day rank is represented in the form of a midlife-crisis Turkish guy in a black leather jacket. That's Murat, played by the very greying Cüneyt Arkın (hair and wardrobe by Johnny Cash), star of *Turkish Star Wars*, a movie that's a galaxy far, far away from anything resembling that classic franchise. And equally as crazy and immune to the laws of physics is *Death Warrior,* where Europe is being invaded by ninjas.

To answer the battle cry, Murat says, "I'm a Turkish policeman. I want to mission!" (The hilarious subtitles are reason alone to check out this Turkish delight.) Off he goes "to mission," inventing a new verb along the way . . . and all the way to Italy. Why Italy? Hmm. The simple answer would be because that's where the ninjas are attacking. A more interesting question is why. Why is it that if ninjas were to attack Italy, would one lone policeman from some random country in any way suffice? And the country's slightly outside his jurisdiction, to say the least.

Luckily, there's a razor-thin coating of some sort of backstory, and that comes courtesy of Murat's mentor, Master Foo. He's some kind of Sho Kosugi kung fu stereotype who appears in flashback, the second-best way for a sensei to appear in a film—the first is getting killed off by goons in the opening frame to kickstart some hackneyed revenge plot. He blathers on about the warrior prowess of Turks and puts forward this rather unorthodox and very testable hypothesis: "Turks can shoot sword!"

While they're not shot here, swords are a fantastic way of entry to see Foo's charge Murat at work. The frenetic beginning of *Death Warrior* features Murat in a to-the-death hilltop curved saber fight that goes on for roughly twelve minutes. It's a pointless (from a narrative perspective) series of back flips, front flips, and "hurricanranas," that flying scissor maneuver which came to us from the world of Mexican pro wrestling, lazily interspersed with lengthy ninja training footage to pad the running time, a genre requirement. White ninja recruits are put through the paces by an evil black ninja—ah, who are we kidding, they're as frequently killed as they are trained—as they seek to become martial arts men of the cloth. And their evil sensei goes above and beyond standard show-offy moves like your whipping a playing card into someone's neck. No, this one can actually fling a match with such force it can embed into a tree.

Clearly Italy has its work cut out for it. That's one evil ninja on Europe's doorstep.

Death Warrior requires keen attention to detail as there's so much of it that's confusing and cobbled from stock footage—itself frequently bookended with other stock footage that it's tough even keeping the stock footage straight. There's a lengthy multi-locale chase scene that gives new meaning to the term "stock car racing," where Cüneyt Arkın and co-director Çetin Inanç deploy toy cars and a cardboard model. It's a two-minute scene that starts in daylight in some random town, ends up somewhere completely different at night, and has Arkın looking over his shoulder to see if his evasive action has proved fruitful. To one extent it has; we certainly have no idea where he is.

One thing's for sure, they haven't left Turkey. (Why would they? It was, as it is now, a cheap place for location shooting.)

It's safe to say that much of *Death Warrior* is "lost in translation"—but way more exciting than Bill Murray bemoaning having to spend time with Scarlett Johansson in one of the world's most fascinating cities. Here are a few fantastic subtitle renderings:

"When bats and ninjas rebirth!" (um, when indeed?)
"Silence tone learning" (all the rage at Montessori schools?)
"Sand grain even weapons!" (a nod to William Blake's "to see a world in a grain of sand?")
"Never ending palsy like a wizard cutting." (Truer words have seldom been spoken.)

Death Warrior is a film so off-the-rails random, it defies most description—for heaven's sake, there are vines telekinetically attacking people! Who those people are is a mystery. There's a solemn meeting between Murat and some shirtless wrestlers on a mountain pass, one of whom he beats the shit out of. Who THOSE people are is a mystery. And ditto, some rando fat guy smoking a pipe. In fact, so much mystery surrounds *Death Warrior*, Neil deGrasse Tyson couldn't fashion a booming narrative out of it. There are sequences clearly sped up, others obviously shot in reverse, and something that can only be described as a flying bag of burning ninja.

But to carry the load, it's all Cüneyt Arkın. Arkın cuts a Richard Gere–like profile as he spins his kicks 180 degrees. And, as per *IMDb*, he has acted in an astonishing 322 movies (or more accurately, has "appeared in"; acting is a bit of a stretch). It's likely impossible for someone named Cüneyt Arkın starring in something called *Ölüm savasçisi* (this film's proper title) to be considered a household name. And yet he should be. The man kicks serious ass.

ABOVE THE LAW (1988)

At some point in the 2000s, Steven Seagal began to morph into a bloated Bobby Baccalà from *The Sopranos*, increasingly draped in overcoats or ponchos to hide the endomorph barrel he'd eaten his way into. Seriously, it'd be wild to put him side by side with Steve Schirripa and see who's got a wider face.

In his debut, *Above the Law*, not only was Seagal a lean, mean, fighting machine, he hadn't even grown out his ponytail. He looks incredible here, causing even Roger Ebert to take notice: "He does have a strong and particular screen presence. It is obvious he is doing a lot of his own stunts, and some of the fight sequences are impressive and apparently unfaked."

And this "strong presence" is in part because of his ambiguous look.

Steven Seagal was the Vin Diesel of his time, able to adopt any ethnicity imaginable. Kind of like Angelina Jolie at the agency.

And in *Above the Law*, he's in peak form, before he launched what would become a staple of his thespianism: squinting, tackling other languages, and garbling accents. Here he's Nico, a Vietnam vet and American of Sicilian extraction—a region which has given us actual legitimate actors like Vincent D'Onofrio, Steve Buscemi, Ben Gazzara, and Chazz Palminteri.

And the globetrotting Seagal treats us to an earful of both Italian and Japanese in the epic opener of flashbacks. And by way of, what else? A martial arts montage! He's wearing a *gi*, while some pan flute is piped in over obsequious bowing. In sepia tones, we get to see Seagal treat us to a bunch of slick aikido under the watch of some Japanese salarymen.

Seagal, in real life, for all his often murky backstory, does come by his martial arts proficiency and Japanese language skills honestly. There's a hilarious YouTube clip of Seagal stuffed like a sausage into a kimono, by all accounts, speaking the language splendidly.

Apparently, before he moved to Hollywood to attempt to act, Seagal's Japanese dojo school was in a rough part of town known for yakuza gangsters and prostitutes.

In *Black Belt Magazine*, long-time martial arts instructor Haruo Matsuoka claims that seeing Seagal doing aikido in his homeland "changed his life." "When I first met Seagal sensei," Matsuoka remarks, "his Japanese wasn't so fluent, but his technique was remarkable—unlike what I'd seen before. He was so fast, very fluid . . ."

Wonder what he'd say about the inflatable body suit that has become of Seagal?

After the Japanese montage, we flash forward to a christening in present day Illinois. And Seagal's breaking language barriers again by showcasing his Italian in a big church and venturing over to a mandolin-infused party straight out of *The Godfather*. This will come into play later when Seagal's parish padre is blown to kingdom come.

More importantly, in *Above the Law*, we get our first glimpse of Seagal in the profession we've come to love him in in countless subsequent roles: an ex-CIA man. If you were to put him in *King Lear*, he'd be a monarch father to three daughters—and an ex-CIA man.

As Chicago PD, Nico, and his "aquiline face" (thanks, Roger Ebert) is busting drug dealers, a rogue cop cliché like Dirty Harry who doesn't let bureaucracy or due process get in the way of administering serious beatdowns. He does this with the help of partner Delores "Jacks" Jackson (the inestimable Pam Grier). And their banter is hilarious: "What is it about this place you don't like? The element!" However, they get more than they bargained for as the drug kingpins are connected to the CIA.

The plot's too convoluted to explore any further, but suffice it to say, there's a big giant conspiracy afoot that requires that Steven Seagal put a foot in the ass of every bad man on the South Side, including a monumental bar fight precipitated when the surprisingly svelte Seagal saunters into the juke joint looking for his niece who has fallen in with a bad element.

His investigation includes the obligatory brandishing of the photograph along with "Have you seen this girl?" Of course, the barfly baddies are less then forthcoming with the info, but perhaps that's because Nico neglected to remove the class photo from the chintzy frame it's housed in. He then deflects his inquiry to the bartender, uttering some nonsensical pigeon-Italian, which to our untrained ears sounds suspiciously close to a slightly accented "Suck a tampon." Equally nonsensical is the barkeep's retort of "Now take some of that money and go buy your momma a condominium." Considering that the median price of a condo in Chi-town climbed to over $331,000 in 2017, perhaps Nico would have been wise to have taken that advice. Sound financial planning advice from a lowlife pint puller; who would've expected that?

Equally unexpected is the adjoining apartment which Nico bursts into after wiping the bar clean of every dago mullet unibrow in the Windy City to the strain of the obviously improvised utterance, "He's crazy!" And there's the niece, lying in bed and smoking some rock with a lowlife piece of linguini, drugs and assorted paraphernalia strewn everywhere. Nico grabs the runt by the scruff of the neck, pulls him out of bed, then slams and rubs his face onto a cocaine-covered mirror before throwing the twerp against the wall for some more choking and bitch-slapping. Way to sully a crime scene and tamper with the evidence, Nico.

Later, a bunch of Salvadoran thugs corral him in an alley with knives and a baseball bat saying, "Don't worry, we won't shoot you, we'll just beat you to death," at which point we get the all-time great action movie cliché: the indefatigable henchman.

The indefatigable henchman will not be denied. He's the last man standing after he's seen his hench-buddies dispatched with such savvy and skill. And yet he STILL thinks he's got a fighting chance. No can do. He and his Louisville slugger are no match for Seagal in a black wife-beater. Above the Law is a dollop of fun. Fellow cops deride Nico's "martial arts hero, chop suey crap," but this is our man at his finest. Seagal doles out some extraordinary beatings. Unlike his acting, these look effortless. And eagle-eyed viewers will spot Ron Dean as a Chicago detective. He's known as the tough-as-nails dad to Emilio Estevez in *The Breakfast Club*.

Above the Law is top-drawer Seagal, before he went into his "continental phase," disappearing into direct-to-video Euro purgatory. Probably a function of age, Squinty McSquintyface began to delegate some of the heavy lifting to costars, which meant more weapons and fewer wrenched extremities for anyone still stupid enough to get in his way and take a swing.

STUPOR HEROES

BY SAVING THE DAY YOU ARE IMPROVING THE WORLD.

—STAN LEE

Departure, adventure, and return are the three components of the archetypical hero myth. To us in Canada, that could mean picking up smokes downtown when it's 20 below. Joseph Campbell's elaborations on the essential elements of a hero's life run through Greek antiquity to today's men and women in leotards.

Superheroes are meant to embody the ideal: the human being (or Kryptonian, or Atlantean, or Asgardian) operating at the pinnacle of perfection and potential. At their best, superheroes are both inspirational and aspirational. They show us that the impossible is possible—if we're a billionaire orphan, we too can dress like a giant bat and prowl rooftops and alleyways at night, looking ineffably cool doing so. At their worst, they're just downright ridiculous. Like when said nocturnal avenger is played by one Mr. Clooney, George.

Superhero movies are huge business now. There's no denying that. In 2019, movies based on comic-book properties grossed an astonishing combined $3.2 billion at the domestic box office alone. But it wasn't always like this. For many years, perhaps because moviemaking technology just wasn't there yet, or perhaps because widespread interest was low, superhero adaptations were the domain of the small screen, often in the guise of made-for-TV movies designed as stealth pilots for television shows that never came. Sure, there were a few notable exceptions along the way, 1978's *Superman* and 1989's *Batman* being two, but there were also dozens upon dozens of misguided attempts to translate sequential art to the big screen. Misguided, perhaps, but for their time and relatively low budgets, nonetheless entertaining and not without some merit. For some, this chapter will be a reminder of those dark days; for others, a celebration of a time when superhero movies were simpler, more joyful, and when Marvel Studios didn't dominate the box office half a dozen times in a given year.

We took on a quest of our own in this very book: to find the wackiest action movies we could. And with great power comes great responsibility. For a genre where silliness and suspension of disbelief are par for the course (Can a domino mask really conceal a person's true identity? Really?), superhero films have to be EXTRA ridiculous to make the cut, and lucky for us, the entries in this chapter are. So, true believers, look up in the sky. Is it a bird? Is it a plane? Nope, it's just a chapter on wonky superhero movies written by your friendly neighborhood authors. Excelsior!

CAPTAIN AMERICA II: DEATH TOO SOON (1979)

Captain America made his four-color debut in 1941, in the pages of "Captain America Comics." Created by Jack Kirby and Joe Simon, Cap was a superhero with a patriotic bent (famously punching out Hitler on the cover of his first issue, one full year before the attack on Pearl Harbor brought the United States into the Second World War). Captain America was born Steve Rogers, a scrawny kid whose pitiful build precluded him from enlisting in the US Army. Undeterred, Rogers volunteered for Operation: Rebirth, and was given a super serum which transformed him from a pencil-necked geek into a formidable warrior of superhuman strength and agility. Now decked out in his familiar red, white, and blue uniform, Cap was given an indestructible shield made out of Vibranium-steel alloy, and into the fray he went, ultimately becoming an integral part of "Earth's Mightiest Heroes," The Avengers.

Though most know Captain America as portrayed by Chris Evans in *The Avengers* movies and his own solo flicks, Evans was not the first actor to carry the shield. In 1990, Matt Salinger (son of J.D.) played the hero in a cheapo flick directed by Albert Pyun (*Cyborg*). That film (ironically) never received a US theatrical release but did see cinemas in France. But even Salinger wasn't the first to don the patriotic spandex on celluloid. It was former college football standout and future star of threadbare Italian B-movies Reb Brown (*Strike Commando*), who was C.A. *primum*, playing the hero in a pair of made-for-TV movies that both aired in 1979: *Captain America* and *Captain America II: Death Too Soon*.

Now, before HBO and Showtime made the medium respectable again, the phrase "made-for-TV movie" was pretty much synonymous with crap; the kind of crap that would appear on network TV. Sure, there was *Roots*, but that's hardly the exception that (dis)proves the rule. Besides, it always carried the imprimatur of "miniseries," something that had the musky odor of a PBS pledge room not hit with Febreze.

"Made-for-TV movie," however, conjured up Lifetime bodice rippers and bloated disaster movies. That'd be disasters even if there weren't fires, crashes, or earthquakes, starring people who couldn't ever make it in "real" movies.

In 1978, *Superman* brought us Brando, Hackman, and Beatty—bankable draws who didn't need first names—and made youngsters leap from tall buildings in a single bound, long before the world of pro wrestling separated the belief-suspending wheat from the kids who became the chaff of Darwin Awards. Of course, producers sunk $55 million into the mega-budget production and it showed. A whizzbang summer hit that also made Christopher Reeve a global star and spawned several sequels (including one that appears in this very chapter. Stay tuned, true believers!).

Then came *Captain America II: Death Too Soon*, hot on the heels of *Captain America*. A sure-fire sign of a cheap cash-in. That these two movies were intended as de facto pilots for a weekly television series which never saw production should speak volumes about the quality therein. *Captain America II* did enjoy a theatrical release of sorts, but again, only in France. Whatever enmity that exists between the United States and France, the French sure do love their *Captain America* movies.

Instead of a marquee name to boost the fortunes of the Marvel adaptation, the film's success fell on the burly shoulders of redoubtable Brown, and along for the ride, 6'5" horror icon Christopher Lee, who'd just left the UK after pal Billy Wilder told him he "had to get away from London otherwise [he] would always be typecast." Probably should've left in 1980.

Captain America II fumbles right from the start, showing Brown as Rogers, not taking down Red Skull, but painting an old lady's portrait in a park instead! His subject admits reluctance in cashing her social security check due to all the muggers in the vicinity. Rogers shoots her a bumpkin smile and urges her to "go ahead and cash that pension check." Of course, she's beset, and of course the Captain saves the day, affirming to one crook that "the old people around here are my friends." Forget the bane of Hydra; this C.A. is champion of *The Golden Girls*.

But every superhero must eventually get around to foiling some nefarious scheme, and in *Captain America II*, that plot is hatched by Christopher Lee's Miguel, a mysterious supervillain not too far removed from his turn as Bond antagonist in *The Man with the Golden Gun*. Here he's a criminal genius of unknown provenance spearheading a lunatic plot to prematurely age the populace thirty days for every single minute unless a hefty ransom is paid. If this meant wasting an audience's time for eighty-three minutes (or two hours, plus commercials), mission accomplished. His gambit involves developing aging drugs to poison the city of Portland, making its residents look bearded and withered and essentially not too different from the hipsters presently there.

To foil Miguel, Rogers has to go undercover in a small Oregon town. And this being TV-movie land, Rogers does not have the *S.H.I.E.L.D.* helicarrier at his disposal, making do instead with a rinky-dink van, a motorcycle, and a ridiculously oversized helmet replete with wings on the side and a visor. And the shield? Forget indestructible Vibranium; this ones made out of extremely pliable, translucent plastic.

Besides less-than-spectacular heroics, *Captain America II* also features another staple of the action film: the "We're not that different, you and I" speech given by the villain to the hero. Here it's Miguel telling the Captain "In any other circumstances, we might have been friends." Huh? In what universe would an erudite, cosmopolitan international man of mystery like Miguel hang around with a musclebound "golly-gee" all-American type that is Brown's Captain? Unless he wanted Cap to paint his portrait, that is.

The *Death Too Soon* tag is an appropriate one. Not for Lee's career though, as he continued to act right up to his death at the ripe old age of 93, but certainly for Reb Brown's dreams of television stardom. But even if Brown was never granted the opportunity to cameo in a big-budget Marvel production like his contemporary Lou Ferrigno, there's just something inexplicably loveable about the "Aw Shucks" galoot. And for that he'll always be the true Captain to us.

SUPERMAN IV: THE QUEST FOR PEACE (1987)

The soaring, bulletproof man from Krypton is the pinnacle of the superhero ideal, and moviegoers flocked to the cinema in droves to watch Christopher Reeve embody the hero in three successful films, making the prospect of a fourth franchise installment a no-brainer. But in the four years between *Superman III* and *Superman IV: The Quest for Peace*, an evil much greater than Lex Luthor or General Zod befell the Man of Steel. No, it wasn't shards of Kryptonite that brought the mighty Superman to his knees. Rather, it was the dynamic producing duo of Menahem Golan and Yoram Globus and Cannon Films, two Israeli immigrants with a dream who knew a thing or two about debasing the legacy of great films (see *Death Wish II* and *3*).

At the time of production, if Cannon wasn't quite teetering on the brink of insolvency, they were certainly racing toward the precipice. With too many films in production, too many box office results that didn't deliver, and too much money spent on securing big stars (the studio paid Stallone a then record $12 million to star in the arm wrestling opus *Over the Top*, a film which barely grossed enough to recoup the star's salary), something had to give. And that something was *Superman IV*. The film's budget was slashed from $36 to $17 million, resulting in the wonkiest effects in the entire series. Furthermore, the run time was cut from 134 minutes to a scant ninety, resulting in Titanic-sized plot holes in the shortest Superman feature since 1951's *Superman and the Mole-Men*. And if the tagline for the first Superman film was "You'll believe a man could fly," for this one it ought to have been "Prepare to have your belief severely put to the test."

As the film begins, a Russian cosmonaut is tinkering outside a space capsule when a piece of debris hits it and sends the spaceman adrift into deep space. And this, a full twenty-six years before the exact same thing happened in 2013's tepid Clooney/Bullock starrer *Gravity*. Luckily, Supes comes flying to the rescue and saves the spaceman. Back on Earth, Lex Luthor (a returning Gene Hackman, whom the Cannon boys must have had incriminating photos of to get him to come back to the series he abandoned) is breaking rocks in a chain gang when his nephew Lenny (Jon Cryer) stages a ludicrous coup to break him out. The future star of *Two and a Half Men* and Luther himself on TV's *Supergirl* sports a ridiculous orange faux-hawk and is resplendent in leopard-spotted jacket and tight pants. He also delivers his lines in an obnoxious, half-hearted Valley-type manner, á la *Bill and Ted*.

Clark and Lois (a returning Margot Kidder) are on route to *The Daily Planet* via subway, but the hapless Clark is unable to board the train before the doors shut. With Lois aboard, the conductor suffers a heart attack and passes out, and the train veers out of control. But fear not, for a phone booth is near. In goes Clark and out comes Superman! (Insert iconic John Williams's theme here.) He swoops in to save the commuters, but everything just looks wrong. The flying is rendered in horribly obvious chroma key compositing, and wires are flagrantly visible throughout the film. Compounding the humiliation, Reeve (who cowrote the film) wore his flying harness underneath his red outerpants, resulting in what looked like a giant, protruding Supergut.

Lex hatches a plot to clone his nemesis, which involves the acquisition of some Super DNA. Thankfully, there's a MacGuffin. The Metropolis

Museum just happens to have a strand of Superman's hair on display, demonstrating the follicle's tensile strength by having it hold up a 1,000-pound weight. Lex saunters right up to the display, smashes the glass, and snips. Even by superhero-movie standards, this scene is completely illogical. To begin, why would a strand of Superhair be in a museum absolutely unguarded? It's not like there might be supervillains lurking about who may think to use it for nefarious purposes, right? Second, forget the guards. Why is the hair displayed behind a single pane of non-reinforced glass flimsier than tissue paper? Third, this is *Superman's* hair: Strong, invulnerable, able to hold up a thousand pounds. Yet Lex is able to snatch it with a single snip of his hedge clippers! Finally, isn't Lex an escaped criminal mastermind convict? Why is no one out looking for him? Instead of hiding like a fugitive from the law like he should, he's walking about carefree in broad daylight without any concern of being re-apprehended. Later in the film, he even says to Superman, "Ever since I escaped from prison . . ." and Supey just stands there. You'd think he'd immediately pick Lex up and fly the crook's escaped ass back to Sing Sing.

This being the '80s and all, nuclear proliferation was the concern *de jour*, so when the president announces that the USA needs to be second to none in the arms race, a concerned (and extremely bratty) school kid writes a letter to Superman asking him to do something about it. After some deliberation, Superman decides to enforce nuclear disarmament. He marches right in to the UN building (in Metropolis? And just as they did with the New York slum in *Death Wish 3*, the Cannon team opted to shoot in England for budgetary reasons, and it shows) and informs a delegate of ethnic stereotypes that he is going to rid the world of nuclear weaponry.

And so the world's nuclear superpowers launch their missiles into space. Supes grabs the missiles and hurls them into a giant cosmic garbage bag which he then tosses into the sun.

There are so many things wrong and/or wonky with *Superman IV*, so before this entry turns into a dissertation, let's just list them, bullet point style:

- Lex creates a Superman "clone." That's all well and good, but this clone looks nothing like Superman. Isn't the very definition of clone "exact duplicate"? Oh well. This monstrosity's name is Nuclear Man, and he was born in the sun. He comes to life fully formed and blond-mulleted, wearing an outfit that looks like something seen on *American Gladiators*. It even has an "N" insignia on the chest (for Nuclear Man, of course), despite the fact that this "duplicate" hasn't even been given that name yet.
- Clark Kent reveals himself to Lois as Superman, then takes her on a whirlwind flight over the best stock footage of the United States the filmmakers could get their hands on. Upon landing back on Clark's balcony, Lois has zero recollection of what transpired. So now the ability to cause short-term amnesia is part of Superman's power set?
- Nuclear Man destroys the Great Wall of China by flying through it. Superman repairs the wall by using a vision that rapidly reassembles the bricks. Is masonry-vision another new power?
- Nuclear Man and Superman wage battle on the moon. The fight is terribly choreographed and resembles two aged WWF jobbers going at it. Steve Lombardi and Barry Horowitz would have provided more hard-hitting action than what we get here.
- Superman defeats Nuclear Man by moving the moon to blot out the sun. Wouldn't that result in worldwide environmental catastrophe by altering the world's tides?

And we can go on. Ultimately, *Superman IV* was a huge flop that grossed less than a quarter of its predecessor and effectively drove the last nail in Cannon's coffin. And yet, for all its numerous problems, it's nowhere near as egregious a crime against cinema as *Batman & Robin* (keep reading!) Christopher Reeve remains charming as ever as the befuddled Clark Kent and heroic as the Man of Steel, and there is nary a Super Nipple nor Super Credit Card to be found.

WONDER WOMAN (1974)

More than forty years before the formidable Gal Gadot embodied Wonder Woman on the big screen, the Amazon from the all-female island of Themyscira was personified by Lynda Carter on the highly successful and fondly remembered '70s television series. Lynda was everything Wonder Woman/Diana Prince should be. She was strong, sexy, fun, feisty, and above all, Amazonian; qualities which can't quite be attributed to *That's Incredible!* host Cathy Lee Crosby.

The New Original Wonder Woman, a TV movie which launched the Carter series, aired in November 1975, but one year before, families were huddled around the tube watching a far different (and barely wondrous) Wonder Woman. Intended as a pilot for a series, the Crosby-starring *Wonder Woman* was an inchoate mess which veered far from W. W. creator William Moulton Marsten's original vision. The film garnered poor ratings and prompted ABC and Warner Brothers to hit reboot.

Starting with a theme more appropriate to a Blaxploitation flick than a movie of this ilk, the film shows a blonde Diana as she's preparing to leave her all-female island for the "world of men." Once there, she's instructed by her mother to "adopt new ways . . . [and] open closed eyes to the genuine value of women." As she touches arms with her sisters and mother for perhaps the last time, an extremely annoying "tchh" sound plays repeatedly over the soundtrack. Yet, in spite of the fantastical origin, there's absolutely nothing wonderful about this particular woman. She has no superpowers, no magic lasso, no bullet-deflecting bracelets, no tiara, and not much of a costume to speak of. Without any of the hallmarks of the Wonder Woman people knew and loved, it really is no wonder viewers rejected this pseudo-superhero.

Now working as an assistant to government agent Steve Trevor, Diana (whom Trevor calls "Dee") overhears a meeting where her boss discusses the successfully pulled-off heist by international super spy Abner Smith and his flunky George. They've managed to steal ten books from around the globe, each one necessary to use the other, which detail the identities, aliases, and whereabouts of thirty-nine active American field agents, thus rendering them vulnerable to "assassination or apprehension." Gentlemen saboteur Smith, who's played with ultimate class as only Ricardo Montalbán can, is far and away the best part of the film, even if Montalbán's continental accent hilariously pronounces "George" as "Zseorsz." Smith will return the books only if paid the hefty ransom of (Dr. Evil voice here) $15 million.

Diana informs Trevor that she needs to see a dentist, which apparently is code between them for "I'm going to go solve this thing." It's just the two of them in the room and Trevor knows Diana's no mere secretary, so there really is no need for them to not speak plainly. She immediately jets off to France and checks into her hotel. Though dressed in tasteful business attire, Diana is spotted almost immediately by one of George's henchmen lurking in the lobby. He picks up the phone and informs George that "Wonder Woman is here." So much for your secret identities and covert operations.

By utilizing extremely tepid martial arts skills, cunning and guile, business-casual Wonder Woman fends off the many attempts made on

her life. And despite the fact that Smith specifically forbade George from messing with her, the attempts keep on coming, the most preposterous of which involves a particularly non-threatening and non-venomous looking snake which George leaves in her room. As the snake coils around her leg, Diana calls room service and orders a container of milk and a saucer. She also explicitly states that the waiter must remove his shoes before coming inside. (Why? Was she afraid of stains on the carpeting?) The waiter does as he's told and slides the milk toward the reptile, which results in it promptly unwrapping itself from Diana's leg and slithering toward the moo juice. Although it's a popular myth in India that snakes drink milk, they're reptiles, not mammals. They can't digest the stuff and doing so would result in death. Yet the snake which Wonder Woman later gives back gift-wrapped to George is very much alive.

Back at home base, the brilliant Trevor has decided to deliver the ransom money in the form of marked bills contained in saddle bags strapped to the back of a donkey! The poor burro is doused in ultraviolet fluid and fitted with four micro transmitters between its hoofs and shoes for easy tracking. The ass is delivered to Smith's lair, located inside the north wall of the Grand Canyon, with Wonder Women following close behind. And she's finally in "costume," although calling it that is rather charitable. The tracksuit/miniskirt combo with stars on the arms and a small eagle insignia on the left upper chest make this Wonder Woman look less like a superhero and more like a flight attendant on American Airlines.

Cash in hand, Smith attempts escape by paddling away in an inflatable raft (you'd think a man with a high-tech lair inside the Grand Canyon would be able to afford something a little more impressive) but Wonder Woman foils him. As the global terrorist and International Man of Mystery is carted off in a marked squad car by two low-level uniformed officers, he exclaims "Wonder Woman, I love you." At least somebody does.

As a movie, *Wonder Woman* is bad, even by made-for-TV standards. But as an adaptation of a comic book icon and a representation of one of the world's greatest superheroes, *Wonder Woman* is wonderfully atrocious.

BATMAN & ROBIN (1997)

Batman is widely regarded to be one of the coolest superheroes ever, probably because of the wicked Fritz Lang urban hellscape he inhabits and the fact that he uses his smarts rather than pure brawn to overpower opponents. Kinda like the chess parts of a chess boxing tournament, but a less terrible analogy that won't have you swiping the pieces away in disgust. But even Batman's most ardent defenders would admit there's something impossibly and undeniably lame about having an effete elfin do-nothing as a sidekick.

Who gives two craps about sidekicks? We do, when it's a movie starring Chuck Norris. But when something is about the likes of Jimmy Olsen, Bucky Barnes, or Robin? If this were late night television, they'd be the expendables you could pay less than the host. After all, you CAN put a price on a catchphrase.

So, *Batman & Robin* is at a disadvantage right out of the gate. The ampersand should tip you off. It was one of the rare instances when a film lived down to its expectations, then put on a hardhat and descended the mineshaft even further.

On the plus side, what the film destroys in terms of minutes lived is redeemed somewhat by the fact that it gave rise to numerous discussions. One of which is that it generates a ready-made and readily defensible answer whenever the topic of "worst film of all time" comes up. This "worst of all time" designation, of course, excludes wedding videos and those made by terrorists to communicate demands.

"Worst" designations are subjective. *Birdemic* and *The Room* are not made by real filmmakers, and vanity pieces like *Battlefield Earth* and their ilk are merely efforts by established screen legends to venture outside their limited ranges or publicity stunts to advance a musical career (*Glitter*). They are judged differently. Likewise, other bad movies are disposable products meant to cash in on a demographic a decade out of diapers—anything that contains "movie" in the title for example (*Disaster Movie, Date Movie, Superhero Movie,* etc.).

Batman & Robin is uniquely versatile and far-reaching in its crappiness. It's a $140 million film that still manages to look like its production design was sourced from an attic.

When the Batmobile is revealed early on, the ever-pathetic Robin red breastplate, solidifying his also-ran status, says "I want a car. Chicks dig a car." He's like a teenager having to go cap-in-hand to pops to beg to get his license.

At this point it's worth mentioning our two principals, the Abbott and Costello of this idiot production. The first is George Clooney as Batman (the third actor in a four-film series to portray the Caped Crusader), doing that thing he does where he makes things look effortless, except in this case, it's not for the positive. He just looks like he doesn't give a crap. His sidekick is Chris O'Donnell, a guy who brings to the role of Dick Grayson/Robin the look and charisma of a PGA tour pro. Burt Ward may have been corny on the old TV series with his "Holy this" and "Holy that" catchphrases, but that show was *meant* to be campy. And at least he didn't give the viewer the compulsion to punch him in the face, unlike our bratty Boy Wonder in this one.

Their chief antagonist is Mr. Freeze. An editorial comment about Arnold Schwarzenegger's mouth perhaps, as the guy never met a syllable he could properly enunciate. Arnold's Freeze has stolen diamonds from the natural history museum, and it's up to the Dynamic Duo to thwart him, maybe by demanding that he say, "Around the Rugged Rock the Ragged Rascal Ran." That would have at least been fun, but instead Schwarzenegger's Freeze character is reduced to uttering a never-ending litany of cold-related puns such as "Let's kick some ice!" and "Allow me to break the ice. My name is Freeze. Learn it well for it's the chilling sound of your doom!" The Governator unleashes a barrage of one-liners that are a bucket of ice water to comedy's head and several Introductory Business English courses short of being understandable. When asked for mercy, Freeze says: "TIE-EM TO WINTAHRIZE YOUR PIE-PPS."

And this Batman isn't any better. At his best, Batman talks loudly by saying little. All Michael Keaton had to do in Tim Burton's 1989 film was pull his quarry close, growl "I'm Batman!" and the poor crim crapped his pants. Here, he's just as pun-happy as his prey, dropping "Hey Freeze. The heat is on!" in the same insouciant register he uses as Bruce Wayne. So much for the Dark Knight.

At the heart of the film, if such a thing could be said when it's so anatomically untrue, is the hockey fight centrepiece at the icy Gotham Museum of Art. It's enough that it pisses off all Canadians, if such a thing were even possible, but it also shares one thing in common with the film that surrounds it: it's unbearably long. *Batman & Robin* is a reminder of that stinging book critique witticism often (and falsely) attributed to short story writer and journalist Ambrose Bierce: "The covers of this book are too far apart."

The hockey fight is a sure sign the viewer is going to take a high stick. But there's more. Also moronic: Mr. Freeze has evil freezing power but it doesn't even induce hypothermia nor death. People can just be thawed out by sunlight. He's basically an icebox you take on a camping trip.

But there are other characters who also deserve to be curbside on garbage day. Too many really. This film is more overstuffed than a Thanksgiving Day turkey. There's Bane, who in the comic book is clever, quick-witted, and cunning. Here, as played by late journeyman wrestler Jeep Swenson, he's a lumbering Frankenstein monster with a similar gift for gab. In the comic, Bane literally broke the Batman, beating him more decisively than any villain before or since by breaking Batman's back over his massive knee. Here, Bane is reduced to being Poison Ivy's monosyllabic chauffeur. But at least he gets a car, unlike Robin.

The leggy Uma Thurman is Dr. Pamela Isley, a.k.a. Poison Ivy. She's a walking high school photosynthesis class, a botanist and eco-terrorist who has chlorophyll skin. She has a venomous kiss and uses pheromones to make men fall madly in love with her, instead of, you know . . . just BEING F-ING UMA THURMAN.

The film's only action movie cred is having arch-Predator Jesse "The Body" Ventura as an Arkham Asylum Guard—his third appearance in a film starring his fellow once-governor buddy Arnie, the others being *The Running Man* and *Predator*. Run far, far away from this one.

ELECTRA (1996)

In his seminal *The Interpretation of Dreams*, psychoanalyst Sigmund Freud wrote that the psychosexual development of all children, regardless of gender, involves some degree of sexual desire for the mother combined with aggression toward the father. He named this the "Oedipus Complex," after the famed Sophocles play *Oedipus Rex*. In response, Carl Jung maintained that only boys contend with maternal lust whereas girls are locked in a psychosexual competition with their mothers for possession of their fathers. He named this the "Electra Complex," after the fifth-century BC Greek mythological character, daughter of King Agamemnon, who along with her brother Orestes plotted the death of her mother, Queen Clytemnestra. But what of mothers who want to get it on with their sons? *Electra* deals with just that icky conceit, but other than the literary allusion of the title, has about as much subtext as the takeout menu of a local Greek diner.

Starring Shannon Tweed, the MILF-alicious 1982 *Playboy* Playmate of the Year and partner to Gene Simmons, *Electra* (not to be confused with 2005's *Daredevil* spinoff *Elektra*) has it all: an inane plot; an over-the-top villain with dreams of world domination; a vaguely defined "super-serum" MacGuffin; and ass-kicking, back-flipping henchwomen clad in leather thong bodysuits and fishnets.

As the film begins, one of those henchwomen is gyrating to some generic "sexy" music on a strip club stage while the other is waiting tables. We'll call them Leather Clad Bimbos #s 1 and 2, or LCB for short. One punter seems especially taken with LCB #1. She tells him to meet her in the alley in ten minutes. There, LCBs both #1 and #2 kick the ever-loving shit of him and drag him into an awaiting car.

The kidnapped man is to be the next test subject for the iniquitous Marcus Roach: a paraplegic who covers his lower extremities with a metallic blanket and tools around in a wheelchair with two large antennae affixed to the sides and a large cockroach painted on the seatback. Roach wants to be restored to his former bipedal self *and* he wants to build a private army of super soldiers to help him take over the world. Naturally. To that end, he has under his employ one Dr. Bartholomew. Bartholomew injects the subject with a serum as they await 100% contamination. Once reached, the subject becomes possessed with super strength and imperviousness to pain, as evidenced by the red-beret-wearing henchman who approaches him only to have his punches shrugged off and his neck brutally snapped. (Which henchmen volunteer for these suicide assignments? Do they have to draw straws?) Nonetheless, the power surge is too great and the man drops dead, spewing forth a substance not unlike Pepto-Bismol.

Roach would have at that point put Bartholomew down too if the bespectacled man of science hadn't diffidently fessed up about a now deceased colleague, Dr. Arthur Duncan, who created a super serum that *does* work. Seems his young son Billy had a congenital form of anemia, took the serum and survived. The now grown Billy of superhuman speed and strength (but not size; that's just average) lives on a farm upstate with his stepmother, Lorna (Tweed). And, Bartholomew informs, if Roach's men can't shake down the Duncans for the formula, it matters not, for the serum can be transmitted from one to another through unprotected sexual congress. "So sex is the key," says Roach as he leers sa-

laciously at his LCBs, ". . . and all we need is the right keyhole."

Cut to Billy chopping wood on the farm, wearing only cut-off jean shorts and a smile and looking exactly like *Kamandi: The Last Boy on Earth*. Lorna approaches her stepson and they exchange this disturbing bit of repartee:

Billy: Ma, you're still young and pretty. You should go out more.
Lorna: You think I'm pretty?
Billy: Prettiest woman in Watertown!

As Lorna is staring at her son's sweaty, chiseled physique, she's almost felled by a falling tree, but Billy pulls her from harm's way in the nick of time. He carries her into the house, helps her out of her clothes, and puts her into a hot bath. "Oh, this feels so good," moans Lorna as she soaks her nude body suggestively with Billy watching the whole time. This wildly inappropriate display is witnessed by Roach, whose henchmen have previously placed surveillance equipment throughout the home. "I know what her weakness is," cackles Roach. "Get the boy!"

While Billy's girlfriend, Mary Anne, is over, Roach's men descend. Both women flee as Billy tangles with the goons, throwing one straight through the air and onto the sharp end of a picket fence. Another chases Lorna on foot, although she's actually running, whereas he looks like he's going to keel over from a heart attack at any second. Nonetheless, Lorna is taken and wakens strapped to a table in Roach's lair. "What are you doing?" asks Lorna as Roach bathes her in red light. "Stimulating your erogenous zone while probing your subconscious," responds Roach. A computer screen shows Lorna bloodily hacking at Mary Anne with an ax, then ravishing her young, innocent stepson. "Yes, I do want him," Lorna admits.

But admission is not enough; Roach wants Lorna to consummate her desires. Billy and Mary Anne invade the compound to stage a rescue. He sees his mother chained to a wall and attempts to wrest her free, but as he's doing this, she licks his face and pricks him with a tranquilizer. Billy wakes up strapped to the same table that once held his mom. Roach attempts to get him to give up the formula, but Billy refuses. "If your mind won't cooperate, perhaps your body will." In saunter both LCBs. They strip each other down, gyrate, and fondle one another, yet Billy still resists. Time to employ the big guns, both metaphorically and euphemistically. In walks Momma, clad in the same thong bodysuit. She effectively rapes her stepson, although how Billy's super-serum could have entered Lorna when they both clearly had their pants on remains a mystery.

Now superpowered, Lorna is to do to Roach what she just did to her son. He dubs her Electra, The Supreme Seductress, and the two engage in the same sort of clothed copulation. Meanwhile, Mary Anne has taken some of the serum and it's Billy and his girlfriend vs. the bimbettes—a battle that culminates with Mary Anne tearing the heart out of LCB #2 with her bare hands, then throwing it into LCB #1's mouth.

They divide and conquer yet again, with Mary Anne now taking on Electra, and Billy throwing down with Roach—the villain now wearing some sort of hybrid helmet/VR device which makes him look like a member of Daft Punk. The battle reaches a crescendo as Roach's wheelchair becomes a flame thrower and Electra shoots blue lightning from her fingers like Emperor Palpatine at the end of *Return of the Jedi*. And all this before Electra mutates!

The central conceit of *Electra* is discomfiting, granted, but director Julian Grant nonetheless imbues the film with great fun. As the super-sexed super-villain, Tweed deliriously devours the scenery, and there are enough explosions and dropkicks to keep any action fan happy. The final credits read "Watch for *Electra II: The Second Coming*." We're still waiting and watching.

THE PUNISHER (1989)

The Punisher, a.k.a. Frank Castle, made his first appearance in 1974 in the pages of "*The Amazing Spider-Man*" #129. Almost immediately, the vigilante anti-hero who utilized kidnapping, torture, maiming, and murder to wage his one-man war on crime became one of Marvel Comics' most popular characters. The Punisher has headlined eighteen comic book series and inspired many a sullen teen (or overweight comic-con attendee) to don a black t-shirt emblazoned with the character's iconic skull insignia.

The character, as portrayed by Jon Bernthal on Netflix, has also become a small-screen sensation. And while many recall his two '00 cinematic adaptations: 2004's tepid *The Punisher* starring Thomas Jane and 2008's kick-ass Ray Stevenson-starring sequel *Punisher: War Zone*, readers of this book know that neither man was the first. Rather, that honor is bestowed upon the 6'5" Swede Dolph Lundgren in 1989's Australian-American coproduction, *The Punisher*.

Now, let's get two obvious debits out of the way. First, the blond, Nordic Lundgren was nobody's first choice when envisioning who would embody the Italian-American Castle. Though he did dye his hair black (and was a heck of a lot more verbose than he was as Ivan Drago in *Rocky IV*), he never truly looked the part. Second, at no time in the film does Lundgren sport the skull insignia, preferring monochromatic, black biker-gear from head to toe. Fine. But putting those two grievances aside, *The Punisher* still kind of kicks some ass.

Whereas in the comics Castle was a decorated Marine whose family was killed after witnessing a mob hit in Central Park, here there is no mention of military service. Instead, Castle is an ex-cop whose family was taken out. Presumed dead, Castle has spent the last five years living in the sewer while waging his war on crime. And doing a damn good job of it too, as the media attributes 125 mobster deaths to the mysterious vigilante known colloquially as The Punisher. (A figure reported repeatedly throughout the film, yet never adjusted for inflation, even as the Castle-abetted body count goes up, up, up.)

The first uptick is when Dino Moretti, lieutenant of the Franco crime family and the man directly responsible for killing Castle's family, is acquitted of all charges. He's back at his palatial estate celebrating his freedom while reporters are huddled outside. As he's downstairs drinking some bubbly with a bunch of low-level goombahs, a black boot is seen entering an upstairs window, a hand reaching in to remove the knife contained therein. Suddenly, henchmen are falling like dominoes, except for the one Castle garroted. He's strung up. As one grievously wounded stumbles outside, the mansion explodes gloriously, sending debris and shrapnel flying everywhere yet miraculously not hitting any one of the assembled reporters.

This creates a state of emergency for the mob, and soon Gianni Franco himself is back on home soil, along with his precocious son Tommy. Meanwhile, the gruff head of the Punisher task force, Lt. Jake Berkowitz, played by Louis Gossett Jr., is on the case.

Franco has designs on uniting the five families by accepting a $500 million drug shipment and splitting it five ways. Castle is made aware of this because of his ear to the ground, a soused former actor who speaks in rhyming couplets. Hence, when the boat carrying the drugs arrives,

Castle is there, but so are a bunch of wetsuit-clad assassins who take out a heap of bagboys by harpooning them through the eye, hurling spiked billiard-sized balls at their faces, and whipping them with chains. Castle gets involved in the melee and takes a knife in the shoulder blade.

He returns to his sewer lair (where twice he's seen meditating filthy and naked) and cauterizes his own wound by applying a soldering hot knife. (Super tough guys in action cinema have no need for doctors and are adept at tending to their own wounds. For further example, please see Johns, both McClane and Rambo.) All that's left of the five families after the dockside massacre are the heads. They take a meeting to discuss what to do next when in walks the head of the Japanese Yakuza, Ediko Tanaka, her goons, and her adopted mute American daughter. She proposes a partnership with the Mafiosi, with a 75/25 split in her favor. Needless to say, this overture is not taken kindly.

When Tanaka kidnaps Tommy and the other children of the family heads in retaliation and threatens to sell them into white slavery, the thespian implores Castle to intervene. He's reluctant but ultimately capitulates, laying the groundwork for the best scene in the entire movie. At an underground casino/brothel run by Tanaka, Castle crashes through a glass roof Michael Keaton-Batman style. He lands on a pool table and growls "Every day the children are gone is gonna cost you money," then proceeds to shoot the shit out of the place for five whole minutes, expending thousands of rounds of ammunition while pursing his lips like a millennial taking a selfie. Later, he manages to steal a city bus and rescue all the kids, save Tommy who's left behind. Unfortunately, in doing so, The Punisher is forced to reveal himself, and Berkowitz, whom we now know is Castle's former partner, arrests him.

Ultimately, all family heads fall to Tanaka save Franco. He busts Castle out of the hoosegow and forces him to aid in rescuing Tommy. The unlikely allies get to work, storming the Tanaka stronghold and taking out dozens of Yakuza. Of course, the question remains: Will the baddie turn on his nemesis once the mission is complete? Is the Pope a Catholic?

The Punisher is derided by many, and yes, it's goofy at parts and not the slavish adaptation that fanboys might have been clamoring for. But it has gigantic explosions, a ridiculously high body count (ninety-one plus), blood, boobs, and tons of henchmen falling forward over railings. Besides, any movie that features kids on a hijacked city bus fighting of Yakuza is aces in our book.

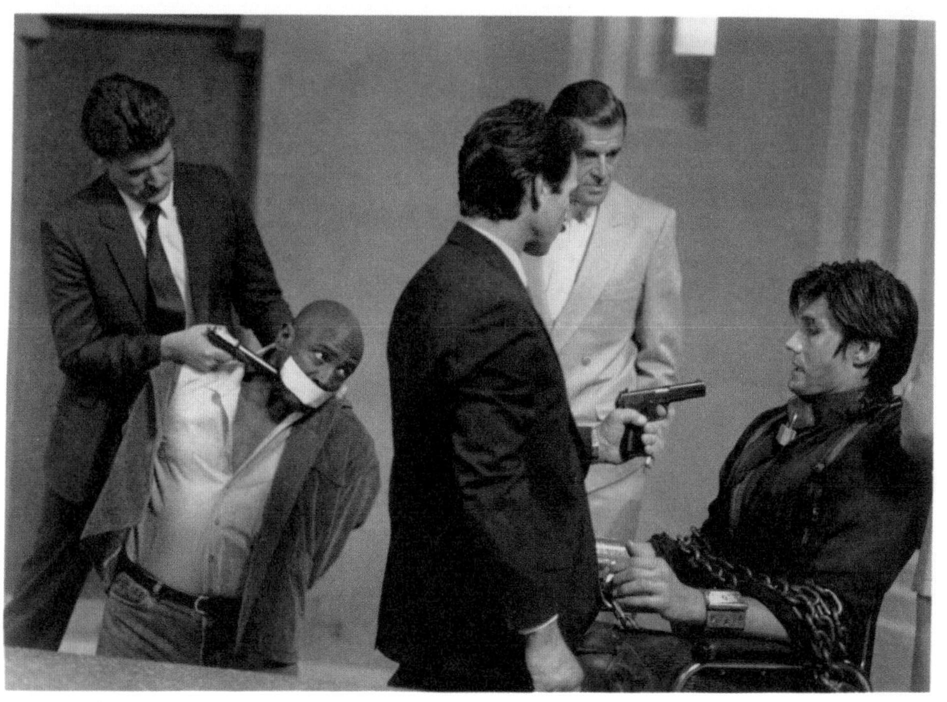

THE PUNISHER

NEW WORLD INTERNATIONAL

STUNT ROCK (1979)

Ask an action aficionado whom they deem the holy trilogy of action stars, and they may name Schwarzenegger, Stallone, and Willis. Others might prefer Seagal, Van Damme, and Norris. Or perhaps Eastwood, Bronson, and McQueen. (If, however, they reply with Damon, Gosling, and Diesel, please take our advice and hurl yourself through a plate glass window. Those people don't know from action.) But would anyone mention names such as Dar Robinson,[36] Vic Armstrong, or Bud Ekins? Doubtful. Yet they're part of that unique group of the unheralded heroes of action—the stunt performers—and anonymity is part of the job. They're the ones who tumble off buildings, crash their cars, and set themselves on fire, risking life and limb in the service of making the topline stars look good. Stunt performers work for the film and its stars, and if they do their job right, no one realizes that it's them they're marveling at rather than the headliner, plus nobody gets sued. Stunt performers have all the guts, but action stars get all the glory.[37]

Brian Trenchard-Smith (*The Man from Hong Kong*, *Turkey Shoot*) hoped to remedy that with his Ozploitation, Stuntsploitation opus *Stunt Rock*. Equal parts action film, concert film, and documentary, *Stunt Rock* is an odd but exhilarating beast. It's a love letter to both stunts and rock (hence the title), and one performer in particular—frequent Trenchard-Smith collaborator Grant Page, here playing himself.

The film begins with a disclaimer more likely seen before a WWE show than a feature film: "This film contains many dangerous stunts. Do not imitate what you see." One particular stunt, the heretofore never-been-done "The Human Catapult," looks like something that inebriated backpackers would pay good money to do in New Zealand, the country whose unofficial motto is "Let's hurl tourists off anything we can find that is impossibly high and ridiculously dangerous . . . and if there's time, *Lord of the Rings* stuff." As Page explains to a reporter, it involves him being "attached to two headlands 200 feet high on 1,000 feet of rope, and the center of which is dragged back much like a bow and I'm the arrow." And like that arrow, Page is pulled back, then soars at tremendous velocity in a sort of miles-long parabola.

After the disclaimer, we see Page in his native Australia in what appears to be early morning. Page nonchalantly strolls toward a massive cliff, and without the aid of any equipment, descends the jagged rock barehanded as waves crash violently against the rocky shores below. Most mere mortals could hardly eke out a push-up or two before a cup of joe, yet this Page guy is descending miles-high rock as if it's something he does every morning after his Egg McMuffin. A chopper arrives and he prepares for his next death-defying feat, "The Thrilling Death Slide."

Although a semi-household name in his homeland and holder of many Australian stunt records, Page has his eyes on the bigger prize: Hollywood success. Hence, he's off to the good ol' US of A to do stunt work on "Undercover Girl in Hollywood," a TV series starring Monique van de Ven, a Dutch actress also playing herself. (Nope, we've never heard of her either.) He's picked up at the airport by his "cousin" Curtis, the afroed, mutton-chopped member of the rock group Sorcery.

Ah, Sorcery. That unholy bastard son of Iron Maiden and David Copperfield, with a healthy dollop of Faustian D&D on the side. Formed in 1976, the LA-based combo was famous for its mind-blowing stage show, which consisted of the band ripping into numbers such as "Mark of the Beast" and "Burned Alive" (and "Stuntrocker," of course) while two magicians in the twin guises of a Merlin-like wizard and Old Scratch himself hurl fireballs at each other and employ other magical feats in service of depicting the age-old battle of good vs. evil. "Ladies and gentlemen, from Los Angeles, California . . . the Doors" kicked off that band's live shows, but Sorcery's is the infinitely more awesome "Prepare yourselves for a night of cosmic combat. A dual to the death to decide the fate of mankind . . . Ladies and gentlemen, Sorcery!"

Cousin Curtis is the magician that portrays the on-stage devil. (Really just by painting his face red. At least the Merlin magician put a little more effort into his look by donning the long white fake beard/hair combo to go with the cosmic-themed robe and conical hat.) As such, there's heaps of Page/Sorcery crossover, including Page joining the band onstage for a climactic stunt where the Devil sets a bound and hooded Page on fire (we're talking total immolation here), yet he reappears completely unscathed to zipline over the rapturous audience.

Because the film is meant as a showcase for Page and his daredevilry, the plot is about as thin as Louise Brooks' negligée.[38] It's all just a vehicle for Page to showcase one crackerjack stunt after another. This includes getting hit dead-on by a car going 60 mph in a televised stunt gone wrong, resulting in Page's head hitting the windshield dead-on, completely obliterating it. He's concussed and ordered to stay at Memorial Hospital for observation. Watching the bit on the local news is journalist Lois who's working on a story about people obsessed with their careers. She's intrigued by the daredevil and drives to the hospital just in time to witness him escaping out the window in nothing but a flimsy hospital gown. As the camera captures him shimmying down the wall, we're *this* close to seeing Page's grapes and sausage. And so is Lois.

It's one crazy stunt after another in *Stunt Rock*, all interspersed with footage of Sorcery both recording in the studio and rocking out on stage. There's also lots of recycled footage from other Page films such as *Mad Dog Morgan* and Trenchard-Smith's *Death Cheaters*. And even a little meta-commentary sprinkled in for good measure, exemplified when van de Ven's smarmy agent declares to Lois that "Stunt men are breakables . . . no one cares if they get hurt."

Ultimately, *Stunt Rock* is a bit of an outlier. The action doesn't come from a shredded, oiled-up combat veteran shooting squibs at a cascade of slovenly extras who then collapse immediately in a comical heap. Rather, the action is embodied in Grant Page himself: a man who, driven by adrenaline, ego, and a boatload of hubris, eschews safety and sanity to realize the moments we gasp at in the films we love. The stunt set pieces are outrageous, Sorcery's stage show is an astounding must-see spectacle unlike any other, and our leading man is a jovial sort of bloke from the land Down Under . . . the sort of bloke who does chin ups off the "H" in the Hollywood Sign for kicks. It's impossible not to be charmed by *Stunt Rock*, a scrappy, exhilarating little film that rocks as hard as it thrills.

THE PUMAMAN (1980)

Pumaman. The greatest copyright-infringing superhero creation of all time, able to run down perps in casual suede runners? Puma cats are speedy, cunning hunters, yet their namesake hero never breaks a stride north of brisk and seems to exist in a perpetual state of befuddlement. So much for a natural shoe marketing cash-in. Then again, bats navigate the world through echolocation and Batman doesn't, so what about that? Except Batman looks damn cool pounding on criminals while slow-of-foot Pumaman looks like a CPA on casual Friday.

Pumaman,
Pumaman,
Does whatever a Puma can,
He can fly overhead . . .

Hold on, pumas don't fly. And they can't teleport either. But Pumaman can. There's really no way around it. As far as superheroes go, animal-inspired or otherwise, you can't get much lamer than The Pumaman.

Dissatisfactory superheroes are as common as un-popped kernels in a bag of butter-saturated popcorn (*Condorman* anyone?), but when a hero's origin involves animals, spaceships, ancient gods, and an extinct civilization, you'd expect the result to be a little more dynamic than this prosciutto-fisted Italian production.

Opening on a glowing orange Christmas ornament spaceship hovering over a Stonehenge-like megalith more Spinal Tap than UNESCO, the camera focuses on a chintzy mask covered in gold-lamé foil as a booming voice bloviates:

> I speak to all humanity.[39] With this mask,[40] I will always be with you. My son will be its custodian as will be the sons of his sons. Through the ages, he will have the powers of a man-god. The power of The Pumaman . . . The Pumaman . . . The Pumaman.

The power of three. Popular even in outer space.

Now it goes without saying that so powerful an artifact would fall into nefarious hands, and indeed, in the next scene, the mask is being examined in the modern-day London lab of pleather-clad Kobras (the great Donald Pleasence, slumming in this Italian production that he cited as the worst film he's ever appeared in—and he was in *Halloween 5*!) and his similarly attired minions. Scientist Jane has discovered that the mask gives Kobras the power to control minds and communicate telepathically with anyone under his command, illustrated amusingly by wax effigies of his vassal's heads replete with red and blue coiled wires attached to the foreheads. And as is any megalomaniacal super-villain's want, he has designs on using this power to rule the world.[41]

But a savior awaits—The Pumaman! Trouble is, no one knows who the current incarnation of Pumaman is. Luckily, Vadinho, the formidable Aztec "high priest of the temple of the God that came from other worlds,"[42] is on the case with a foolproof, if not foolhardy, way of sussing out the current embodiment of the Aztec space-god warrior of truth and justice, and it involves throwing every American who has the misfortune of being the son of doctors *and* whose parents

perished in a plane crash out of high-rise windows until he finds the one who can survive the fall. And this is one of the good guys! Seems a little Draconian to us (a few simple questions really would have sufficed), but hey, you can't make that proverbial omelette without breaking at least a few eggs. (Or in this case four "americans" [*sic*] as the grammatically incorrect expository newspaper headline exclaims.)

Enter American in London Tony Farms. He's a paleontologist working in a London museum, and when Vadinho gives him the old heave-ho, he lands on his feet. Just like a cat! The one, the only, the preposterous . . . The Pumaman!

Now, there are a lot of stars-and-striped themed superheroes who look ready to throw down with "Japs" and "Krauts." But with his costume of khaki pants, an ugly brown shirt with an Aztec face sewn to the front, and a two-tone reversible cape which doubles as a poncho, Pumaman Tony looks like he's waging a war for '70s décor.

A hideous goblin-faced belt that looks like a cheap Chinese wresting belt replica completes the outfit, and suddenly Tony can fly. Trouble is, this "flying" is more like drowning in mid-air since this incarnation of Pumaman never seems to get the hang of zero gravity. ("You do not fly but your mind does," says Vadinho. Tony's mind must have been stuck on those plastic dinosaur bones he barely seemed to be working on back at the lab.)

Pumaman and Vadinho join forces to take down Kobras. This leads to laughable sights such as Pumaman (who now has—if not quite super—at least moderate strength) punching his way through conspicuously precut plywood walls. Witness also as Vadinho proves to be the much more powerful and capable fighter of the two. Makes you wonder why he even went to the trouble of finding Tony (and taking those innocent lives in the process) in the first place when it's blatantly obvious that the towering Aztec could have taken on the squat Kobras and his minions all by himself.

Pumaman the film earns a participation trophy, God bless it, but in the end, it's just too goofy to take seriously. The hero's powerset is laughable and not consistent with his animal namesake. ("Your hands are claws!" sure, but what mountain cat ever popped in and out of rooms like Salem S. on *Sabrina the Teenage Witch*?) Pleasence is game as always, but when he's holding an Aztec mask that seems to increase or decrease in size depending on the scene or trades in his pleather for a gold shark's tooth Nehru jacket, you can't help but snicker. Still, any movie that features a superhero flouncing mid-air with sci-fi "pwew-pwew" noises accompanying his heroics is worth at least one viewing, if only to verify that such an oddity actually exists.

THE ADVENTURES OF HERCULES (1985)

We can thank Cannon Films, that plucky, now-defunct studio owned by Israeli-expats Menahem Golan and Yoran Globus, (one of whom, sadly, is also defunct) for some of the goofiest films of the 1980s. Never meeting a genre they didn't like (or at least felt they could exploit for maximum lucre), Cannon pretty much single-handedly ignited the Reagan era's ravenous appetite for all things ninja with Sho Kosugi's *Enter the Ninja* and its subsequent sequels. In 1983, hoping to capitalize on *Conan the Barbarian*, Cannon stepped into the sword and sandal world with its rendition of *Hercules*. Looking to reap Cimmerian sword-sized grosses with a film budgeted for less than the cost of three of James Earl Jones' Thulsa Doom wigs, producers tapped the second-most famous former Mr. Olympia turned terrible actor, *Incredible Hulk* Lou Ferrigno, to portray the umpteenth cinematic incarnation of the Greek mythological hero.

Hercules the first was a delightful medley of subpar acting, ridiculous exposition, atrocious special effects, and Sybil Danning's heaving bosom, themselves a kind of special effect. Despite a tepid box-office reception, the film did eke out just enough to warrant a sequel, much to the delight of the two-dozen or so who didn't get enough Ferrigno sweaty-pic action in the first film. Those special people were rewarded with 1985's *The Adventures of Hercules*, and anyone who suspected that the makers of the 1983 film were a little cukcoo-for-Cocoa-Puffs had their suspicions confirmed completely and then some, for *Hercules* the sequel is even more stupendously demented than its already pretty-damn ludicrous predecessor.

Like the original, *Adventures* begins with a wonky, blah-de-blah-blah-blah prologue detailing the origin of the cosmos. The gods still reside in space, but Earth has been circling the drain for the last several years because Zeus's seven mighty thunderbolts were stolen from him during an uprising of jealous gods. The bolts have been hidden away and the destructive forces of anger and chaos have been unleashed on Earth. As if this isn't enough, the moon is on a collision course with Earth which will lead to the destruction of all planets and living things. Somewhere Neil deGrasse Tyson is shaking his head.

We soon see a bound slave girl taken toward an altar where she is to be sacrificed to Antius the Firemaster. Resplendent in his red wig, feather boa, and haphazardly applied makeup, the one who controls Antius bears a shocking resemblance to late comedienne Phyllis Diller. Antius is summoned, and what could be best described as a giant blue cartoon consumes the poor slave girl whole. This act of unbridled brutality is witnessed by two scantily clad females who are lamenting their fates among the gods, Urania and Glaucia. Besides having monikers that sound like painful medical conditions, the ladies also serve to propel the plot much more than Herc in this one.

The fairer haired of the two, Urania, treks to a blood-red Stonehenge replica where she prays to the fairies, referred to as "little people" throughout the film. Two horribly rendered optical effects appear and spout a bunch of nonsense about destiny, cosmic forces, and the way to properly prepare and cook a Thanksgiving turkey. (OK, maybe not that last one, but in a movie as insane as this, if it were to be included, it wouldn't seem a damn sight out of place.)

Meanwhile, Zeus finally decides to get off his skinny tush and send his champion Hercules

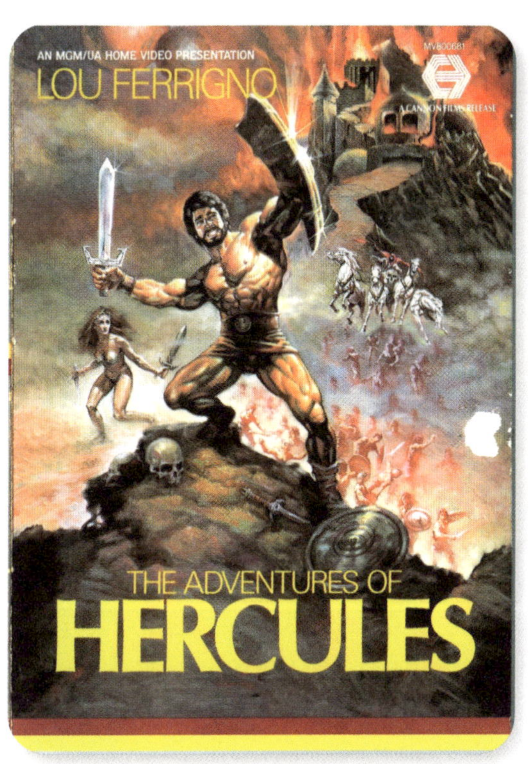

back to Earth to retrieve the seven thunderbolts and prevent chaos from engulfing the planets. Why now? What in Olympus's name was Zeus doing in the last seven years while Earth was going down the shitter? Binge watching *Game of Thrones*?

Herc teleports from space to Earth, and before he is given even a single second to recover from what must be a severe case of space lag, he is beset upon by a giant shag carpet with a baboon face. He dispatches the monster with ease, which then disappears into the ether, leaving behind one of the thunderbolts. One down, six to go!

But do the gods take kindly to this act of heroism? Heck no! Instead, they take conspiratory meetings on an intergalactic mesa situated in front of what looks like a giant bagel hanging overhead. They even go so far as to resurrect Minos, the big baddie from the first film, to assist them. Yet Minos has designs of his own and plots with Dedalos, the goddess of Chaos, Disaster and, um, Science, to overthrow the gods in Science's name. Dedalos, another refugee from the first film, is a beautiful woman clad in a ludicrous costume which features a highly distracting bulbous codpiece as its most prominent design feature.

In their continuing quest to retrieve the bolts, Herc, Urania, and Glaucia encounter rubber-suited slime monsters, human glow sticks, masked Amazon warriors clearly portrayed by men, and a Claymation Gorgon. Eventually, Hercules meets Minos in a climactic space battle where they summon "pure energy" and transform into early Atari 2600 video game characters. During the battle, Hercules's energy avatar becomes a giant gorilla, and Minos's, a dinosaur, thus giving the audience the cheapest version of King Kong vs. Godzilla ever committed to celluloid.

The Adventures of Hercules is one of the more ludicrous films in this book (and that's really saying something!) Nonetheless, like eating Taco Bell when high as fiddlesticks, it's so audaciously bad, it transcends badness and becomes really, really tasty. And you won't hate yourself afterward.

CONQUEST (1983)

In Lucio Fulci's *The Senator Likes Women*, a.k.a. *The Eroticist*, there are elaborate dream sequences where the protagonist humps giant behinds and plays with apple bottoms (actual apples) in some "Baby Got Back" Garden of Eden. And yet the Italian director who also did kid's movies (!) (*White Fang*) and westerns (*Four of the Apocalypse*) didn't become infamous for bigging up butts—it was for horror.

His 1979 opus *Zombie*, a gorefest *sans pareil*, shocked audiences worldwide with a sanguinary splatterfest chock-a-block with rotting, maggot-infested corpses, rendered flesh, body parts munched on like hors d'oeuvres at a dinner party, and ocular trauma aplenty. It was far beyond George A. Romero's relatively genteel *Night of the Living Dead* and created a subgenre all its own.

Then it was one stone-cold classic gothic gore pic after another, with movies such as *The Beyond* and *The New York Ripper* earning the director both raves and derision in equal measure, as well as the sobriquet "Godfather of Gore."

Perhaps sensing a break from horror was needed, Fulci turned his hand to the *peplum* genre with 1983's *Conquest*, his first action film. Peplum, in a nutshell, are Italian films featuring characters in animal furs and leather tunics who wield giant swords, and buxom babes who wear serpent bustiers to highlight heaving bosoms. And for some reason, there's also a preponderance of squawking birds. And even when armed with bows, arrows, and the finest steel-forged weaponry around, people still gnaw meat right off the bone as if they've never heard of a knife. But it's more than that. Peplum is basically a deity smoothie. Throw in as many mythical figures from antiquity as you like and hit "puree."

The idea of melding Fulci's gore and exploitation sensibilities with Italy's cottage industry of *Conan the Barbarian* rip-offs was one perfect in theory but perhaps a bit flawed in practice, and *Conquest* left many an audience member scratching their head. Now Fulci was never the most literal-minded storyteller to begin with, even in his prime, but *Conquest*, both aesthetically and narratively, is pretty darn inscrutable. To begin, there's the cinematography. Fulci and his cinematographer used soft-focus lenses and a plethora of fog machines in an attempt to achieve a dreamlike atmosphere. Dreamlike it might have been, but it also resulted in images so muted, most viewers would spend their entire viewing time adjusting the picture settings on their TVs. And that's during the daytime scenes. For the nighttime scenes, well, good luck making out anything at all. It's all just one hazy shade of Hyboria.

We begin right in the thick of the effluvium, like Queen's "Fat Bottom Girls," with "*just a skinny lad/never knew no good from bad.*" That's Ilias, standing there with his *Welcome Back Kotter* coif as he's fitted with a leather tunic and bequeathed a magical, ancestral bow. He's a so-called exemplar of "bravery amongst men," and his gift-giver is his Zeus-like father Cronos. And with a hearty "fare thee well," Ilias is sent off on a heroic quest so indeterminable, someone named Cronos should've known to put a time limit on it. But it's also likely Cronos deemed it high time that his freeloading bum of a son leave the house already and assumed that vague talk of "path[s] of courage and sacrifice" would be just the key to do it. For his part, brave Ilias looks about as disoriented as the audience surely must have felt.

Then there's the evil queen Ocron (sword-and-sandal regular Sabriani Siani), ruler of the sun "who can make night into day," a power which doesn't sound evil at all. It's actually quite nice. She prances around a mountaintop in nothing but a G-string—attire that easily transitions from day into night, even if the cinematography doesn't—her identity concealed by a mask of gold. (Her only outfit for the entire film. Now that's how you save on wardrobe costs!) She also commands a hirsute army of wolf warriors that meld the body of post-transformation *Teen Wolf* Michael J. Fox with the face of Chewbacca. The pack attacks Ilias's homestead for reasons unknown, and in a gloriously violent scene, one of the lupine warriors knocks Cronos's scalp clean off with one awesomely swift blow of a club. The pack then grabs a fleeing naked woman (presumably Cronos' wife) and quarters her with their bare hands (not wanting to waste any time drawing her). All this to bring her severed head back to Ocron, who bashes in the skull and consumes the brains with relish (as in her manner of consumption, not the condiment, although one does tend to wonder from time to time how human brain would taste between a bun).

Anyhow, whether it's a result of eating grey matter so perilously close to bedtime, the effects of the unexplained substance she snorts, or a combination thereof, Ocron's nighttime repose is far from restful. She writhes around in orgasmic ecstasy as a snake slithers atop her nude body, fantasizing of a future time when "the wanderer" Ilias will assassinate her with one of his magically manifesting blue arrows, which, according to Cronos, are made of flames and come straight from the sun, making the fact that they're baby blue and look and sound like lasers rather befuddling. Obviously unnerved, the queen puts a hit out on young Ilias.

Now, any youngster out alone on his first heroic journey (and really, you never do forget your first) could really use a friend, and it's just that that Ilias finds in tall, chiseled lone-wolf warrior Mace, a character whose looks are much more suited to a film of this ilk than the raw-boned dilettante we're supposed to follow. He even has a cooler weapon: not a mace as his name would imply, but a nunchuck-like device made from human bones, which he uses to take out the entire wolf army while our ostensible hero, who has done little to nothing heroic thus far, gets knocked out faster than Michael Spinks taking on Mike Tyson. Nonetheless, the much more formidable Mace takes a shine to Ilias and offers to take him to the not-at-all-inscrutable destination of "wherever our feet can carry us."

This, of course, shall not do, so to stymie the happy wanderers, Ocron turns her pet dog—a sweetly panting husky—into the all-powerful Zora, the cactus-faced commander of "the darkest and most dreadful creatures of the earth." He agrees to help her as long as she pledges herself to him, body and soul. Which she does . . . to a dog. We'd say that's wrong but who are we to disparage the sexual proclivities of scantily clad masked demigods? For his part, Zora has our heroes do battle with muck encrusted zombies of the deep and a bunch of white silly-string covered monsters that bear more than a slight resemblance to Frosty the Snowman.

It's all gonna come down to a *mano e mano* between one of our heroes and the evil queen. In the climactic battle, Ocron gets her mask knocked off, revealing that she too is a dog. Literally speaking, of course, as actress Sabrina Siani is an exceedingly beautiful woman.

Despite it's considerable eccentricities, lack of discernible storyline, and myopic *mise en scène*, the super-brutal *Conquest* is still fifty shades of awesome, even if those shades can't be distinguished from one another.

SINBAD OF THE SEVEN SEAS (1989)

Sinbad of the Seven Seas is yet another adaptation of that intrepid sailor of Arabian lore and legend. You know, the *othe*r famous sailor (not the spinach-eating one). The one who sails the high seas engaging in magic and adventure, resplendent in his golden turban and MC Hammer parachute pants. The one who uses his chiselled physique, cheese grater abs, and superhuman strength to . . . Wait. Let's back up a bit. Never in the history of Sinbad adaptations has the character ever displayed anything more than a whit of strength beyond slightly above average. Unique fashion sense sure, but super strength? Never.

But if you're going to deviate that far from the source material, you might as well get the strongest guy you can find. Yes, Hercules's Lou Ferrigno is also Sinbad, here minus a turban, but sporting a fulsome Hasselhoff-style bouffant 'do while running about half naked with nothing to keep him warm during those Arabian Nights. Alas, the sartorial splendor of Sinbad has been jettisoned along with all fidelity to the source material. Also, like Ferrigno's *Hercules*, it's a Cannon production shot in Italy with an Italian director and a predominantly Italian cast. (Enzo G. Castlellari, director of the original *The Inglorious Bastards*, is the credited director. He handed in three hours of what the studio deemed un-releasable footage, so Luigi Cozzi, *Hercules* director and *Sinbad* cowriter, was brought in to clean up the mess.[43] And that's probably why *Sinbad,* like *Hercules*, is nuttier than a squirrel's hidey-hole in the doldrums of December.)

The film kicks off with a static shot of legendary scribe Edgar Allan Poe and that hoary standby of cinematic exposition, the text crawl, informing us that the tale we're about to witness is based on Poe's atypical non-horror story "The Thousand and Second Tale of Scheherazade." Great! We love ourselves some Eddie. Yet what follows bears little resemblance to the yarn in any shape, form, or fashion. So why the deception? This is a Cannon film starring a guy most famous for throwing Styrofoam boulders around while slathered in green greasepaint. Knowing that, there really is no need to appeal to the literati. Ferrigno plus Cannon invariably equals *fromage*, so invoking and besmirching (by association) the good name of "The Raven" writer is gratuitous at best and befuddling at worst.

And speaking of both literature and befuddling, *Sinbad* opens with a gender-swapped framing device lifted wholesale from *The Princess Bride*—here a young girl tucked into an extremely uncomfortable looking bed demanding her mom read her a bedtime story. Happy to oblige, Mom pulls a hefty tome off the shelf and regales her (Cozzi's real-life daughter) with a tale from a time when "our earth was such a very little lonely grain of sand lost in a myriad of stars." A poetic description to be sure, but it makes our planet sound like a cosmic Orphan Annie. There, "the greatest man ever born"[44] sails the seven seas, accompanied by his "brave friends," who a) are pretty much useless on their own, continually getting captured and requiring rescue, and b) have names that when put together sound like the most poorly conceived, politically incorrect boy band ever: The young prince Ali, the bald cook Ahmed, the Chinese Soldier of Fortune, the Viking Warrior, and the *pièce de résistance*, Poochie the Dwarf, really just a man of slightly below average height.[45]

While Sinbad and crew were away, the evil wizard Jaffar, trusted vizier to the kind and wise Kalif of Basra, unleashed the forces of the Lord of Darkness upon the land, marked by winds knocking over stalls in the market, people running around haphazardly while bumping into each other, and little else. Soon, Jaffar is controlling the Kalif's mind. And he has the Kalif's daughter, also betrothed to the young prince Ali, abducted and strapped to a machine that looks like something out of a seventh-grade science fair exhibit. The wicked Jaffar has also appropriated the source of the Kalif's strength, the sacred gems of Basra. Thus, it falls on Sinbad and his merry man to retrieve those gems if order is ever to be restored to their fair city.

Good setup for an adventure, no? Well, it's serviceable at least, if not a bit road-tested since the retrieval of magical doohickeys also propels the plot of *The Adventures of Hercules*. And before Sinbad can even hoist sail, he must escape from Jaffar's trapdoor dungeon. Luckily, this Sinbad also has a little Dr. Doolittle in him, making fast friends with a cobra. Sinbad bonds with his "new friend" by opining that snakes have gotten a bad rap ever since that no-good Eve took that verboten apple bite. Finally understood after all these years, a dozen blatantly rubber-looking snakes soon surround the jacked-up Pied Piper, and Sinbad commemorates his new friendship by tying the poor reptiles together into one long rope for escape. That he ties the creatures together using what has to be extremely painful knots, then leaves them in that state once he's escaped, says a lot about this Sinbad's conception of friendship. At least he rescues his other friends from certain death by piranha, using his incredible might to break the painfully obviously plastic chains (sensing a trend here) that Jaffar's guards attempt to bind him with.

Most of the film depicts Sinbad and his crew sailing from land to land, trying to retrieve the magical gems and fighting all sorts of bargain basement looking monsters, including a creature made of rock who is bested by having rocks hurled at him. Wow. You'd think a giant piece of living rock would be impervious to his own makeup. But that would make sense, and truthfully, little in this movie does. There's also evil dancing amazons to contend with, reanimated knights perched atop ghostly steeds, and the big boss, a potbellied creature that looks like an assemblage of slime-covered Hefty bags. Sinbad's men do help when they can—the Viking Warrior wields a pretty nifty weapon that has a club on one end and a mace on the other, and the Chinese Soldier of Fortune, when not spouting maxim malapropisms wrongly attributed to Confucius, is no slouch with his fists and feet[46]—but it's really all the Sinbad show. So, if you've ever longed to see Lou Ferrigno swing a human battering ram over his head, wrestle a horse, or take on his own evil doppelganger in a homoerotic grappling contest, then either your clozapine has worn off or you're the right audience for this film. It's a toss up.

And no discussion of *Sinbad of the Seven Seas* would be complete without bringing up the glory that is actor John Steiner (*Yor, the Hunter from the Future*) as the villainous Jaffar. Here, Steiner devours the scenery like Kobayashi guzzling hot dogs. With his pointed nails and goatee, black robe and eyeliner, Steiner certainly looks the part as he delivers preposterously purple prose such as "The city of Basra . . . is a great ripe plum waiting to be pluck [sic]. Grant that it is my hand that plucks it," with Shakespearean gusto. He even has a sidekick in the form of a female bodybuilder, *The Alienator* herself, Teagan, as the sorceress Soukra, who stands around in a dominatrix outfit, not doing anything else of value except for continually chiding Jaffar that all his machinations are useless anyway since Sinbad is gonna get him in the end. With sidekicks like that, honestly, who needs enemies?

Sinbad of the Seven Seas is a goofy blast that would make a tremendous triple-bill with the two Cannon *Hercules* films. All are wonderfully daft, and you have to wonder which legendary hero Ferrigno would have been tapped to play next if Cannon Films had managed to avoid insolvency. Captain Nemo, perhaps? Beowulf? The Big Bad Wolf?

NINE

COVERT OPS

AND THE LORD SPOKE TO MOSES, SAYING, "SEND MEN TO SPY OUT THE LAND OF CANAAN."

—BOOK OF NUMBERS

Cyber espionage and spy satellites mean that, these days, the oft-used technique of finding attractive foreign agents, bedding them, and then pressing them for intel is a thing of the past. And that's a shame, as erectile dysfunction meds have easily kept up with advances in cyber technology. Still, there's nothing like boots on the ground, a passable accent, cunning, and—let's be honest—a death wish. Crimes against the state are taken very seriously, indeed. So, while action stars of other chapters may get off with misdemeanor assault or a lifetime ban from owning firearms or having a driver's license, that's nothing compared with courting US military detention, the death penalty, or worse. Actually, that's just an expression: there's not much worse than that.

Luckily, there are slightly less dangerous options than espionage in covert ops that don't require passports, foreign language mastery, or adjusting to international time zones.

"Covert" is a weird word in that, if you take the "c" away, it means the opposite. Regardless, clandestine operations are common in action movies, and we're not talking about midday trysts when the husband is away (although those sometimes occur, too).

Covert ops can take many forms. There's the guy who tries to stuff himself with bologna sandwiches to get in good with the mafia right down to the special ops forced to be a con to infiltrate a nasty prison gang.

In this chapter, the suspension of disbelief is so great you'll need a crane. For example, in *Crackerjack 3*, ex-intelligence ops go undercover as garden gnome deliverymen to infiltrate a high-stakes *G7* meeting in Germany, using only two German language words.

Our favorite undercover gambit by far is donning doctors' scrubs for one of those finish-the-job hospital assassinations. Putting on medical attire means automatic carte blanche access in any hospital in the world. Add a clipboard and stethoscope to the disguise and you could probably infiltrate the Centers for Disease Control. After all, who needs photo ID in a place where life and death literally occur when you can just waltz around in a lab coat?

Use an assumed name, get a fake passport, and join us as we dive into the world of cloak-and-dagger.

INVASION USA (1985)

Matt Hunter leaves so much destruction in his wake, he should come with a weather warning. It's Chuck Norris, for Chrissakes.

Hunter is a sure-shot former CIA man with roundhouse kicks so formidable, they could instantly annihilate all Chuck Norris Fact memes.

When we're first introduced to him under the blazing Florida sun, he's doing every manly activity possible short of punching out a bear—and probably would've done that too if the lumbering mammal wasn't the focus of state conservation efforts. Either way, Hunter chops wood, lassoes a gator, and then steers an air boat through a smelly ammonia swamp, his chest protruding like a conquering white trash general.

That's certainly enough to work up a macho appetite.

Back at his Everglades homestead, Hunter grouses, "God, I'm sick of frogs," when a sociable rube of a neighbor offers him the Bayou delicacy three ways *Master Chef*-style: "fried, steamed, barbecued—your choice."

But anyone who rocks that formidable a beard and full denim; who blows away baddies with twin Uzis fired from custom shoulder rigs (with nary a pit stain to be seen), can eat when and what he wants.

Invasion USA is peculiar, with a wacky and very paranoid premise—the product of Cold War-era braindead brainstorming—a Cannon production cowritten by Chuck's younger brother Aaron.

Just so we're all clear, this is what happens: Communist guerillas dressed as US Coast Guard personnel butcher a bunch of Cuban boat people, trade blow for high-powered weapons, and attempt the movie's title . . . an "Invasion USA" right there on the sandy beaches.

The guerillas are led by, what else, an evil Russian mastermind named Rostov, who orchestrates the beach landing, which then morphs into an urban massacre as Cuban expats are gunned down by perps in disguise as Miami's finest.

This by land assault is an odd strategy to say the least.

Last time we checked *Wikipedia*, the US Army had 475,000 active personnel. Exactly what kind of offensive two hundred ethnic stereotype militiamen could mount against such a global superpower is unclear. Still, it's not really about half a million fighting men or the invaders. After all, Chuck Norris alone is worth a thousand enlisted men and then some.

Still, you can't fault the plucky commie upstarts for trying, as they blow up every third suburban Florida homestead with rocket launchers before the reticent Hunter guns and glowers them into submission, forced out of CIA retirement to do what only Chuck Norris can do.

In two off-the-charts scenes, a barfly who messes with Hunter gets his own beer bottle crushed in the vice that is a Norris handshake, and a hooker gets a coke straw rammed up her honker by an evil goon.

But those unforgettable set pieces don't even crack the medal podium, as this is a movie where Hunter, after gunmen storm a shopping center, drives a pickup truck through a Christmas mall-Santa display, making hood ornaments out of a dozen useless henchmen. Step aside *Die Hard*: this is the quintessential Yuletide film for the ages.

The Sunshine State quickly declares martial law, which shouldn't be too tough to enforce as most of Florida's residents are retirees or illegal. Regardless,

Hunter IS the law. No baddie is safe from this aggressively trigger-happy an opponent, a guy who makes Bronson look retiring and measured.

He sends bad men to kingdom come with steely glares and Uzis, 'Nam-era anti-tank ordnances, M16s, grenade launchers, fists, elbows, roundhouse kicks, and finally, side kicks (he even front-kicks an antagonist through an office cubicle). The insurance claims levied against this man must number in the millions of dollars, and all this carnage while calmly promising one helpless ruffian "I am gonna hit you with so many rights, you are going to beg for a left."

Valour, thy name is Matt Hunter, a man so formidable he is literally a nightmare to deal with, plaguing the dreams of even the most battle-hardened of Russian supervillains. And we failed to mention, he also saves a school bus full of innocent kids from being bombed to oblivion by chasing down the vehicle and disarming the incendiary device, all from the comfort of his pickup.

Chuck Norris can diffuse IEDs without even leaving the confines of his own vehicle. Take that, *Hurt Locker*.

CRACKERJACK 3 (2000)

Not prejudiced by having watched either of the first two *Crackerjacks*, we came at this film fresh, albeit expecting the drop-off that usually occurs in any film's third installment. But boy is this one Victoria Falls. (And we're going out on a limb here by saying *Crackerjacks 1* and *2* were not exactly *The Godfather*). We did, however, tap into the notoriously fickle *IMDb* brain trust where one armchair faultfinder opined, "If I see another film that's worse, I'd be very surprised."

While a lot of verbal inflation is commonplace on that site's reviews, he (or possibly a she) hit the bull's-eye on this misfire. Even after dredging up the worst of the worst, we still somehow suctioned *Crackerjack 3* from the muddy river bottom of bad movies.

Genre legend Bo Svenson stars, a guy whose face needs dry cleaning, it has so many creases. And we say this with all due respect to the ex-Marine and judo black belt who could likely lob us through drywall. He's a veteran of hundreds of TV and film roles over four decades of near-constant work, most notably in *North Dallas Forty, The Inglorious Bastards* and *Walking Tall Part II.*

Here, Svenson is Jack Thorn. He's exiting a high-profile CIA gig to retire to his shack in the Vermont woods for some fly fishing, contemplation, and days spent wearing cable knit sweaters. His replacement, the puffed-up Marcus Clay, is part of a "new wave of money managers" the CIA is hiring—and is CANADIAN. Now we realize Drake and Justin Bieber are undercover ops invading our stateside neighbors from deep within the bowels of the entertainment industry, but this is ridiculous. The *absolute minimum* requirement when it comes to working for the civilian foreign intelligence service of the United States should be holding an American passport. Still, when you've already cast French kickboxer Olivier Gruner in the role, you have to explain him and his accent away somehow. (Although they could've done one better and explain his dialogue; the man makes Van Damme sound like Demosthenes, emphasizing the second syllable in "eCONomic," for example, making it sound like someone is swindling an Irishman with an ethnic slur.)

Part of the Agency's new MO, apparently, is not only hiring foreign nationals with English diction poor enough to disqualify them from leading bus tours but also phasing out all covert ops maneuvers. And that means putting the likes of Jack and his old-school spying methods out to pasture. (One of the sad running gags is Jack's inability to use a cellphone, which does not auger well for anyone in the intelligence community.)

On Day One of retirement in New England, Jack is fishing in what looks like a sump or a tar pond, which speaks to *Crackerjack 3*'s low budget and resolute lack of location scouting. Two assassins skulking about and not yet felled by fumes emitted from the toxic remediation site passed off as a fishing hole are hot on Jack's tail. Luckily, bombshell assistant Kelly saves the day, as she's been tracking her ex-boss with high-tech satellite systems after he'd tossed his newfangled phone technology into the Vermont woods in frustration.

She shoots one assassin dead, and angler Jack casts his lure into the mouth of the second hiding behind a tree, reeling him in like a large mouth bass.

He hauls the catch into his cabin, ties him to a chair, then calls in a group of comrades for assistance: a rag-tag group of retired Eastern bloc spy types from East Germany, Cuba, and Russia, none of whom convincingly hail from any of those places but come complete with accents that might materialize after bar shots with frat guys.

They hold a lengthy debate on how best to torture, then extract information from the prisoner, whom we find out is the improbably named Griswald. Not quite the surname of choice for a global financier conspirer nor an assassin.

After much reminiscing about torture methods they specialized in before these fell out of favor . . . oh wait . . . Gitmo . . . ah, never mind, the spy vets eventually decide on a potent drug cocktail that makes Griswald think he's dancing at the Bolshoi! But luckily, not before they extract pertinent info from him about the theft of a neutron bomb by a Griswald associate, part of a scheme to short-sell the international markets after causing a financial meltdown, in this case blowing up a meeting of G7 finance ministers in Germany.

All signs of the warhead theft point to an inside job, the new CIA hire, obvious to anyone who by this point hasn't keeled face first into the sofa from boredom. Besides, Marcus has got a French accent, so he's all but doomed to action movie villainy. But the Gallic schemer has beaten Jack to the punch, incriminating the old-timer because he has the clearance level to know where and when the nuke was being transported and also happened to have the day off when the heist occurred! We have to keep reminding ourselves that this is a film dealing with matters of intelligence. You'd think the CIA would've investigated matters further, asking for Jack to provide an alibi that day, you know . . .an alibi—"a claim or piece of evidence that one was elsewhere when an act, typically a criminal one, is alleged to have taken place."

Jack immediately regrets ceding control to the crooked Canadian. Now it's up to the retiree, his brunette assistant, and his four Cold War holdover buddies to rush to Europe, clear Jack's name, and save the day.

Crackerjack 3 is no prize when it comes to visual style. Our heroes fly to Germany aboard "Air Fidel," a commandeered Cuban jet with a high school boiler room interior. Maybe commie austerity can be forgiven, but when it comes to *mise en scène*, the CIA hub makes the digs in *Glengarry Glen Ross* look like Facebook headquarters. It's decorated with cheapo *National Geographic* maps and looks more like somewhere stolen credit cards are processed.

But what really puts *Crackerjack 3* into another stratosphere of oxygen-depleted stupidity is the scheme to infiltrate the G7 meeting and disarm the bomb. This involves the crack team going undercover as garden gnome deliverymen!

The German spy has a side business, as a kind of Kris Kringle of child labor exploitation, getting youngsters to paint porcelain gnomes in an abandoned warehouse which also conveniently happens to have a cache of weapons. Speaking *"Ja und Nein"* German you usually get from a bunch of Englishmen in a WWII period piece, the group bypasses G7 security detail, who have no questions for the guys in German or otherwise, setting up a big showdown between Marcus and Jack.

And FYI, Jack eventually does develop cell phone end-user competency. More competency than *Crackerjack 3* director Lloyd A. Simandl developed in his entire career, which encompassed films as diverse as the post-apocalyptic *Empire of Ash III* (which was the direct sequel to the director's dreadful *Empire of Ash*; *Empire of Ash II* being the original film rereleased and retitled the following year) and the depressing Brigitte Nielsen starrer *Chained Heat II*.

SKIN TRAFFIK, A.K.A. A HITMAN IN LONDON (2015)

It's said that neurons that fire together wire together. That's the basis of learning. And what we learned is that *Skin Traffik* is as braindead as they come.

Mickey Rourke, Michael Madsen, Daryl Hannah, Eric Roberts, and Jeff Fahey would have been an all-star cast—in 1983. Oh, how the mighty have fallen. Once, Rourke, Hannah, and Roberts toplined the critically acclaimed and Oscar-nominated *The Pope of Greenwich Village*. Thirty years later and they're barely keeping their heads above water in this straight-to-video stinker, all three the unfortunate victims of a cut-rate cosmetic surgeon's knife. And their punch-the-clock acting is no better than their horrific, begging-to-be-featured-on-an-episode-of-*Botched* visages. *Skin Traffik* (a.k.a. *A Hitman in London*) has so much scenery chewing, it needs a dental plate.

The promotional artwork is Seagal-esque. Never a good sign. But instead of the ponytailed Guru of Glacial, the more Expendable (and less expensive *Expendable*) kickboxer Gary Daniels stars. He plays Bradley, a hitman mixed up in a human smuggling ring that is so dangerous, it manages to displace the letter *C* with a *K* in the film's title.

We're embarrassed to say we're quite familiar with Daniels' work via his appearance alongside ex-pro wrestler "Stone Cold" Steve Austin in the appalling straight-to-video clunker *Hunt to Kill* (as if there's ever any other type—until sustainable hunting becomes a thing, no big-game hunter will ever venture forth with the intent to merely graze an elephant or leave an antelope with a flesh wound.) Here, Daniels is burdened with executing the entire range of his craft—first by looking stoic, then pensive, back to stoic, then pensive again while occasionally leaping sideways and firing off some rounds. That's our favorite action cliché. Well, that and nameless henchmen flying face forward in a parabolic arc off a fire escape or catwalk after being shot rather than simply crumpling into a bloodied heap as common physics would dictate.

In *Skin Traffik*, Mickey Rourke is Vogel, which means bird in German. Appropriate as Rourke, like the proverbial phoenix, was reborn in *The Wrestler*. It seemed then that his career was back on track, but like that other figure of myth Icarus, he soon came crashing down with a thud. Here he flames out badly. And his face is so pancaked with foundation, it needs a cascade of syrup and a side of blueberries.

Vogel is a London gangster in possession of a "disk" (basically the other spy movie MacGuffin that isn't a secret dossier). And hitman Bradley's job is to procure the disk. But something (as always) goes terribly wrong.

There's an obstacle in Bradley's path besides Vogel: a slew of goonish human trafficking baddies. Bradley lays waste to most of them, then finds himself the unwilling guardian of a Russian prostitute whose sister has been turned out in Amsterdam.

She has a Russian pimp named Sergei whose accent is more *Star Trek*'s Chekov than Chekhov, and this film boldly goes to various locales (Holland/UK) as if it were some kind of internationalist spy caper. It isn't. It's more bomb than Bond.

Mickey Rourke is *literally* in this movie for a cup of coffee. He takes a few swigs, mumbles an inane speech, and then summarily disappears (probably to fire his agent).

From what we can gather (and it's *all* we can gather for wont of a hearing aid), Hannah's Zhanna and Madsen's The Boss oversee a global sex trade ring. They meet in a London bar to discuss their nefarious operations, but it's nigh impossible to hear their dialogue over the cacophony of the eardrum-crushing soundtrack. In some movies, *Dolemite* a prime example, the boom mike sneakily worms its way into the frame. That gaffe is more forgivable than *Skin Traffik*, where the boom mike appears to have been forgotten entirely.

Through some complex machination, we find out that the trafficking *cappo di tutti cappi* is Eric Roberts, who leads an Illuminati-type organization called The Executive. If he were a member of an acting executive, the Board of Directors would seek his replacement. He mostly sits behind a desk grinning that unsettlingly toothy grin that is a trademark of the Roberts' acting clan.

With a body count rivaling The Bard's finest work, this tragedy ends up in a showdown between Bradley and The Executive in an airplane hangar. Why? Because it's an alternative to an abandoned warehouse, the lousy action movie locale *de rigueur* when a bunch of people need to shoot each other. Guns drawn, pistols at dawn. One big yawn.

Skin Traffik is worth seeing if only for Madsen's zany World War II speech about a German army division's hats! That and Robert's quizzical

inquiry as to whether Bradley has access to the "World Wide Web." In 2015!?! Never mind the fact that every soul on the planet has Internet access right in their purse or pockets, but honestly, who other than perhaps Al Gore refers to the internet as the World Wide Web? If only we were making this up.

ANGEL OF DESTRUCTION (1994)

What's scary is just how un-scary action villains are. Bombastic sure. Megalomaniacal, of course. Insane, yes. Cool? Always. Some are. Think Andrew Robinson as the unhinged Scorpio in *Dirty Harry* or Brian Thompson as the relentless Night Slasher in *Cobra*. But soil-your-undergarments, I-better-cross-the-street-if-this-guy's-coming scary? Rarely. That's probably why they need to hide behind "muscle," a strange word to describe henchmen in the '80s and early '90s, as nobody seemed to be acquainted with free weights.

Robert Kell in *Angel of Destruction* is *scary*. He's a hulking ex-mercenary with a blond buzz who just oozes malevolence, or as much malevolence as you can ooze wearing pleated dress pants. He wreaks business casual destruction. Kell is played by Jimmy Broome, whose mob name would surely be . . . Jimmy Broome. He's an actor who never appeared in any other film. And that's too bad as he acquits himself sublimely here.

We begin with Kell entering a hotel, lady of the evening in tow. He tells her to wait on the bed; he forgot something in the car. But instead of heading to his vehicle, he knocks on another door, then utterly destroys the room's occupants. He kicks one unfortunate over a table, judo-flips another onto a nightstand, and punches one guy so many times, it starts to look like a *Three Stooges* bit. Kell's quarry is Karl. "You left my men to die in Angola," sneers Kell. He then slugs him flush in the face so hard, everything we know about forward momentum goes out the window, along with Karl. For some reason the punch sends Karl hurtling outside face forward even as his back was to the pane! Luckily, many viewers will already be distracted by the fact that there was an obvious visible roof there earlier which would've broken his fall. Kell also kills his female companion and cuts off her finger.

But the film is called *Angel of Destruction*, so there must be an angel. And in action films, "Angel" in the title invariably means there'll be a darn formidable female protagonist. (See *Angel Fist, Avenging Angel,* and *Angel Terminators*.) This *Angel* is undercover cop (or as undercover as you can be in a parade of midriff baring outfits) Jo Alwood, capably played by Maria Ford. Jo works in Hawaii, but standing in for the fiftieth state is that most chameleonic of countries, The Philippines. What do you expect? This film was produced by both Roger Corman *and* Cirio Santiago. The Philippines is a given with that combo.

To the apparent rescue? Brit, a private investigating ballbuster in aviators on the hunt for a girl roped into the sex trade. She's strong, adept, and efficient, able to handily beat the five guys holding the girl she's seeking. Might have made sense to have her the hero, but this is a Corman production. He may be the King of the Bs but only a C cup will do!

Also, because this is a Corman production, the next scene will take place in a strip club. Actually, just a regular nightclub, but there soon will be some stripping. For on stage is international pop superstar Delilah, a singer whose stage show features a blonde in skimpy lingerie tied to a wooden chair, trussed, and gagged. As Delilah sings the ear-splitter "Are You Chained?" she removes the girl from her tethers, then removes the girl from her top. The identically clad Delilah is then helped out of her top while she keeps singing. And in which world would an act like

this be allowed to put on shows anywhere outside of a gentleman's club? Forget it Jake, it's Corman-Town. Of course, an act such as this might attract the wrong sort of fan, and oops, psycho Kell is one of them. He sneaks into Delilah's dressing room to leave her a giftbox containing that severed finger.

Now fearful, Delilah and her blonde stage partner Reena hire the tough damsel from before to guard their bodies. Turns out she's Jo's stepsister. And the two are talking on the phone when Kell walks into Brit's office and ferociously beats her down, then snaps her neck—a scene particularly shocking considering how tough Brit was portrayed earlier.

Bringing down Kell is obviously personal for Jo, but it gets even more personal when Delilah asks her to take over bodyguarding duties. Jo agrees even though she's an undercover cop (that's seriously her job title), and she really should ask her superiors for permission before agreeing to take on freelance work.

Delilah even wants her as part of the act. Also in the job discription is staying the night at Delilah's mansion, really just so the filmmakers could include a topless Maria Ford kicking the stuffing out of some invading redneck mercenary types doing Kell's bidding.

Angel of Destruction never wastes an opportunity to get our heroine naked, including the utterly implausible scene where Kell kidnaps Reena and demands that Jo does a full striptease act in lieu of Delilah performing, a demand that Jo seems almost too eager to agree to. Don't know what Kell's endgame was here, other than just disappointing the audience that paid good money to see a performance by a hitmaking pop act and got a not-so-great strip performance instead.

But Maria Ford (a trained martial artist) is one B-action vixen who's more than just, to quote David Brent, "a pair of tits." She can throw down with the best of them. And she's never less than convincing in her quest to bring down Kell. She's one super cop who's able to outrun bullets fired at her at near distance from an M16 *and* leap away from an explosion, not just unscathed, but also unmussed.

Angel of Destruction is gratuitous and ludicrous, but it's also a bit of a blast. A terrifying villain matched with a hero who can convincingly kick tush never fails to entertain. And its gratuitousness only ups the entertainment value. Not only does this angel earn its wings, but it also would make a fantastic double-bill with 1987's also Corman-produced *Stripped to Kill*. That's the one where the cop played by *Death Wish 4: The Crackdown*'s Kay Lenz goes undercover as an exotic dancer to apprehend the culprit behind a slew of gentleman's club murders. The one that inhabits some kind of Bizarro-world '80s TV hell by costarring Greg Evigan from TV's *My Two Dads* and Norman Fell, *Three's Company*'s lecherous landlord. Oh Roger, how we love you so!

VIRUS, A.K.A. SPILL (1996)

If "with a special appearance by Eric Peterson" means anything to you, you're probably Eric Peterson. No slight here, but you've gotta question the motivations behind this as a selling point in *Virus*'s opening credits. Even as Canadians, the name didn't ring a bell, though he's been a continuously working actor up here in shows like *Corner Gas*, a comedy that revolves around a small-town petrol station that requires huffing fumes to find funny.

But the movie is not about him; it's all about bad movie staple Brian Bosworth, a man with strangely supple lips and a wishbone jaw who studio execs tried to turn into a bankable movie star once he'd fumbled his football career. The *Virus* star was once one of the most highly regarded linebackers in NCAA football history, then proceeded to annoy everyone at the professional level with his unprofessional antics, which included attending Seattle Seahawks' practices by helicopter and out-peacocking Miami coke dealers when it came to attire.

He burst out of the blocks in the hilarious *Stone Cold* (1991), a swaggering badass with a crew mullet cut at right angles, and wraparound blue shades.

He was more WWE than NFL, but bridged the gap between sports entertainment and sports by way of what's become common to both: juicing. When asked, he offered up this old yarn to the *New York Times*: his 'roids were "prescribed by a physician," an excuse that hasn't become any more legitimate-sounding with the passage of time. You could call Bosworth a big pharma trailblazer in a way, as he was busted long before the current crop of cheating footballers and wrestlers. (We're looking at you Brock Lesnar—but not directly into your eyes. You're terrifying.)

In *Virus*, he's ex-football star turned secret service man[47] Ken Fairchild. He's known for his honesty and forthrightness, character traits that should "put him on the endangered species list," according to a jokester reporter who wears a trench coat and smokes a stogie—a headline-grabbing hard-bitten cliché of clichés who files bylines for the fictional *New York Tribune*.

At a presser at Camp David, the US presidential retreat in Maryland (represented in this budget-hampered film by a campground just north of Toronto), Fairchild's steely eyes catch a miscreant plotting to peg the POTUS with an egg.

He thwarts the assault with a chokehold, then hilariously shoves it down the would-be assailant's throat.

When location scouting for an upcoming ecological summit at Thermal Wells National Park in Oregon, with geothermal springs replicated for the silver screen by spouts used to water golf courses, Fairchild gets stuck in the mud and is ridiculously dragged out of the mire by a lassoing horse-riding veterinarian.

The cute veterinarian is required so she can later perform lifesaving tracheotomies on humans (using a pen, of course)—because hamster and human medicine is transferable—and because, naturally, Fairchild needs a + 1.

After her horse drinks from a nearby stream, it goes apeshit, and locals also start becoming afflicted by a waterborne pathogen whose side effects include . . . wait for it . . . bleeding from the nose. This is such a cheap copout for a contagion flick, where the big payoff should be bleeding out of every orifice, creating new ones, or at the very least, developing some nasty sores. But then again, we shouldn't be surprised by the glaring absence of practical effects. This is a low budget stinker with cinematography that wouldn't pass muster as a jury duty training video.

Naturally, we find out the chemical spill is part of a secret government weapons program, and with geysers opening all over the grounds, the president's life is in peril. And the "death by splash" has to be foiled by boiling the water or something.

As the UN press conference is happening, attended by fewer journalists than you'd see at an H&M ribbon cutting, Fairchild has to figure out what's going on and save the day.

There are some dynamite action clichés here: the black friend whose life expectancy is counted in the minutes pirouetting through the air post-explosion, the wheelie motorcycle riding, the copious stock footage, and when a long-haul truck is careening over a cliff edge, a different view of the chasm depending on the cut. And you can't forget the lazy trope newspaper headline exposition constantly rearing its ugly head. EXTRA, EXTRA! This career-killing contagion movie tanks!

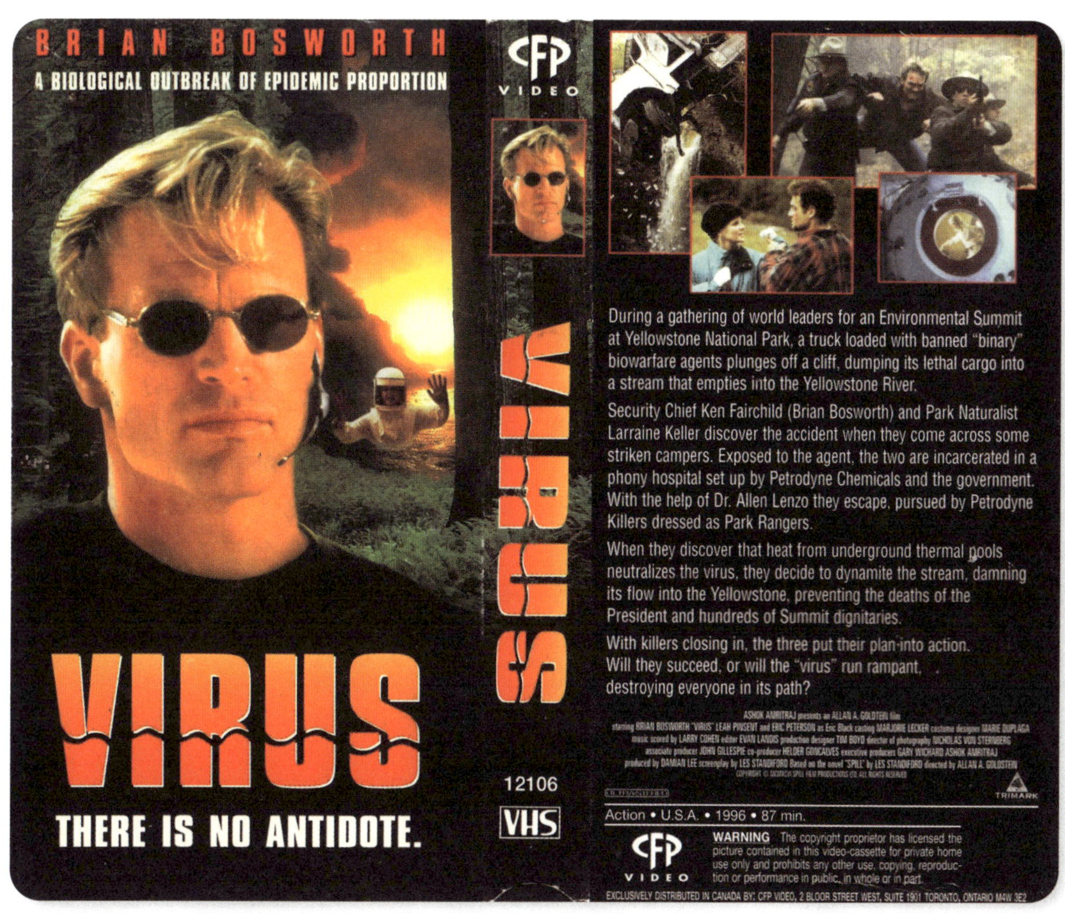

HALF PAST DEAD (2002)

Later Seagal film titles double as editorial comments about his career, like *Half Past Dead*, a jail break film based on a weird phenomenon frequent enough that it even has a *Wikipedia* page devoted to it: chopper-assisted prison escapes.

In the film, there's a "new" Alcatraz, which calls to mind Monty Burns' confused question about there being a "New" Mexico. The structure was reopened by a tough-on-crime California governor, so blinkered he's willing to overlook the fact that Alcatraz's original structure crumbled because of sea salt and exposure to the elements. If there's a business case for reopening an island prison there, we'd love to hear it.

The warden is a short man, "Il Fuego," who claims he's "harder than all the inmates" (in terms of toughness that is, not what's happening below the waist). And his New Alcatraz, like the old one (which housed a bitter, syphilitic Al Capone), has its own high profile occupant. He's Lester, a death-row bank robber who's squirrelled away hundreds of millions somewhere. But instead of singing like a canary, this jailbird ain't talking, much to the chagrin of law enforcement.

An evil gang called the 49ers—evil gangs are often named after successful sports teams—hatches a plan to spring the old fart one-percenter from jail, have him lead the gang to his secret stash, and then run off to somewhere tropical so gang leader Donny can "work on his tan." This sentiment sounds better espoused by African American actor Morris Chestnut than say, tacky corrupt offense-monger Silvio Berlusconi.

Their strategy is to descend on the prison via helicopter to spring the newly minted billionaire because there's a sound plan to make millions—rob an institution known to be heavily well-armed and then bank on the fact that a guy who's already on death row will be so petrified of dying, he'll blab all the info required to rob him of his fortune.

Unfortunately for the gang, they have an even bigger problem than a stupid ill-conceived plan, and he's barrelled shaped. Standing in their way: the past-his-best-before-date, ponytailed martial arts murmurer, Sasha (Seagal), who seems partial to prison food given his considerable girth.

Sasha had been undercover to find out more about who was behind the murder of his wife (a Euro gangster it turns out, who makes hackneyed pronouncements like "I am a soldier trained in the art of killing"), when he, along with career criminal Nick (Ja Rule) were busted and sent to the infamous San Fran island pen.

They bonded over their different levels of melanin and exchanged banter about black colloquialism diction (for the record, it's "Ah-ite," a phrase that stumps the ethnically equivocal Seagal, who Nick opines is "whiter than I thought!")

While Seagal is more of a threat to a banquet hall buffet at this point in his career, he's still occasionally kicking ass and taking names, even if he has to repeat those names just in case he forgets. The gang finds out how true this is, as they have to battle the man when their helicopter crashes, trapping them on the island prison.

Just how will they all escape? Use a bloated Seagal as a flotation device?

To add some intrigue, the ill-timed helicopter scheme occurred at a time when a Supreme Court justice and head of the Federal Bureau of Prisons (since kidnapped) were to witness Lester the embezzler's execution. Freeing the duo gives Seagal a time-sensitive mission other than simply twisting the forearms of a bunch of undifferentiated cons.

Seagal is so slap-happy and downtempo with his martial arts, yet opponents do pirouettes when they're merely touched. But that's not the only inanity that abounds: despite this being a "state-of-the-art" prison, doors aren't bulletproof.

OF NOTE:

Half Past Dead was Seagal's last film to be given a theatrical release until he played the Hispanic heavy (no pun intended) Torrez in 2010's Danny Trejo–starrer *Machete*.

NEVER TOO YOUNG TO DIE (1986)

A couple dozen or so stereotypical '80s toughs wielding torches gather in a small quarry to listen to the musings and machinations of their beloved leader. A hush falls over the beer-guzzling crowd as he begins to speak. He's the diabolical Velvet Von Ragner, sweet transvestite, musician, and domestic terrorist. He begins his missive by castigating his faithful, addressing them as "my little turdballs; my little scumbuckets" before detailing his nefarious plan to poison the city's water supply. And as is standard in films of this type, all crucial information pertaining to how to carry out this sabotage is contained within a single disk.[48] And the disk is now in the possession of international superspy Drew Stargrove. "Get me Stargrove, I want Stargrove!" shrieks Ragner, looking just fine in a full face of Cruella de Vil makeup, satin robe, and lace fingerless gloves.

And the actor playing Ragner: none other than de facto KISS leader and owner of the worst hair plugs in rock 'n' roll, Gene Simmons. Now, the God of Thunder may be an atypical choice for an action movie villain, although at six feet two, he does have the physical presence. But when you pair him with John "Have Mercy" Stamos as our hero, Drew Stargrove's son Lance, Prince protegee Vanity as the partner/love interest, and a special appearance by one-and-done Bond George Lazenby, well that's certainly one of the strangest action movie casts ever assembled. And speaking of strange, what's with that title? *Never Too Young to Die* sounds more like an ABC disease-of-the-week tearjerker. Heck, even "Stargrove"[49] would have made for a more suitable moniker.

Lance is a gymnastics star at an unnamed private highschool who believes that his frequently absent superspy dad (Lazenby) is a globe-trotting "troubleshooter for oil companies." So when Stargrove Sr. misses his son's gymnastics meet, Lance is disappointed but not surprised. What Lance doesn't know, however, is that while he's showing off his prowess on the gymnastic rings, dad is on a super-secret government mission to "flush out Ragner." Unfortunately, the mission goes sideways and Stargrove ends up dead from a Ragner shotgun blast.

He attends his father's funeral where two things of note occur. First, dad's lawyer tells Lance that he's inherited the family farm. Second, he spies a mysterious and very distraught woman standing off in the distance. She's Danja Deering, Stargrove's former partner. When Lance goes to the farm, Danja is there, fending off the attack of two of Ragner's lackies looking for the disk, one of whom looks like he stepped right off the set of *Conan the Destroyer*. Lance arrives just in time to witness Danja blow one of them away. After the requisite scene or two of teenage angst and ennui, Lance begins to accept that Dad may not have been entirely truthful regarding his employment.

In a meeting with point person Carruthers, Danja learns a bit about her deceased partner's arch nemesis (maybe a bit too much). First, he performs a nightclub act at a club called The Inferno, and he's not just a transvestite but an actual hermaphrodite! And yet, even as a half man, he's still twice the man Tom Cruise is. She goes to the club to investigate, unbeknownst that Lance is following her on his pathetic scooter. The Inferno is a biker bar in the most literal sense, with bikers constantly riding their rides in and out of the building, yet somehow not disturbing

the generic hair metal band on stage nor the audience assembled to watch the performance. Even Lance takes a spin inside on his less-than-impressive motorized transport. Soon, the moment arrives. Live on stage, ladies and gentlemen . . . Velvet Von Ragner! And when performance time arrives, well, you may have wanted the best, but you're getting Velvet Von Ragner instead. And there he is: Gene Simmons, effulgent in a giant pink feather boa headpiece and a peekaboo nylon full-body unitard that would make even Cher blush, with just enough groin coverage to keep the "Love Gun" in check. Too bad we can't "Turn Back Time" to unsee this.[50]

When Lance is kidnapped by Ragner's thugs, an interrogation beatdown triggers something inside, and he transforms on a dime into a more-than-capable fighter despite showing absolutely zero combat prowess before, almost a post-pubescent Jason Bourne. Stamos, or rather his stunt double, kicks all sorts of ass—leaping, flying, and roundhouse kicking the baddies into submission. He also finds Daddy's secret lair where all the cool, big-boy weapons are kept. So it's goodbye Lance Stargrove, high school gymnast; hello, Lance Stargrove, super-spy! Guess he's Daddy's boy after all. And if anyone is going to stop Ragner from carrying out his diabolical designs, you know it's gonna be a Stargrove!

Never Too Young to Die has a twist everybody can see coming, an icky sex scene between Lance and the much-older Danja, an even ickier scene of Simmons forcefully jamming his trademark massive tongue down Danja's throat, and ickiest still, the revelation of Ragner's hermaphroditic C-cups.

Never Too Young to Die is a weird one, there's no denying that. The inclusion of Stamos as top-billed star could only have served to limit the appeal of the film to the *Tiger Beat* set, yet the film's surprising level of violence, homoeroticism (and homophobia), nudity, and entendres galore (we'd say double entendres, but the film really isn't clever enough for those) ensured that it was out of that demographic's reach. But take our advice and see it. It may be something those involved would rather have forgotten, but it's far from the worst nor most embarrassing thing that either Stamos or Simmons ever did. For that, look no further than The Beach Boys' "Kokomo" video and *Gene Simmons: Family Jewels* respectively.

FOR Y'UR HEIGHT ONLY (1981)

Ernesto de la Cruz was born in 1957, in the Baclaran *barangay* of the Philippines. Afflicted with primordial dwarfism, he entered the world the size of a "bottle of Pepsi-Cola . . . so tiny we had to feed him by dropper." The name on his tombstone may be Ernesto, but to Filipino moviegoers and lovers of strange cinema everywhere, he is the incomparable Weng Weng,[51] "superspy, karate expert, and ladies' man." From his two-feet-nine frame to his cherubic face and trademark bowl haircut, Weng Weng is, if nothing else, the most unusual-looking action star ever.

In the late '70s and early '80s, Filipino audiences were nuts for Bond . . . James Bond. To satiate the craving for more superspy adventures (and naturally to make a quick buck) local producers rushed in with their own homegrown versions of 007. Actors such as Tony Ferrer, who enjoyed remarkable success portraying Tony Falcon in the *Agent X-44* series of films, were given suave makeovers and a license to kill. But no other ersatz secret agent man was as indelible or incredible as the pint-size Pinoy Weng Weng.

Discovered by producers Peter and Cora Cabellas, Weng Weng appeared in small roles in a string of low-budget films before capturing the public's attention as the sidekick to Philippine comedy king Dolphy. Looking to capitalize on their little star's newfound visibility, the Cabellas gave Weng Weng his first leading role as Agent 00 in 1981's *For Y'ur Height Only*, an obvious riff on 007's latest big-screen opus, *For Your Eyes Only*. If the title alone didn't alert audiences that they were in serious rip-off territory, the opening frames certainly did. Looking dapper in his white Robin Gibb-inspired disco jumpsuit, Agent 00, framed in a circle, walks toward the camera accompanied by a carbon copy of John Barry's iconic Bond theme. He points his gun toward the screen, fires, and the circle fills with red.

Mere moments after setting foot on Manilla soil, esteemed scientist Dr. Van Kohler is kidnapped by goons working for the nefarious Mr. Giant, an international terrorist whose identity is shrouded in mystery. Mr. Giant, who communicates through a small circular makeup-sized magic mirror with flashing lights like some dollar-store *Snow White* queen, demands that Kohler give him the formula for the (assumedly highly destructive—it's never made entirely clear just what exactly it's capable of) "N-Bomb." Meanwhile, Agent 00 is busy singlehandedly taking out the henchman of nasty Boss Columbus, using his surprisingly effective mini-martial arts.[52]

He's called into his superior's office (played by Tony Ferrer himself) and is briefed on the Kohler kidnapping. He's also given a slew of gadgets, Q style, including a pendant he can use to communicate with the "pretty broad" agent who's managed to infiltrate Mr. Giant's crime syndicate. He's also given a ring that has the dual function of controlling a weaponized whirly hat (shades of Oddjob) and detecting poisons placed in drinks! Finally, he's given a pen that doubles as a blowgun and a pair of X-ray specs that 00 wastes no time in testing, using them to cheekily ogle the pretty receptionists in the office without their garments.

Agent 00 is tasked with bringing down both Mr. Giant and Boss Columbus, and Weng Weng goes about the task like the exhilarating dynamo that he is. In various scenes, he's seen exuberantly taking out bad guys with marksmanship-like precision, sliding across a floor while shooting

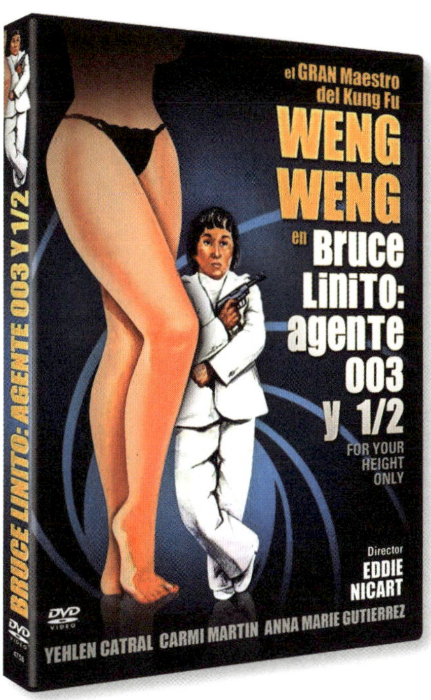

his gun before bumping his head against a wall ("Oh, my little head!"), ziplining off a carousel for a quick getaway, and leaping from a top-floor hotel window, his descent softened by an umbrella used as a makeshift parachute. Amazingly, Weng Weng did all his own stunts, Jackie Chan style, as there were no stuntmen his size who could convincingly double for him.

It wouldn't be a Bond rip-off without the ladies, and Agent 00 certainly has the eye for them. Like a shrunken Richard Dawson, he runs around coercing every woman he meets to give him a smooch. And no lady can resist Agent 00's charms. When a seductive lass asks, "Are you a sexual animal?" the innocent yet mischievous twinkle in Weng Weng's eyes confirms the affirmative.

Tensions intensify as the baddies (who nefariously smuggle bags of coke stuffed in fresh-baked loaves of bread to push in "every kindergarten and sandbox" in the vicinity) realize that Agent 00 is continually one step ahead of them, "[making] a monkey out of the forces of evil!" Ultimately, Agent 00 straps on a jetpack (a miniature version of the type Sean Connery used in *Thunderball*) to sputter and soar into Mr. Giant's hidden island compound where both Van Kohler and the exposed agency mole are being held. He also takes out dozens of henchmen using a sword.[53]

For Y'ur Height Only was a smash and the character was reprised in 1982's *The Impossible Kid*. But sadly, Weng Weng-mania was short-lived. As the '80s gave way to the '90s, roles for Weng Weng became scarce and his health started to deteriorate. He moved back to Baclaran as poor as he had left, a victim of the Cabellas, who had purloined all of his films' profits. In 1992, at age thirty-four, Weng Weng died of cardiac arrest in his childhood home, his fame in his homeland already forgotten.

Weng Weng's legacy is not an easy one to encapsulate. Some may take issue with the exploitative elements inherent in his film. Indeed, in the doc *The Search for Weng Weng*, Tilman Baumgärtel, film academic at the University of the Philippines, describes Weng Weng's films as "personally unsettling to me because [he] is a handicapped person that was put in front of audiences because of that very handicap. . . It's not politically correct to show people like that or put them in the foreground." Baumgärtel's assessment is at best problematic and at worst highly reductivist. Audiences loved Weng Weng neither because of nor despite his handicap. They flocked to his films because of the infectious enthusiasm and *joie de vivre* he brought to his roles. He triumphed over adversity and managed to pack seven feet of entertainment into just shy of three. Or as no less an authority than ousted first lady Imelda Marcos said, "He entertained us. He could make us laugh and make us happy." And what more could you ask for from a hero than that?

NIGHTFORCE (1987)

If you put a handful of college students together, their capabilities would range from being able to organize a kegger (likely) to founding Facebook (less so). It would not include dropping a full course load, packing up a cache of weapons in a U-Haul, and driving south to battle a terrorist army. It wouldn't happen even if the professor gave them an extension on their poli-sci essay, and it certainly wouldn't happen in any universe we're aware of—except of course, the bad movie-verse.

There's a reason the films that fill this book usually feature revenge plots and trained professionals—they're grim-faced killers and martial artists who'd score high on competence and low on verbal acuity, and unlike the average college undergraduate, not the other way around.

It's enough to make your head spin. Speaking of spinning heads, enter Linda Blair as Carla. When her friend Christy, a US Senator's daughter, is kidnapped by a communist gang and taken over the border into Mexico, Carla enlists the help of four classmates to go get her. Because there's nothing Mexican cartels (both then and now known for decapitating vics and dumping them into open graves) fear more than a group of well-heeled psychology majors.

Be that as it may, they prep for the business at hand. This includes firing weaponry in the woods. Hey, there's no time for basic training when exams are due. Carla is joined by a team that includes Henry (played by Chad McQueen, son of Steve), and three transposable frat guys. Comedic relief comes when a member of their party packs an inflatable sex doll for the long journey south, and when the team tests out a bazooka, saying, "Now let's fire a real man's gun!" It's that kind of cavalier attitude that lead to the debacle in Iraq, we're guessing.

Someone once said, "A goal without a plan is just a wish" and these kids have no friggin' plan whatsoever. Luckily for them, they run into someone who does, a pasty figure in khaki skulking about in the Mexican desert. Pet monkey in tow, he just happens to be hanging around the far-flung cantina our team of Gringo coeds brawl in. Could've been worse; could've been Greedo (who we all know shot second).

That's the splendid Richard Lynch who plays the battle-hardened, pockmarked mercenary Bishop. Lynch was a Brooklyn-born bad movie maven who was Chuck Norris's Russian antagonist in *Invasion USA* and who made a career out of doing films that are natural fits for our book such as *Deathsport*, a dystopian thriller with a title that leaves little to the imagination about a bunch of "destructocycles" used in a fight-to-the-death combat arena.

Bishop gathers his young team around a table in his backwoods shack for a mission debrief and tempers their youthful enthusiasm with a message about how that nasty cartel, "castrates their victims alive." (That kind of goes without saying. Who gives a crap what they'd do to you if you were dead?) Perhaps to help the medicine go down, he busts out a flute and starts serenading them in front of a roaring fire. Wait, what? And why the F a flute? Bishop admits later it's "To confuse the hell out of people." When it comes to us and to the average viewer, to quote George W. Bush, "mission accomplished." Flutes are for *Smurfs* and Warner Brothers cartoons, silly rabbit.

But don't underestimate a man and his flute. And Bishop is just the kind of world-weary General Patton a team of neophytes would require. He draws out battle maps even while mocking the kids' weapons, saying "This is fine for World War II, but this is the '80s!"

And if it's one thing the '80s was known for, it was fightin' commies! (And with all the hairspray, you could also say the decade was about fighting follicular gravity.)

The terrorist guerrillas are a nasty bunch, led by a stogie-gnawing Fidel lookalike with an accent so heavy, "trouble" sounds like "travel." And he's not one to be trifled with. He's got a battle-hardened group of rapist goons under his command as well as the Senator's daughter held captive in a bamboo jail by a circus dwarf with a heart of gold who just wants a green card. Yay, ethnic stereotyping!

However, Fidel doesn't know what he's up against: a bunch of well-to-do college students with no combat training who are miraculously able to mow down hundreds of his best after being told how to mount an M60 to a jeep. The people who complained Rey from *Star Wars: The Force Awakens* could do anything instantly have clearly never seen *Nightforce*, where grenades are lobbed with Major League Baseball precision by people who likely wake up hungover at the crack of noon.

For a movie called *Nightforce*, next to none of it takes place at night, except for the sleeping bits. And it's amazing that a film this bereft of plot is so full of exposition, including the classic from the world of journalism: "this just in. . ." Hey, it sure beats "EXTRA, EXTRA! RUTHLESS CARTEL KIDNAPS GIRL."

DEATH MACHINES (1976)

When you look at a title like this one, you might think of H. G. Wells's "spiderlike machines nearly a hundred feet high . . . able to shoot a beam of intense heat." But this isn't a macro battle between Martians and humans. Rather, it's more a mundane earthly fight over who controls the always-booming assassin business.

Crime boss Mr. G., basking poolside with naked ladies as was the custom of the time, orders two hits. One to take out some bank VP, and because this is an action movie, the other one of the most common professions in the action business—the ubiquitous and ever-present dojo owner. But somebody is knocking off Mr. G's assassins before they can go about their grisly business. And in spectacular fashion too.

Hit #1: A marksman with eyebrows thick as shoeshine brushes sets up his high-powered rifle atop a tower and quietly lies in wait as if a presidential motorcade was about to glide by. To boost the tension, the target is obscured by the occasional tree branch. Then . . . a free shot. But as he's furrowing his Scorsese brows and is about to depress the trigger, he's jumped. Three assailants heave him over the railing, hurtling him to his death, something that would've been nice to see had the director not cut away and graced us with a Wilhelm scream instead.

Hit #2: The next assassin is an unassuming baldy fixin' to waste the bank exec while he goes for his morning job. He's calmly smoking a pipe while unwrapping his rifle from its swaddling blanket, taking aim, and crouching behind the hood of his car. Before he can get off a shot, a car rolls up, and three assailants pull out a bazooka and blow him to smithereens with a stopover in Kingdom Come.

Hit #3: Mr. G's second-in-command calls his *Capo di tutti crappy* from a phone booth, and the two get in a heated exchange about what the hell is going wrong. But before THEY can come to any sort of conclusion, one of those stealthy silent bulldozers bowls over the henchman, somehow without him hearing anything to alert him before it's too late.

Hit #4: Mr. G is left to ponder another call, maybe to Mafia Human Resources to see if there are any underboss resumes lying around. As he dines in a restaurant so stereotypically Eye-talian, it comes with gingham tablecloths and Chef Boyardee accents, HE narrowly escapes a Last Supper as a truck plows through the trattoria window.

So who's behind all this? A rogue cop, maybe one wearing one of those leather chest holsters that that kind of officer was contractually obligated to wear in every film? How about a mild-mannered civilian vigilante with a *Death Wish*? Or perhaps a mysterious stranger in a Kevlar onesie?

And the answer is . . . none of the above! No, it's an underworld Dragon Lady with a 'do that would crush Tracy Turnblad's from *Hairspray*. Madame Lee can control both her bouffant from the ravages of gravity and her minions, three trained killers who always do her bidding, no questions asked. Why? Because they were tested with an experimental brainwashing serum. If you saw that one coming, please agree to meet with us at an undisclosed car park garage.

In the '70s, it was revealed to a Senate Committee that the CIA had been doing evil brainwashing experiments in the early 1950s, attempting to create assassins who'd bear unquestioned allegiance and have no memory of their actions. The so-called MK Ultra or CIA mind control program subjected patients to so many hallucinogens, they'd be able to make sense of, or hell, even direct this movie. So mind-controlled assassins aren't as ridiculous as they may first appear.

However, when they appear here, these assassins are pretty ridiculous. Madame Lee has hand-picked three ethnically correct killers (black, white, and Asian), "The most deadly assassins the world has ever known," after a fight-to-the-death tournament that takes place on a wooden bridge and features a bunch of chiselled combatants armed variously with spears, swords, and sticks. The Caucasian proves his guile by slipping a pistol inside his pant leg and blowing away one of the others who'd been busying himself with simple kung fu. Take that, Indiana Jones!

With Madame Lee firmly in control of the assassin business, all mob requests must go through her, and the next hit, orchestrated from an island compound only accessible by stock footage of a Cessna landing, is massacring everyone at a martial arts school.

The three mind-controlled Death Machines, clad in black tanks and skinny pants as if they're rehearsing for the Bolshoi, bust in while the *gi* geeks are sitting cross-legged taking in a fighting stick demo. Rule of thumb: If you're wearing a white *gi* and practicing group punches/kicks, you're not long for this earth. And that's proven correct here. They're all killed in the ensuing melee,[54] with one student electrocuting himself by swinging a sword and connecting with electrical equipment on the wall.[55]

The police are baffled by the body count as well as the calling card "Red Buddha Statue" that the three stupidly leave at every crime scene. Luckily, there's lone survivor, Frank, who had his hand lopped off in the attack. He claims he can identify all three perps but doesn't give any descriptions to the homicide squad. But that's more an example of sloppy directing work than sloppy detective work.

As he's convalescing in hospital under police guard, we get proof that the Death Machines weren't just selected for their fighting prowess or by affirmative action, but also for their cunning. The black and Asian Death Machines wheel their Caucasian comrade into the hospital in a gurney—literally going undercover—as they attempt to finish the job on poor Frank, who now probably winces whenever he hears the phrase "all hands on deck."

The rest of *Death Machines* is basically seeing whether Frank, now sporting a black glove like he's in a *giallo* film, can, with the help of an inept police force, bring down Madame Lee and her doorway-eclipsing hair.

Death Machines is a depository of inept set pieces, with dialogue often drowned out by a face-melting synth. There's a poolhall throw down where Frank becomes a human strike zone as he's pelted with billiard balls; a strip club patron who complains to the manager that he's "seen better entertainment in the zoo," (reviewers of this one felt similarly on *IMDb*); and a Death Machiner eluding capture by feigning a stomach bug, then kicking the crap out of an entire police precinct. And it should be noted that while we're not sticklers for verisimilitude, *Death Machines* does not, in fact, contain any actual machines of death (unless you count that bulldozer).

STONE COLD (1991)

A lot of thought goes into what's put where on a supermarket shelf. "Top-shelf" may be a handle for something of high quality, but it's actually not as coveted because it's out of sight. The stuff in plain view, such as the brazen product placement and marketer's wet dream stuffed into the opening frames of *Stone Cold*, is where it's at. Here, the baddies' hold-up strategy seems to be to linger in front of grocery displays long enough for Nabisco to get their eyeballs. Little do they know, a rogue cop is lying in wait—Joe Huff, a bad man with a bad name, a bad trench coat, and an even worse haircut.

He bats a henchman into a dairy fridge and goads another into slipping on broken glass, sending the poor greasy bastard hurtling into a conspicuous Coca-Cola display.

Huff (Brian Bosworth) is A COP ON SUSPENSION, reprimanded by his superiors for his reckless conduct, but which could've just as easily been for his "clean up in aisle four" insolence.

He's then blackmailed by the FBI into undertaking a dangerous undercover mission, where he has to infiltrate a nasty biker gang that blows away priests through stained glass displays and amuses themselves by William Tell-ing cheap domestic beer off one another's heads and shoulders.
Their exploits are so notorious, Huff gets wind of them via EXTRA EXTRA, newspaper exposition! (This while he's in the kitchen making a not-exactly-healthy Minute Maid/Snickers bar smoothie. We really weren't kidding about the product placement.)

To infiltrate the gang, Huff has to frequent titty bars, race bikes, and fight in a sand pit to prove he's man enough to be considered a biker prospect.

The Brotherhood gang is led by "Chains," played by none other than genre stalwart Lance Henriksen, whose threats are so vicious they come served with a side of more threats: "I will peel your skin off with a knife dipped in shit. . .," and William Forsythe does his bidding as cigar-chewing sergeant-at-arms, Ice.

Gang members in '80s movies may be defined by their lack of definition, but bump ahead a decade and the gangsters here are rippling muscle, as menacing a bunch of bikers as you'll ever see.

Still, Huff takes no guff. He tosses two greasers onto billiard tables and hoists another two up above his head by military press (Being lifted up by the neck and groin seems more painful than finally being dropped on your back or head). Huff pitches another guy headlong into a well-stocked bar, wasting hundreds of dollars of watered down strip club booze.

Stone Cold proves that just one gang is never enough. Hence, a bunch of Jersey dagos and greasy Chicanos get their faces rearranged. Huff's though, remains intact, as does his beaver tail do, a hairstyle so formidable it not only takes you out of the movie, but out of the Earth's atmosphere as well.

OF NOTE:

The money shot in *Stone Cold* is a staple of action films: the helicopter that blows up. This time, they up the ante with a flying motorcycle that crashes into said helicopter.

AFTERWORD

So there you have it. A journey through a world of crippled avengers, one-armed executioners, and no-legged mafia hitmen. A world where cops supposedly versed in the ways of the Samurai know absolutely nothing about the ways of the Samurai. A world where musical groups fight to the death for prime stage time in the streets of Orlando, even though the film has the word "Miami" in the title. A world where Reb Brown is king, and Cameron Mitchell is more ubiquitous than Diet Coke.

We hope you enjoyed taking this walk on the wild side of action with us. Hopefully reading this volume evoked some enjoyable memories and reinforced why we all love this zany genre as much as we do. And if you're inspired to seek out some of these films—all the better! And the good news is, there's more—so much more! These films are like rivers with thousands of tributaries. Are you intrigued by the cut-and-paste filmmaking technique of Godfrey Ho? If so, there's 150 Ho-directed films to delve into. Does the dashing yet doughy presence of Cüneyt Arkın float your boat? You're in luck! Three-hundred-and-twenty-two films in his filmography and counting. The action genre is vast and varied, and, like a box of your favorite cereal, offers rewards for digging to the bottom. Countless wacky and WTF moments are scattered among the bulging biceps, bullet bandoliers, buxom women, and explosions big enough to level five city blocks.

Every film starts off as an action film. After all, the director yells "Action" before every scene. But only the best of the best are ACTION films. And as long as they keep making them, we'll continue to gleefully watch them. We certainly hope you do, too.

And remember: even if your opponent's weapon is bigger than yours, it's not the size of the weapon that counts, but rather what you do with it. BAM!

ENDNOTES

1. Not to be confused with *The Human Tornado*, the 1976 cult Blaxploitation film and sequel to *Dolemite*.

2. The first of many firsts, apparently. On their respective *IMDb* pages, it states that the twins were also the first sanctioned professional kickboxers in Ontario, the first to air live kickboxing on Canadian pay-per-view, the first to promote legal amateur kickboxing and MMA on the same card, the first to televise kickboxing on Canadian TV, and the first to promote, manage, and train six Canadian World professional kickboxing champions. Surprised it doesn't say they were the first Canadians to throw a punch.

3. In 2007, the McNamaras slapped the Ontario government and Hayashi with a $100 million civil suit for, among other things, "Use[age] of inflammatory language, including the word 'bloodsport' to describe kickboxing." No strangers to litigation, the brothers also sued Miramax and two other companies for $37 million for "tarnishing [their] image with a silly movie" and failing to "obtain clearance" when the studio released the Jackie Chan vehicle *Twin Dragons*.

4. In action films, there are a surfeit of them, usually outfitted with a various assortment of railings for henchmen to fall over when shot. It makes one wonder, however, if every urban action flick is set in a poverty-stricken milieu since there's just so many abandoned buildings. Although the city in *Psycho Kickboxer* is unnamed, there's no doubt that it takes place in an economically devastated locale, as evidenced by the sheer abundance of crimes committed in what looks to be no more than a five-block radius.

5. For some odd reason, JCVD's character's name is given as "Ivan" in the opening credits, but "Karl Brezdin" in the closing. In the film, he's only referred to as "The Russian."

6. *The Joys of Yiddish* author Leo Rosen hilariously defined chutzpah as "that quality enshrined in a man who, having killed his mother and father, throws himself on the mercy of the court because he is an orphan."

7. *American Kickboxer* is the title this film was released under. However, on the official DVD release, it's entitled *American Kickboxer 1*. This is strange because *American Kickboxer 2*, released in 1993, shares nothing in common with its "predecessor." The official sequel to this one was released in 1992 and is entitled *To the Death*. Barrett reprises his role, but for some reason, producers changed his character's name from B. J. to Rick Quinn. Furthermore, the tile *American Kickboxer*, while technically not a misnomer, is somewhat disingenuous as there's nothing about the film that renders it patriotic. There's even an "International" kickboxing tournament held, yet all the participants are American. But hey, *American Ninja* did well as did *Kickboxer*, so why not a portmanteau of two previously successful films?

8. That the newspaper looks like a photocopy of a photocopy is indicative of the cheap-as-chips nature of the film. And of course, the majority of exposition in *American Kickboxer* is delivered through the mechanism of the on-screen newspaper headline, that time-honored device of lazy storytelling employed by so many of the films included in this book.

9. Denard is played by South African kickboxer Bruce Morris. All his dialogue is ADR dubbed, leaving poor Morris sounding like Van Damme after taking a mouthful of Quaaludes. He's also fond of uttering hilarious malapropisms such as "Your mother's the dog."

10. Action films are notorious for their uber-generic titles, but this may be the most generic of them all. Makes *Hired to Kill* sound like *Eternal Sunshine of the Spotless Mind.*

11. The montage was popularized by Russian director Sergei Eisenstein and best demonstrated in his masterful "Odessa Steps" sequence in *Battleship Potemkin*. The word denotes a series of short shots used to condense space and time. In action films, training montages are typically used to depict a hero enduring rigorous training which transitions him or her from inadequate to primed and ready for the struggle that lies ahead and are usually set to a chart-topper power ballad sung by the likes of Survivor or Joe Esposito. The montage in *Run Like Hell,* however, has no musical accompaniment since music costs money. It does, however, conclude with the requisite demonstration of triumph. In *Rocky*, it was the titular fighter's jubilation upon reaching the top of the steps of the Philadelphia Museum of Art. In *Run Like Hell*, it's the girls engaging in a brief group hug upon conquering a small hill.

12. Not a fruit or vegetable smoothie

13. According to no less an authority than *Urban Dictionary*, Pervert's Row is the seating area directly in front of (or around) the stage at a strip club. The courtside seat for gentlemen's entertainment, and we're using that term loosely.

14. Amanda MacMillan, "Why Men Are Much Worse At Being Sick Than Women," *Time Magazine*, February 2017

15. Oliver Reed's drunken exploits were as legendary as André the Giant's. According to the late film critic David Hemmings, Reed could drink twenty pints of lager with a gin chaser . . . and still run a mile for a wager. And his behavior was no better on the set of this one, reportedly ruining the most expensive shot in the film by pulling out his "little Ollie" and urinating all over the set.

16. PJ Soles, who charmed everyone in *Rock 'n' Roll High School* and *Halloween*.

17. Played by Teagan Clive, a female bodybuilder. In 1985, it was reported that Clive filed a civil rights suit against the Anaheim PD after she was allegedly placed by a police officer in a chokehold after the officer mistook her for a man using the women's restroom.

18. Luciano Pigozzi, a.k.a. Alan Collin and Alan Collins, was an Italian actor and veteran of one-hundred-plus films, including *Werewolf in a Girls' Dormitory* and *Yor, the Hunter from the Future*, a movie featuring his *Strike Commando* costar Reb Brown, "trotting across the pseudo-prehistoric terrain looking genial and speaking fluent Californian," according to the *New York Times*.

19. Never once in the entire film is our group of trained killing machines ever once referred to as "The Annihilators," but since that's the title of the film, that's what they will henceforth be collectively known as. This is not uncommon practice. In the similarly plotted Vetsploitation *The Executioner*, nobody ever says "Hey look, there's the Executioner," but we ascribe that name to the character anyhow. Say what you will about *The Expendables*, but at least the group referred to themselves as such.

20. Obviously a name meant to strike fear in the hearts of the neighborhood, but a more fitting moniker for a tartan-clad boy band from the '70s. And they don't even don skates, unlike, say, The Punks in Walter Hill's *The Warriors*. Interestingly, The Punks, who do wear roller skates, don't reference their footwear in their nickname. And denim overalls and rugby shirts don't exactly scream "Punk" either. Oy, the mind reels!

21. Again, neither squibs nor bullet wounds were employed. Come to think of it, there are no bullet holes anywhere. This is especially evident when vehicles belonging to our heroes and the henchmen are shot up.

22. There's only one other feature film in the Sellier Jr. oeuvre: The T&A comedy *Snowballing*. Before his death in 2011, Sellier Jr. was known more for producing religious TV documentaries such as *Miracles in our Midst* and *The Case for Christ's Resurrection.*

23. Katherine Harmon, "Does Revenge Serve an Evolutionary Purpose?" *Scientific American*, May 2011

24. Of note: it turns out Belgium has contributed more to the action world than the Muscles from Brussels, Jean-Claude Van Damme. Belgian-born inventor/huckster John Joseph Merlin (b. 1735) is the brains behind the inline skate. Merlin, who is also responsible for something else on wheels—a prototype wheelchair for people with gout—would glide up and down the boulevard wearing his invention to draw attention to the London museum he founded.

25. Not for nothing does Z'Dar's character share a name with a *Masters of the Universe* villain—a literal cross between a man and a cobra. MOTU's Kobra Kahn had the ability to spray a "sleep mist," which immediately rendered the recipient unconscious. Unfortunately, many of Z'Dar's over-one-hundred films had the exact same effect on the audience.

26. Played by Chiang Sheng, Shaw Brothers regular and member of the Peking Opera School acrobat/martial arts troupe known, so coolly, as the Venom Mob.

27. University of Utah researchers, from 2015 from: In vitro strain in human metacarpal bones during striking: testing the pugilism hypothesis of hominin hand evolution by Joshua Horns, Rebekah Jung and David R. Carrier.

28. And we don't mean Eric Roberts, although we're sure he would have fit the bill quite nicely.

29. Hogan has been known to take liberties with the truth when it comes to his own legend. He claims to have once auditioned for Metallica after the band lost their bassist Cliff Burton in a tragic bus accident. His quote: "I was big pals with Lars Ulrich and he asked me if I wanted to play bass with Metallica in their early days, but it didn't work out." Lars' response: "I don't know Hulk Hogan . . . [and] I certainly have no recollection of doing anything with [him]." Hogan has since amended his story, saying that he merely sent the band audition tapes but never heard back.

30. On his role in *No Holds Barred*, the *Ghostbusters II*, and *The Running Man*, the actor told *A.V. Club*, "You know, there are some things you can't unsee, and there are some movies you can't get off *IMDb* no matter how hard you try. That's all I'm going to say."

31. The purported attendance figure for Wrestlemania III, held in 1987 in Michigan's Pontiac Silverdome and main-evented by Hulk Hogan vs. André the Giant—at the time an indoor attendance record. However, many have accused Vince McMahon, the friend of hyperbole that he is, of inflating that number. Wrestling journalist Dave Meltzer puts the actual attendance at closer to 78,000. An impressive number nonetheless, and arguably the peak of "Hulkamania."

32. Prima was born Humbertus Knoch to a Dutch father and an Indonesian mother, just like the Van Halen brothers. But the similarities end sharply at genealogy. Sure, Prima could kick butt with the best of them, but could he rip out blistering renditions of "Eruption"? Didn't think so. Then again, Prima has the physiology of a Greek God while the Van Halens look more like sticks of souvlaki, so it's a toss up, really.

33. Considering their inauspicious beginnings, the Rhees ended up doing pretty well for themselves. Simon became a lauded fight coordinator, stunt performer, and Hollywood martial arts instructor while Phillip is best known for producing and costarring in the *Best of the Best* series.

34. For all the martial arts pedants out there, Tanaka is actually a *shidoshi* or ninjutsu instructor. But sensei sounds so cool and it's a more accessible term.

35. The story goes that Jean-Claude approached Cannon producer Menahem Golan as he came out of a Beverly Hills restaurant and gave him an impromptu martial arts demonstration that so impressed M.G. that JCVD was cast in the above role.

36. Widely considered the greatest stunt performer of all time, Robinson held nineteen world records, including one for highest paid stuntman ever. He also invented a device called "the decelerator" which allowed stuntmen to jump from great heights without the need of an airbag. In addition, Robinson is famous for being the only man to jump off Toronto's CN Tower (formerly the world's tallest free-standing structure) when, doubling for actor Christopher Plummer in the film *Highpoint*, Robinson freefell 700 feet before a tiny parachute opened at the very last moment. Sadly, Robinson died at age thirty-nine in a freak motorcycle accident on the set of the forgotten film *Million Dollar Mystery*. He had completed stunt work on *Lethal Weapon* shortly before his death, and the archetypical buddy cop film is dedicated to his memory.

37. There are action stars who do opt to perform their own stunts, Jackie Chan being the most notable example. Tom Cruise does his own stunt work too, but no one of sound mind would consider Tom Cruise an action star—even though you can tell he really, really wants to be one. Guess Scientology can't give you everything.

38. Obligatory *Simpsons* reference.

39. Great, except there's no one around for miles, so who's really listening?

40. That looks like a third-grade art project.

41. Again with the world. Why does every supervillain endeavor to take over the world? Seems like a lot of hassle to us. Look at how much being the President of the United States ages somebody in just eight years. Now multiply that by the world and for life. They should just conspire to take over a small tropical island, live out the rest of their years in luxury, and be done with it.

42. Imagine how cool that title would look on a *LinkedIn* profile!

43. Just how crappy does a film have to be that the guy responsible for the looney *Star Wars* knockoff *Starcrash* is the last-minute savior?

44. OK, now the hyperbole's starting to get laid on a little thick. Greatest man ever born? Obviously, Mother never heard of Jesus or Buddha. Then again, those two never battled rubber-suited monsters or had impressive pec cleavage.

45. Blame *The Simpsons* for besmirching the good name of Poochie forevermore.

46. Just once it would be refreshing to see an Asian character in one of these films whose specialty was *not* the martial arts. Greco-Roman wrestling, just as an example, would make for a wonderful change of pace.

47. If you have any designs on joining the Secret Service . . . no designs for you. If you have visible body markings, you will be required to remove them at your own expense. That's gotta limit the talent pool considerably.

48. The all-important-disk-containing-all-the-information-needed-to-propel-the-plot-forward is a trope that has reared its head in many an action or espionage film and continues to this day, evolving only so far as to accommodate changes in technology (the disk is now the flash drive). That the conceit has survived for so long, despite its inherent implausibility, is all the more impressive. Why implausible? Because these are criminal masterminds. If they're smart enough to devise plans to take over the world, they're also clever enough to make backup copies of any and all important data.

49. One suspects that this may have been the original intention, especially considering the theme song playing over the opening credits, with lyrics like "*Stargrove/Flying like you've never flown/Stargrove/Running in a danger zone.*" Then again, the closing credits are set to a tepid ballad entitled "Never Too Young to Die," so who knows?

50. And for this and other mediocre films, Simmons all but abandoned KISS in the mid-'80s, leaving most of the song writing duties to Paul Stanley. Not a good idea as Simmons' film career went nowhere, and the two albums from this era, 1985's *Asylum* and 1987's *Crazy Nights* rank among the band's very worst.

51. According to Andrew Leavold's fascinating documentary, *The Search for Weng Weng*, producer Peter Cabellas named his actor after a particularly strong alcoholic beverage popular in the Philippines. Others say the drink is named after the actor. Still others insist that Weng Weng is a local idiom for "totally wasted." Regardless, if you'd like to make a Weng Weng, you'll need vodka, rum, gin, tequila, whiskey, grenadine, and a variety of juices. Serve it over ice in a short glass, for obvious reasons.

52. The signature Weng Weng fighting style was to knock the assailant to the floor, usually by tripping or kicking the knees. The snack-sized scrapper would then leap on top of his prone attacker and pound the stuffing out of him. This was usually enough, but should it not be, Weng Weng was never above delivering a good old-fashioned blow to the nether regions.

53. They say you should never bring a knife to a gun fight and Agent 00 heeds that maxim. But when it becomes evident the flurry of assailants are all sword-wielding, Agent 00 does as the Romans do. Interestingly, by the time 00 picks it up, the sword that he appropriated from a downed combatant appears to have shrunk at least a foot from the time it was in the enemy's hand.

54. Director Paul Kyriazi claims this scene was inspired by Kurasawa's *Sanjuro*!

55. Laurence Olivier reported that he was nearly electrocuted when his prop sword nearly connected with a light dimmer switch and studio soundstage electrical equipment.

ACKNOWLEDGMENTS

Chris and Jeff wish to thank friends, family, and the army of action movie fans all over the globe. If ever a crack mercenary force needs assembling, we'll know where to turn.

For images, the authors would like to give a special thanks to the following: Elisabetta Volpe and worldwide distributor Variety Distribution for the cover image, Paul Zamarelli (VHSCollector.com), Nico Mastorakis, Brian Trenchard-Smith, Brent Huff, Cinema Epoch/CineRidge Entertainment, Alamo Drafthouse, Arrow Films, and October Coast Publicity and Publishing. Other images come from MoveStillsDB.com and IMDb.

ABOUT THE AUTHORS

Kirschner and Lombardo are the hosts of the *Really Awful Movies* podcast, and authors of *Death by Umbrella! The 100 Weirdest Horror Movie Weapons.*

Jeff Kirschner grew up wanting to be either Indiana Jones, Rocky Balboa, or some demented hybrid of both. His room was plastered with dozens of photos of Harrison Ford and Sylvester Stallone in their respective heroic alter egos. And lots of posters of Bruce Lee, whom he wanted to emulate despite never making it past white-belt level in his karate lessons. *Robocop* made him an action freak and *Die Hard* an action fanatic. And it's been all about the henchman ever since. He's a Toronto author, writer, and college professor.

Christopher Lombardo has studied aikido, shot guns, done Muay Thai, and boxed—and is terrible at all of them. He's simply not henchman material. Luckily, he has been able to vicariously enjoy all things action through the wonder of cinema. Lombardo is a Toronto author and writer who's written for the CBC, *Toronto Star*, and *Globe & Mail.*